MW00333957

THE POLITICAL PHILOSOPHY OF NICCOLÒ MACHIAVELLI

THE POLITICAL PHILOSOPHY OF NICCOLÒ MACHIAVELLI

Filippo Del Lucchese

EDINBURGH
University Press

© Filippo Del Lucchese, 2015

Edinburgh University Press Ltd
The Tun – Holyrood Road, 12(2f) Jackson's Entry, Edinburgh EH8 8PJ

www.euppublishing.com

Typeset in 10.5/13 Sabon by
Servis Filmsetting Ltd, Stockport, Cheshire,
and printed and bound in Great Britain by
CPI Group (UK) Ltd, Croydon CR0 4YY

A CIP record for this book is available from the British Library

ISBN 978 1 4744 0427 3 (hardback)
ISBN 978 1 4744 0429 7 (webready PDF)
ISBN 978 1 4744 0428 0 (paperback)
ISBN 978 1 4744 0430 3 (epub)

The right of Filippo Del Lucchese to be identified as Author of this work has been
asserted in accordance with the Copyright, Designs and Patents Act 1988, and the
Copyright and Related Rights Regulations 2003 (SI No. 2498).

Contents

Introduction

Novel 84 of the *Novellino*, the most important collection of short stories before Boccaccio's *Decameron*, narrates the encounter between the *condottiere* Ezzelino III da Romano and the Holy Roman Emperor Frederick II:

> It is recorded how one day being with the Emperor on horseback with all their followers, the two of them made a challenge which had the finer sword. The Emperor drew his sword from its sheath, and it was magnificently ornamented with gold and precious stones. Then said Messer Azzolino: it is very fine, but mine is finer by far. And he drew it forth. Then six hundred knights who were with him all drew forth theirs. When the Emperor saw the swords, he said that Azzolino's was the finer.[1]

In the harsh conflict opposing the Guelphs and Ghibellines – a conflict of utter importance for the late medieval and early modern history of Italy and Europe – the feudal lord Ezzelino sends the Emperor a clear message: honours, reputation, nobility, beauty ultimately rest on force. Gold is not important, good soldiers are, because good soldiers will find gold, not the contrary.

This anecdote, in all its simplicity, well summarises a concept that will guide our reading of Machiavelli in this book, namely the concept of 'realism'. Machiavelli has been blamed, since his death, for his pessimism, his amoralism and his influence in corrupting minds and causing people to deviate from a straight, ethical and honest concept of politics towards a corrupted and immoral concept of selfishness at the expense of others. Notwithstanding a parallel movement that, since the sixteenth century, has tried to re-establish a true picture of Machiavelli's thought, 'Machiavellian' still represents, in ordinary language, the wicked character, treacherous and unfaithful, who does not accept the shared common rules of politics, the outsider, the traitor, Evil.

In this book, I will not try to defend Machiavelli from these accusations. Many have done this already, much better than I could. Moreover, I think that focusing on Machiavelli's realism contributes to changing the focus of the question in the right direction: what is at stake, in Machiavelli's thought, is not so much the alternative between morality and immorality, but rather the conception of reality that influences what we think about men, society, politics. Rulers knew well enough how to be immoral long before the publication of Machiavelli's *The Prince*. Machiavelli has not taught them anything they did not know already. Or, if he has, he learnt it from the political reality he observed, both in his own time and in the past.

Realism, in this sense, means talking about men as they are, rather than as they ought to be, because any wish to transform evil into goodness would be a matter for alchemy rather than for political thought. This does not mean, for Machiavelli, that an objective, natural dimension of humanity rigidly determines men's action in history. It means, rather, that history unfolds for causes, and these causes depend on both the natural dimension and the social and political dimension of human action, strictly intertwined. Rather than preaching a better world, the political theorist should understand those causes, explain their influence and action, and suggest how to play a role within the world – a world where the causal necessity has to be understood not as a static and rigid series of chained events, but rather as a dynamic and fluid field of occasions and forces acting upon each other.

Although this is a book on the history of political thought, then, it can and should also be read through the lens of political theory. In fact, Machiavelli is not only one of the most important political thinkers of the early modern European tradition – the inventor of political science, as it is often said. Machiavelli is the first author who poses the problem of politics in a new form, a form which is still the one that concerns us today, no matter how much of his thought or how many of his problems are still directly or indirectly relevant for us (and many of them are). Moreover, through his work, he shows a revolutionary approach to the interpretation and comprehension of the relationship between the knowledge of history and theory itself.

Theory, on the one hand, can make sense for Machiavelli only if, from the abstract heaven of ideas, it is brought down to the earth of the actual dimension of human life and of men, existing and living in a particular time and place. There is no advancement of learning if there is not a solid comprehension of history, of how similar circumstances can or can not produce similar outcomes, of how rules – however fluid and elusive this concept can be in Machiavelli – always have exceptions, whose comprehension, though, does not destroy the rule itself, but rather enriches our own understanding of it. Historiography, on the other hand, is not a neutral reading of facts, an impartial narration of how things did happen, an unbiased accumulation of erudite and uncritical knowledge. The knowledge of history can be effective, for Machiavelli, only when it is guided by a partisan and critical curiosity, when it is driven by questions that concretely affect people's lives. Politics is, for Machiavelli, at the confluence of these two conceptions of historiography and theory.

Politics is also, in this sense, a challenge against the claim that authors, theories, thoughts should be studied within their disciplinary boundaries. Machiavelli represents one of the most powerful antidotes against this blind and harmful conception of knowledge, largely based on outdated and untopical ideas about learning and teaching. There is no theory, for Machiavelli, without a comprehension of history, and there is no knowledge of history, for him, without theory. He learned this from his ancient sources; we can learn this from the modernity of his thought.

The old question of whether Machiavelli is a political 'scientist' or merely a politician – a question itself driven by disciplinary concerns rather than by a serious approach to the author's thought – is thus wiped out. If one means by 'scientific approach' an attitude concerned with a comprehension that constitutes the basis for action, the building of intellectual 'tools' to understand and act within reality, then of course Machiavelli is a political scientist and not only a politician. If one means, on the contrary, an analytical attitude, constrained within a formal language, rigid categories, a specific set of problems and 'technical' issues, then of course he is not a scientist.

A meaningful and respectful approach to his work, however, will precisely reveal that, for Machiavelli, there is no true knowledge without politics, and no politics without a deep study of history. I am not proposing a sceptical solution, trying to satisfy scholars who support both positions. In fact, both kinds of scholars will probably find my reading of Machiavelli partial. This is precisely what I have learnt from Machiavelli: every reading is always partial. No observer can claim to be neutral and outside the field of problems that Machiavelli points out. On the contrary, we are necessarily within this field, both part of the problem and the solution, in the same way that Machiavelli was trying to elaborate, within the early modern crisis of Italy and Europe, both the comprehension of the crisis and its solution.

The partiality of my reading also influences my methodology and, in particular, the use of secondary sources. Within a (supposedly) neutral introductory work, the reader would expect to find an exhaustive illustration of at least the main historiographical interpretative schools. At the risk of deceiving this potential reader, interested in a good handbook's chapter or in a Wikipedia-like essay with a more solid background, I have decided not to take this approach. The partiality of my reading of Machiavelli also produces a partiality in the engagement with secondary sources. The major schools and secondary sources that I have referred to are of course in the background, and are mentioned whenever it is necessary for the comprehension of the aspects of Machiavelli's philosophy that I consider pivotal. However, they are not necessarily in the foreground, if they do not also consider these themes as pivotal.

One of the most important cases in this sense is the very influential 'Cambridge School'.[2] Mainly concerned with the rhetorical nature of Machiavelli's work, for example, this school has not extensively focused on Machiavelli's treatment of social struggle and political conflict – a theme that deserves, in my view, the highest attention. For this reason, my engagement with the Cambridge School is not central in this introductory work. More broadly, and to put it in other words, in this book I will not discuss topics merely because they have been discussed by the major and most influential interpreters of Machiavelli, but I will discuss these scholars' interpretations whenever they touch on the themes that I consider crucial to the understanding of Machiavelli.

The suggestion I can give to the reader of this book, especially to students, is to move to a direct reading of Machiavelli's text as soon as possible. As Italo Calvino points out in a text that cannot be too highly recommended, 'no book that talks *about* a book says more than the book in question'.[3] This should be what schools and universities 'ought' to help us understand. Calvino's is a harsh truth for those who teach in universities and therefore must publish in order to survive as teachers and researchers. I thankfully remember introductory reading and secondary sources that helped me by throwing light on extremely difficult pages of, for example, authors such as Aristotle and Spinoza, Descartes and Hegel. It is a truth nevertheless: like all of them, Machiavelli still freshly speaks for himself.[4]

This also points to a question I am very keen on: the imperative of listening to the author's voice. An introductory work, such as the present one, should never be a substitute for direct engagement with the author's text itself. Such an engagement is a necessity, not an option, if the reader wants to really grasp an author's spirit. Hence, I make extensive use of direct quotations from Machiavelli's text and, in the last part, from his interpreters' works. Modern readers might find Machiavelli's prose difficult. Let me reassure them straight away:

Machiavelli's text *is* indeed difficult. Rewriting his prose for the sake of our understanding would not contribute to making it easier. It would only contribute to making it more 'homogenised', namely closer to our language, our culture, our understanding of politics and history. It would be an illusion: it is precisely in the distance between our language and culture and his language and culture that we can find useful tools for the comprehension of both.

Modern anglophone readers, moreover, might find Machiavelli's prose difficult because of the extremely difficult enterprise of translation. Let me reassure them as well straight away: Italian readers too find Machiavelli's prose difficult nowadays.[5] Machiavelli stretches categories, and does violence to old concepts, words and expressions, in order to build his own new theory of politics. Rather than Latin, he decides to employ the Italian vernacular, a language still young in his own days, and hence more malleable, but also more ambiguous and sometimes enigmatic. My preference, therefore, is for those translations that are closer to the literal sense of Machiavelli's language. Again, this choice probably makes the reading more difficult, but avoids the illusion of clarity, whose undesirable effect would be only an illusion of comprehension. When necessary, I slightly modify the existing translations, and when useful for the understanding of a passage, I also discuss the reason for this modification. By doing so, I hope to contribute to a better understanding of Machiavelli's thought. Most of all, I hope to contribute to familiarising the reader with his theories, concepts and language.

In this book I have tried to point out those themes, arguments and thoughts that seem to me to be the backbone of Machiavelli's political theory. In Chapter 1, I briefly describe Machiavelli's environment, as well as his cultural, political and religious background. Machiavelli's work stands out as an original intellectual enterprise, and yet this enterprise can be better understood when it is framed in its historical context. I will suggest that the dramatic historical events following Lorenzo de' Medici's death in 1492 and the French invasion of Italy in 1494 ignite an epochal shift of consciousness as regards men, their role in the world, their possibility of action, and the very meaning of history. I will also suggest, though, that such an epochal shift happens at the heart of a much longer historical process that had already started transforming and shaping men's consciousness: humanism and the Renaissance. My aim is to show to the reader that this long historical process and these dramatic and sudden events *together* explain the exceptional nature of the Florentine milieu, within which Machiavelli develops his revolutionary thought.

Such a milieu is not only geographical, i.e. Florence and Tuscany, one of the main cradles of European civilisation. It is also political, in the sense that the 1494 crisis opens up the possibility of experimenting with a more radical form of democracy and popular participation in Florence's government. I will discuss the role that Machiavelli plays in this exceptional historical period, and how his first-hand political experience forms the basis of his major works, written after he loses his office, following the fall of the Republic or, as he says, *post res perditas*.

I have decided to explore Machiavelli's thought through his major works: the *Discourses on Livy*, *The Prince*, the *Florentine Histories* and the *Art of War*, without forgetting to mention other works that contribute to the understanding of his political thought. They are respectively analysed in Chapters 3 to 6. Devoting a chapter to each of his books allows for the preservation of the works' unity and coherence. In each of his books Machiavelli is urged by a different political situation to analyse politics, history and their connection. Yet in no way do I intend to suggest, as many scholars have done, that Machiavelli's position changes following the changing political circumstances. On the contrary, he repeatedly confirms his political stance, reworking it in different contexts and with different methodologies. In order to grasp the theoretical basis of Machiavelli's political thought and its consistency, I have decided to introduce the major works by devoting Chapter 2 to his philosophical ideas, ideas that underlie all his production.

The history of Machiavelli's political thought is also the history of its appropriation, its uses and misuses, the history of its faithful interpreters and its denigrators. It is a history that goes along the very genealogy of modern European political thought and philosophy. In the last two chapters of this book I will briefly reconstruct this history, through the major interpretations of Machiavelli's thought from the sixteenth through to the twentieth century. I will show how the most important political philosophers of Western history engage with Machiavelli's thought and heritage. My aim is not to summarise their political philosophy in its entirety. It is rather to follow them on the specific interpretations and illustrate the responses that they feel compelled to give to the challenge represented by Machiavelli's theory. As had been the case for Aristotle, or Plato, or a few other groundbreaking thinkers, Western political thought would not be the same again after Machiavelli.

Machiavelli is also a literary author. His poetical work is generally considered of limited importance. One will easily find in his poetical works many of the great themes that characterise his historical and political works as well as, more generally, his philosophy and, of course, his own biographical experience: *Capitoli*, devoted to *fortuna*, ambition, occasion (written before 1512), poems on the historical period, like the two *Decennali* (1504 and 1514), and poems on the corruption of the present world, like the unfinished *L'Asino* (*The Golden Ass*, written probably around 1512). After the fall of the Republic and the political exile in San Casciano he also wrote a novella, *La favola di Belfagor Arcidiavolo* (*Belfagor*, 1518), and also a theoretical text on language (or at least an early version of it, composed around 1521 and eventually modified by other authors), the *Discourse or Dialogue on Our Language*, and some of the funniest and most ironical letters to some of his closest friends, like Guicciardini and Vettori. Machiavelli's masterpiece, however, is undoubtedly the comedy *La Mandragola* (*The Mandrake*, 1518), one of the funniest and most daring comedies of the whole early modern European theatre.

La Mandragola speaks about love, sex, cheating, treachery, men's naivety and men's guile. Like many other literary works, one can read it as a metaphor or even as an allegorical rewriting of Machiavelli's political thesis, developed in his major works. I do not think that this is the right approach, though. This metaphorical approach will compromise the appreciation of the real artistic value of these works. Furthermore, the literary works' content, even if read with allegorical lenses, will not add anything to the comprehension of Machiavelli's political thought and philosophy. Even if one wants to consider Machiavelli's poetry, comedies and novellas a rewriting of his political theory, they are no more than a rewriting. Hence, I prefer to leave them out of this introductory work, which is devoted to Machiavelli's political, historical and philosophical ideas. This also means recognising that Machiavelli's mind is wide and open enough to focus, in different moments of his life and in different personal circumstances, on different intellectual outcomes. The author is the same, while the intent varies. Rather than exploring Machiavelli's whole production, I will guide the reader through his political, historical and military works, leaving aside his literary works.

Some of the themes analysed in this book have already been pointed out by other scholars; some of them have been repeatedly and consistently underestimated by the existing literature, especially by mainstream scholars. I try, in this case, to throw a different light on Machiavelli, and to present his work for what I think it is: a revolutionary foundation of modern political thought.

PART I: THE RED DAWN OF MODERNITY

1. The Storm

1494

In the twelfth canto of the *Orlando Furioso* (*Mad Orlando*), one of the masterpieces of Italian and European literature, published in 1516, Ludovico Ariosto describes the hero's search for Angelica in the enchanted palace of the sorcerer Atlantes. It is a palace apparently rich but in fact completely empty, where lost people frantically look for something they can not find:

> [Orlando] jumped from his horse and stormed through into the living quarters. He dashed hither and thither, never stopping until he had looked into every room, every gallery [. . .]. While vainly pursuing his quest hither and thither, full of care and anxiety, he came across [. . .] other knights who were also searching high and low, pursuing a quest as fruitless as his own. They all complained about the malicious invisible lord of the palace [. . .] and none of them could tear themselves away from this cage – some there were, the victims of his deception, who had been there for whole weeks and months.[1]

The castle of Atlantes, one of the *Furioso*'s most powerful metaphors, perfectly describes the state of deep crisis, uncertainty and confusion that characterises Ariosto's and Machiavelli's time, during the dramatic evolution and redefinition of the whole European political scenario of the late fifteenth and early sixteenth century in Italy.

The year 1494 can be easily defined as the 'beginning of the end'.[2] When Charles VIII, king of France, entered Italy with his powerful army and his revolutionary artillery, all the principalities and republics of the peninsula knelt before him. A reaction against the French avalanche would be soon organised, and the king would have to escape Italy, risking his own life at the battle of Fornovo sul Taro in 1495. An unprecedented event, though, had happened. Italy, the cradle of civilisation, had been invaded by a foreign army, and had revealed all its powerlessness. It would become the prey and the stake of the conflict among the rising European countries for the following decades. This is the tragic scenario that Machiavelli experienced in the early years of his life and diplomatic activity.

The causes of this crisis, though, were profound and rooted in the pluri-secular and peculiar evolution of Italian societies and institutions, both on the internal front and on the foreign dimension.[3] The conflicts that shook the peninsula between the fifteenth and the sixteenth centuries were at the same time Italian and European. The fall of Constantinople in 1453, for example, had reshaped the balance in the Mediterranean Sea and dramatically reduced the power of the Republic of Venice, largely based on trade and commerce with the East.[4] The powerful oligarchy, ruling the Republic since the closure (*Serrata*) of the Great Council, the ruling assembly of the city, in 1297, had progressively focused on hegemony and expansion over the northeast of Italy, rapidly coming into conflict with the neighbouring state of Milan. The ephemeral success of this internal expansion testifies to a crisis of the older economic system rather than a growth of the Venetian influence over Italy.

The peace of Lodi, signed in 1454, established a long-lasting situation of balance among the main Italian regional states: Milan, Venice, Florence, the Papal State, the kingdom of Naples. Francesco Sforza, the powerful *condottiere* who became Duke of Milan, and Lorenzo de' Medici, the humanist poet and leader of the most powerful family of Florence, assumed the role of guarantors of the treaty and opened up a period of peace and prosperity for the whole peninsula. Instead of fighting each other, with a few exceptions, the princes and rulers could devote all their energies to building the architectural, artistic and cultural treasures of the late Renaissance.[5] However, this period of peace also contributed to negligence in cultivating the art of war and the culture of defending one's own country against the enemy. During this period of flourishing of the liberal arts, and decline of the martial arts, several enemies were growing more and more powerful outside the boundaries of Italy.

The rise of the great European nation-states, then, was the cause of the collapse of the Italian political and military world of the early sixteenth century, but it was also its consequence. France, Spain and the Empire fought their conflict *in* Italy and *over* Italy because they found themselves more powerful than any Italian state at the time. But they also became more powerful as a consequence of the bitter conflict of these decades, which reshaped their institutions, apparatuses and foreign policy agendas for the following decades. The Habsburgs' dream of connecting the papal territory with the Spanish domain in South Italy, via the conquest of Milan, was opposed by France, the only European power able to resist this project. The question would be settled only when Charles V, a few decades later, renounced this project and definitively separated the German Empire and the Kingdom of Spain, giving birth to the European political landscape of the balance – and the conflict – among the European countries that would last for several centuries afterward: the Europe of the nations was born in the fire of the Italian wars of the late fifteenth and early sixteenth centuries.

The 'discovery' of America by Columbus, the achievement of the Reconquista by Ferdinand of Aragon and Isabella of Castile, and the death of Lorenzo de' Medici in Florence mark 1492 as a crucial year in the history of Europe. The death of Lorenzo seems a fact of minor importance compared to the two other events, which would have dramatic effects on a global scale. It should not, however, be underestimated, because it represents the breaking point of the fragile balance of power that had presided over the Italian – and therefore European – situation of peace for about forty years.

This event also helps connect the internal history of Florence with the Italian and international situation which would be the theatre of Machiavelli's diplomatic career. Precisely when a strong and capable prince was needed to face the storm that was about to break over Italy, the pillar of the Italian balance died, revealing the dramatic effects of the power vacuum that marked the Italian situation.[6] In this vacuum, several forces appealed to the king of France, Charles VIII, inviting him to descend on Italy and restore peace and order, which meant, in fact, to reinforce their own political power against that of their enemies: Cardinal Giuliano della Rovere against the Borgia pope, Alexander VI, the usurper Ludovico il Moro against the legitimate heir to the Milan throne, Gian Galeazzo Sforza, and against the alliance between Florence and Naples. In such a divided country, Charles VIII fully conquered Italy in a few months, 'with chalk', as it was commonly said. Machiavelli himself named the 'chalk', with which Charles's representatives marked the doors of the Florentine houses suitable to accommodate the 18,000 soldiers coming from all over Europe while they were marching toward Naples.

After the death of Lorenzo, Piero de' Medici became leader of the family and of the whole patronage system through which the Medici had been able to control all the institutional key roles, and therefore rule Florence as a de facto principality, without changing the formal republican status of the city. Piero, however, did not have Lorenzo's skills and did not enjoy the same reputation that was unambiguously accorded to the 'Magnifico'. Tensions rose fast among all the social strata of the Republic against the Medici regime, and especially among the aristocratic families who saw their power being eroded by the Medicean system.[7] When Charles VIII entered Italy, he was seen as the liberator who would finally restore justice against Piero's regime.

The tension among the aristocratic families, and between them and the people, though, made it difficult to unify a common front against the Medici. Whereas the main aristocratic families aimed at restoring a true oligarchic system, possibly with the Medici as *primi inter pares*, the lower strata of the population pushed for the restoration of a more egalitarian regime, and a government based on the rule of the *popolo*. However, when the inept Piero de' Medici, who felt the collapse of his power to be imminent, rushed to welcome Charles VIII and surrendered the Florentine fortresses to the invader without consulting anyone in the city, the reaction against him was strong and the regime was overthrown. The Republic was finally set free from the Medici regime.

The French entered the city with their threatening army, and the people of Florence generally welcomed them, but not at all costs: when Charles demanded the restoration of the exiled Piero de' Medici, the city fiercely refused. The resistance has been made famous by the speech of Piero Capponi, who responded to the king's threat with his famous words, 'If you blow your trumpets, we'll ring our bells.'[8] Charles left the city with his army after a few days, and the Florentine Republic was finally born.

CULTURAL AND POLITICAL BACKGROUND

The role of secretary of the chancery, within the institutional apparatus of the Republic, was extremely important. The secretaryship was not a political position in itself, but rather a diplomatic and, we would say today, administrative role.[9] Two chanceries dealt with both the internal and foreign affairs, often providing continuity to a volatile and instable system with short tenure even for the most important offices in the government. The men in the Signoria and the other governmental bodies changed continuously, thus making the secretaries of the chancery the only persons to have a real awareness of the internal and foreign policies.

In 1498, Machiavelli was appointed secretary of the second chancery of the Republic of Florence, the city where he was born in 1469 and where he would die in 1527. He was appointed four years after the expulsion of the Medici, and immediately after the fall of

Girolamo Savonarola, the Dominican friar who de facto ruled over Florence between 1494 and 1498. Machiavelli was not involved with Savonarola's regime. This fact certainly contributed to his election. It would have not been sufficient, however, for appointment to one of the key institutional roles of the new regime. Someone in charge must have actively wanted Machiavelli in office. The person who played an active role in promoting Machiavelli's candidature was Marcello Virgilio Adriani, secretary of the first chancery, who succeeded Bartolomeo Scala in 1498. The historian Paolo Giovio suggests that Adriani had been not only Machiavelli's mentor, but also his teacher.[10] Adriani thus represents the link between Machiavelli and the humanist world and culture.

A humanist and classical education was a traditional characteristic of the Republic's chancellors and secretaries. Coluccio Salutati, Leonardo Bruni and Poggio Bracciolini had covered this role in the past, and were widely recognised and remembered as pillars of the Florentine civic and cultural life.[11] Humanist secretaries, moreover, played a fundamentally important role in shaping the political memory of the city. Political humanism was a fundamental ingredient of the republican spirit and the civic life of Florence, especially in the ideological conflict opposing the city to the Italian principalities.

Political humanism was indeed an active force against traditional powers and institutions. Humanism was a wide and multiform international movement, which grew in both republics and princely courts. Especially in Florence, though, the humanists were able to build a powerful defence of the republican spirit by using cultural, historical and ideological tools. Grounding their arguments on Latin and Greek political thought, men like Salutati, Bruni and Bracciolini celebrated Florence and its freedom as the heir of republican Rome. At the end of the thirteenth and the beginning of the fourteenth centuries, the *florentina libertas* was opposed to the Visconti's absolutism in the ideological fight accompanying the actual war between Florence and Milan.

Holding the office of secretary of the chancery, Machiavelli naturally followed in the footsteps of these illustrious predecessors. More indirectly, though, his cultural and political role was strongly connected not only to Florentine civic humanism, but also to the critical philological humanism that, in a different political environment, had challenged power itself in the name of culture, reason and truth. Lorenzo Valla, who had had a great impact on Erasmus of Rotterdam, had elaborated a critical spirit that challenged the concept of authority itself, through a direct attack against scholasticism and the authority of Aristotle.[12]

In his *De falso credita et ementita Constantini Donatione declamatio* (*On the Donation of Constantine*, 1440) Valla proved, on the basis of a new philological analysis, that the donation with which the emperor Constantine supposedly granted the Pope of Rome authority over the Western Roman Empire could not have been written in the fourth century, and unambiguously revealed that it had been forged in a later era.[13] Valla's method and spirit, though, proved something even more important to generations of humanists, namely that culture can not and should not blindly serve power. A political and ideological engagement became for him a necessity that also resonates in many pages of Machiavelli and the radical republicans defending freedom against authority.

Machiavelli's political work is based largely on a radical use of his classical sources, politically bended toward a defence of a popular republic and freedom. The ancients are not for him authorities, but rather teachers of freedom and critical thought. This humanism was a threat: when the bones of Titus Livius were believed to have been found in Padua, a monk crushed the skull, fearing that the people would have been moved against religion.[14] Machiavelli himself would write that 'whoever reads of the modes taken by Saint Gregory and by the other heads of the Christian religion will see with how much obstinacy they persecuted all the ancient memories, burning the works of the poets and the historians, ruining images, and spoiling every other thing that might convey some sign of antiquity'.[15]

Another political actor who played an extremely important role in the cultural and political environment of Machiavelli's early years of activity was Girolamo Savonarola.[16] A Dominican friar from Ferrara, Savonarola had been called to preach in the convent of San Marco in Florence by Lorenzo de' Medici, following the suggestion of the philosopher Giovanni Pico della Mirandola. San Marco's convent had traditionally had strong ties with the Medici family. Savonarola's sermons were strongly critical of the style of life of the Florentines. He chastised Florentine culture for not being sincerely Christian. Over the years, his preaching became increasingly driven by prophetic and apocalyptic tones. It was also driven by a profound and sincere attention to the needs of the poor, and he was quickly identified as a defender of the lowest strata of the population.[17]

During the 1494 crisis due to the passage of Charles VIII through Florence, and the threat of an open conflict with the powerful French army, Savonarola played a primary role of mediation, taking part twice in a delegation to the king.[18] His successful role boosted his participation in the active political life of the city following the exile of Piero de' Medici. From that moment on, he acted as the real leader of the republican regime, until his fall, condemnation and execution in 1498. The friar's fall was due to the pressure of the internal aristocratic opposition, and the external threat of Pope Alexander VI, who had excommunicated him the year before.

Friar Savonarola contributed to the rediscovery of the republican spirit, formally maintained, but actually crushed under the Medici yoke for several decades. His main achievement, which also played a fundamental role in Machiavelli's political position, was the reopening of the Consiglio Grande (Great Council). The Consiglio was an inclusive governing body, in which about three thousand citizens sat, including many of the middle and lower classes, with real and concrete powers over political and financial issues. A new large room had to be built to host this new body, and it quickly became the symbol of the new popular regime.

Savonarola grounded his influence largely on his personal charisma, deriving from an inflaming and inspiring prophetical spirit. Masses of citizens regularly attended his preaching and enjoyed the peculiar mix of denunciation of the irreligiosity and immorality of his enemies, within and outside the city, and his political arguments in favour of a popular regime.[19] The young Machiavelli himself often listened to these sermons, which undeniably had a strong influence on him, especially in terms of the political role of religion, and of a clear understanding of the influence that a prophetic stance could have on the people – a stance, though, that, coming from an 'unarmed prophet', would soon reveal the weakness of the friar and, in the time of crisis, would not be enough to save him.

Savonarola's political thought was based on an eclectic, and sometimes consciously confusing, mix of traditional positions.[20] If he is clearly inspired by a Thomist view concerning the primacy of a princely government, he often refers to Venice as a possible model of republican regime. If he openly endorses the people and the poor in his sermons, he is definitely inspired by a Platonic idea of the philosopher-king, without dismissing, at the same time, the idea of a mixed government along the line of political Aristotelianism.

This latter element is particularly important as it would offer Machiavelli a perspective on what seems to be revolutionary in the friar's politics, but is in fact in continuity with a more traditional Aristotelian and Thomist inclination toward the common good and the preference for a non-conflictual political life. Machiavelli would harshly criticise this stance in his later writings, but, most of all, would not support or be involved in the friar's regime. This anti-conflictual position is consistent, in Savonarola, with his celebration of the myth of Venice as a stable, peaceful and powerful republic, a myth that would be dismissed by Machiavelli in the early chapters of the *Discourses*.

Savonarola's regime would not last long. The Republic did not die with him, though, because the aristocratic families were not able to reach a stable compromise on how to administer power and, most of all, on the position to assume toward the Medici family, still in exile, but now actively working against the Republic. In this troubled and unstable political environment, Machiavelli was nominated secretary of the second chancery.

THE YEARS OF THE CHANCERY

During the early years of his tenure, the Republic was engaged mostly in reconquering Pisa, strategically important for the commerce and therefore the economy of the city, and lost with the passage of Charles VIII. Machiavelli's early experiences were therefore at the siege of Pisa, where he witnessed the repeated defeat of the mercenary armies paid by the Republic. This experience would have a profound influence on him, and would make him aware of the importance of developing a militia composed of citizens rather than of mercenaries. This would be one of his main concerns during his tenure, and would leave powerful traces in all his major writings, from the *Discourses*, through *The Prince* and the *Art of War*, to the *Florentine Histories*.

Machiavelli also began in these years the long and intense series of international diplomatic missions that deeply shaped his political awareness and formed the backbone of his 'experience with modern things'.[21] Whenever he could, Machiavelli brought with him his beloved classics, Caesar and Plutarch, Livy and Tacitus. Their reading was always intertwined with the great events that were changing the face of Italy and Europe, and in which he was consciously taking part. He was proud of both his origin and his culture, but also aware of the weakness of Florence's position in the new political scene. When Cesare Borgia, the son of Alexander VI, began conquering the Romagna and seemed to direct his forces against Florence itself, Machiavelli was at the French court, and he was well aware that France's friendship was the only protection Florence could count on. On the one hand, he made this clear in the secret letters he regularly sent to his magistrates. On the other, he responded to the arrogance of France and the powerful cardinal Georges d'Amboise. He would proudly remember one of their dialogues in the last months of 1500, when Valentino (for so Cesare Borgia, son of Pope Alexander, was called by the people) was occupying Romagna. For when the cardinal of Rouen said to me that the Italians do not understand wars, I replied to him that the French do not understand the state, because if they understood they would not have let the Church come to such greatness.[22]

In 1502, Machiavelli met for the first time the man who would have a great impact on his idea of a new prince, Cesare Borgia. Cesare had started, with the pope's support, a successful military campaign to build a large and powerful state in central Italy. He had of course worried all the existing states, especially Florence, which was so close to the Romagna, where the Borgias' enterprise had started. Like a thunderstorm, the new *condottiere* struck quickly and powerfully. When he conquered Urbino, Machiavelli was immediately sent to him. This was the beginning of a relationship of fascination and repugnance at the same time. Repugnance, because the duke represented a terrible threat to the already weak position of Florence in the Italian political scenario. Fascination, because the Duke embodied precisely those qualities that Machiavelli thought a powerful and virtuous prince should embody, in order to resist the adversities of the present times. The letters received in Florence were signed by Francesco Soderini, bishop of Volterra, who accompanied Machiavelli in this difficult mission. However, as Machiavelli's biographer Roberto Ridolfi underlines, the language and spirit of Cesare's portrait, sketched for example in the letter of 26 June 1502, largely stem from Machiavelli's pen:

> The lord is very splendid and magnificent, and is so courageous in arms that even the greatest undertaking appears small to him, and both for the acquisition of glory and for more territory he never rests nor recognizes weariness nor danger. In battle he arrives at a place before one can even realize that his men have been moved; he has hired the best soldiers in Italy. All of which make him victorious and formidable together with his perpetual good fortune.[23]

Later in the year, an attempt was made in Florence to overcome the instability due to the neverending quarrels between the aristocracy and the people, as well as among the aristocratic families themselves. The institutional reform implemented seems a move toward a more authoritarian regime: the standard-bearer, or *gonfaloniere*, formerly elected for a short period of time, was turned into a lifelong office. The reform was not implemented without resistance, as the idea of having a single person in office for life was clearly modelled on the *doge* of the Republic of Venice, and was seen by some as a threat to the collegial administration of power. However, the fight was strong between the pro-Medicean families, more or less secretly working for the reintegration of the powerful family into the city, and the *piagnoni*, the advocates of a more popular politics, following the pattern of the former Savonarolian regime. The stalemate allowed Piero Soderini, member of one of the most prominent aristocratic families, to be elected first *gonfaloniere a vita*. His regime would last ten years, until the fall of the Republic and the reintegration of the Medici.

This event was of capital importance, because Machiavelli and Soderini would collaborate on some of the most delicate issues of Florentine politics. Elected with the favour of the aristocratic families, Soderini unexpectedly turned his back on them and promoted a government in favour of the people, supporting the role of the Consiglio Grande, instead of diminishing its importance as the aristocracy desired. Machiavelli and Soderini were linked by a sincere friendship. Although the secretary would not spare the standard-bearer some criticism for his hesitant attitude in his actions, Machiavelli would become one of the key figures and one of the main supporters of the Soderini regime.

Between Soderini's election in 1502 and his fall in 1512, when the Medici finally regained the city and crushed republican freedom, Machiavelli carried out difficult missions in the Italian territories, as well as in France and Germany. Following Cesare Borgia, he saw the cold violence with which the duke effectively controlled his territories, tamed his ministries and reshaped the conventional means of politics.

In 1506 Machiavelli was finally able to see his project of a civic militia voted on and approved by the Consiglio Grande. Machiavelli had been working on this project for several years, tirelessly looking for the support of key figures in the Florentine administration, including Piero Soderini. He also worked to build an argument to respond to those – the aristocrats – who were afraid of a national militia and, for this reason, preferred to pay – with public money – unfaithful and ineffective mercenaries rather than giving arms to the people of Florence.[24]

He personally took care of the enrolment of the new infantry in the Florentine domain. He acquired military experience and, most of all, the awareness that military practice and political theory must go hand in hand. In support of his project, he writes to the Florentine authorities, that

> everyone knows that anyone who speaks of empire, kingdom, principate, [or] republic – anyone who speaks of men who command, beginning at the top and going all the way down to the captain of a brigantine – speaks of justice and arms. You have very little justice, and of arms, none at all; and the way to reacquire both is simply to order up an army by means of a public decision and a good order, and then maintain it. Don't be fooled by the past

one hundred years when you lived differently and you preserved yourselves, because if you carefully consider the difference between your present times and those of the past, you will see that your freedom cannot possibly be preserved in the same way.[25]

Machiavelli's effort was rewarded when, in 1509, the Florentine army finally achieved the mission and Pisa was retaken – a small event in European history, but a great success for Florence and a huge personal achievement for Machiavelli.

In these years, Machiavelli experienced politics in one of the most critical scenarios of the early modern period. In 1512 the Republic fell. Machiavelli was undoubtedly recognised as one of the key men of the Soderini regime, and therefore marginalised. He was also accused of having prepared an anti-Medicean plot, organised by Agostino Capponi and Pietro Paolo Boscoli. Tortured, Machiavelli would not confess. Still he would be kept out of office, and never seriously employed again in active politics. In this time of forced idleness, though, he would write his masterpieces, that now keep alive his memory, as well as that of his enemies.

PART II: A POLITICAL PHILOSOPHY

2. The Philosopher

THE EFFECTUAL TRUTH

Is Machiavelli a philosopher? And why is such a question even important, if Machiavelli himself does not seem interested in presenting his work as a philosophical system, and himself as a philosopher? He is certainly a political philosopher, and insofar as political philosophy is considered a part of the general philosophy of a period, he finds his place within it as one of the main intellectual figures of his own period.[1] Yet the question is more complicated: can Machiavelli be considered a philosopher in the full sense of the word? Does his political work contain a philosophy or at least point to a philosophical system whose values and principles have played a role in shaping the peculiar political conclusions he draws?

The question is not asked merely to satisfy intellectual curiosity. What is important, in fact, is not to place Machiavelli on the right 'intellectual bookshelf', or within the right academic discipline, but rather to critically evaluate the meaning and potentialities of his discourse within the framework of his own culture. In particular, it is essential to understand the way he is able to transform the paradigms of political theory, the intellectual tools he exploits to do so, and the outcome and heritage of this cultural enterprise. Machiavelli claims the absolute novelty of his political work, having taken 'a path as yet untrodden by anyone'.[2] Many among his followers and his critics acknowledge this novelty, in order to either praise it as the dawn of political modernity[3] or blame it as the sunset of the traditional influence of ethics and morality on politics itself.[4]

These followers and critics speak of course from within a particular philosophical position, situating their critique within the wider ideological battlefield that shapes their own time: for example, materialists or libertines on the one side, late-scholastics or Neoplatonists on the other. Their philosophical ideas are often mingled with political beliefs: republicans or democrats on the one side, monarchists or absolutists on the other. It is essential, therefore, to grasp the philosophical questions that – sometimes openly, sometimes not – go along with Machiavelli's principal interest, which is mainly political. This must be done before analysing Machiavelli's individual works, and as a sort of necessary condition for understanding them as individual works. The philosophical ideas that guide Machiavelli's reflection, in fact, often underlie all his writings, and therefore are better illustrated together, as a sort of conceptual fabric that embraces his own production.

Even if Machiavelli does not seem explicitly interested in philosophy itself, yet a powerful and coherent set of philosophical ideas emerges from his works. These philosophical ideas exist not only to serve the political positions. It is difficult (and sometimes impossible) to determine if the former affect the latter, or vice versa. In fact, what seems to me really new and original in Machiavelli is that they powerfully work together, and this contributes to making his prose so effective and his ideas so striking, both for his contemporaries and for us.

One of the most striking expressions of this revolutionary thought, for example, is the famous assertion on the necessity of knowing the 'effectual truth' ('*verità effettuale*') of things rather than their 'imagination'.[5] This maxim probably summarises and concentrates in itself the core of Machiavelli's philosophical ideas, as well as all the difficulties in interpreting it. On the one hand we have a category – truth – that has a long and complex philosophical history, on the other hand a term – '*effettuale*' – that has no story, and is coined by Machiavelli. This could be read as a sort of generic realism opposed to idealism and utopianism, spanning from Plato's *Republic* to More's *Utopia*. But in fact, Machiavelli's implicit reference to the fact (*factum*), to the effect (*effectus*) and to the idea of doing (*facere*), summed up in his neologism '*effettuale*', alludes to a powerful set of philosophical ideas that not only rejects the idealistic tradition, but contributes to the development of an original vision of nature and the world.

Machiavelli actually does engage with the philosophical tradition. True, he very rarely quotes philosophers. Yet he is clearly familiar with the main political and philosophical systems of the Greek and Latin tradition, including of course the two main classical traditions: Platonism and Aristotelianism.[6] We also know that, early in his life, he became deeply interested in the Epicurean system. His early education and public life, moreover, took place in an environment where those ideas widely circulated. Undoubtedly, then, philosophy played a role in the formation and development of his ideas about nature and men.

Yet the historian Felix Gilbert is boldly unambiguous when he writes that 'Machiavelli was not a philosopher. He intended neither to outline a philosophical system nor to introduce new philosophical terms.'[7] Nevertheless, this is quite a restrictive definition of what a philosopher is: one can think and write 'philosophically' without producing a new system or coining new terms. More important, then, is to determine if the philosophical language and approach is used as a mere subsidy for the sake of expression,[8] or if philosophical ideas substantially contribute to the formation of one's political thought. In the case of Machiavelli, one can also argue that politics heavily depends on the philosophy of nature, and that Machiavelli's revolution – the bulk of his modernity – has been to place politics and history in the realm of nature,[9] somehow following, but at the same time overcoming, the traditional Aristotelian framework.[10]

In order to clarify this point, it can be useful to explore the main philosophical questions both arising from and underlying Machiavelli's text. These questions touch upon the so-called Machiavellian naturalism, or the role and notion of nature in his system. Time and the historical unfolding of events play a great role in Machiavelli's mind, and therefore have also to be explored with the greatest attention. This will bring the focus to two further and strictly related questions: the capacity of men to interpret history (the 'truth' of history and the possibility of grasping it) as well as the possibility of action within history (the *virtù* of men).

NATURALISM AND PHILOSOPHY

The first, and perhaps clearest, allusion made by Machiavelli to the traditional philosophical language is in the use of the concepts of 'matter' and 'form'. They appear throughout his works, from the early chapters of the *Discourses* to the late *Discursus florentinarum rerum*. The terms are clearly borrowed from Aristotle's philosophical system, where they are two of the four causes operating in nature (the other two being the mover or producer of a thing, and the thing's end or purpose). Yet Machiavelli avoids imposing an Aristotelian point of view on the structure of the events he considers. He does not use them in a purely metaphorical sense either, though; for Machiavelli, matter and form constitute the ground of political events upon which men are called to act.

Matter can be corrupted, and resists the form that men want to impose on it, for example with laws and ordinances given to a city.[11] However, matter can – and in fact must – be moulded by men.[12] What counts for

Machiavelli is not matter itself as a static element, but rather its inclusion within the movement of history. One could say that form is not a cause acting upon matter, but rather the unfolding of historical events and the outcome of a specific interaction of different forces acting upon it.[13] The fact that human products, like cities, states and people, are treated as 'matter' suggests that men are not the only 'actors' in this game. In fact, they are part of a wider interaction of natural and artificial forces, acting one upon the other. Men are only one of these forces. Sometimes their action is effective, and creates a matter capable of resisting the transformation imposed by the movement of history. Sometimes, however, their efforts are powerless, and this moves the matter toward corruption.[14]

So we already have two powerful philosophical notions operating within Machiavelli's naturalism. The first is the rejection of anthropocentrism: man is not at the centre of the universe, and his action (helped or guided, as it was for the Christian tradition, by God's providence) is not the only driving force. The second powerful idea is that everything – all matter – is constantly exposed to the ceaseless interaction of forces and forms, and therefore to the unavoidable possibility of corruption. Corruption is in fact one of the key concepts of Machiavelli's naturalism. His whole philosophy can be interpreted as the attempt to elaborate intellectual and political tools in order to resist corruption, as much as possible.

Although using the traditional language of 'matter' and 'form', Machiavelli is clearly reshaping the paradigm, and reinventing the old dialectic of 'nature' and human-created 'convention' (or, as the Greeks would say, of *physis* and *nomos*). It would be an oversimplification to say that he sees human force and will as a 'form', freely acting over the passive element of matter;[15] or that he puts the couple 'matter/form' on the side of nature and necessity, and sets human action, on the other hand, in the realm of freedom. In such a context one could ask whether the human world and politics are determined by nature, or whether they are on the contrary autonomous and independent. But in Machiavelli's framework, humans are a part of nature, and a force acting within it. Human action does not take place in an abstract realm, but within nature. And similarly, nature itself is not separate and unchanging, but exists only within history and is made of corruption and regeneration. Thus, the natural and the human should not be considered separately.[16]

Machiavelli does not subordinate or reduce politics to the same laws operating in the natural world, nor does he make politics autonomous and self-determining. Nature and history are thought of together; neither is subordinate to the other. They are defined according to common categories that explain and illustrate the functioning of both realms.[17] Within this vision, however, Machiavelli is interested mainly in exploring and reflecting upon the world of men, history and politics. In this sense, he consciously decides to be a political philosopher in the full sense of the term.[18]

Because of his focus on politics and history, many scholars have seen his naturalistic language (such as the image of the state as a tree or a plant[19]) as merely metaphorical. I believe, on the contrary, that in addition to the rhetorical impact of such metaphors, Machiavelli tries to establish a stronger connection between natural processes and human events. He uses such metaphors for the sake of developing tools of interpretation and mechanisms of knowledge of this entangled reality, which is at the same time natural and human.

Thus, he brings to the forefront the arts and techniques available to men for gaining access to nature. For instance, he not only uses the human body as a model for states and societies, but rather he uses medical arts and knowledge as a paradigm of interaction between men and the environment they live in. Machiavelli is especially interested in this insofar as politics closely resembles medicine as a circumstantial art, strongly based on the interpretation of signs according to experience and knowledge.[20] Wise princes should deal with present issues, but also forecast those problems that might arise and develop later:

> When one foresees from afar, one can easily find a remedy for them but when you wait until they come close to you, the medicine is not in time because the disease has become incurable. And it happens with this as the physicians say of consumption, that in the beginning of the illness it is easy to cure and difficult to recognize, but in the progress of time, when it has not been recognized and treated in the beginning, it becomes easy to recognize and difficult to cure. So it happens in affairs of state, because when one recognizes from afar the evils that arise in a state (which is not given but to one who is prudent), they are soon healed; but when they are left to grow because they were not recognized, to the point that everyone recognizes them, there is no longer any remedy for them.[21]

Medicine, then, becomes a good model of wisdom for the politician, precisely because it requires both the interpretation of current symptoms and a sound framework of knowledge based on the past and the study of history. Just as the 'experiments performed by ancient physicians' serve as the basis for present physicians, so must ancient laws and orders serve as the basis for understanding present times.[22]

This allows Machiavelli to develop his peculiar relationship between nature and history, as well as between the methods of studying and interpreting them. The human world is not only similar to the natural world, but is part of it, and therefore they function in one and the same way. Although politics and nature may respond to different norms, and require different skills for their interpretation, they are still parts of the same reality. Machiavelli is thus able to build the knowledge which is peculiar to the part (politics) by exploiting the resources, teaching and experiences inspired by the knowledge of the whole (nature itself).

The relationship between the part and the whole, therefore, constitutes the peculiar object of Machiavelli's theory of political knowledge. It must be seen in its dynamic movement rather than in its static description. How do things change over time? How important can this change be? And conversely: do things repeat themselves? What degree of permanence can be recognised, by the wise observer, under the surface of an apparently ever-changing world? This is another philosophical question which Machiavelli tries to answer.

In the same way that nature is one and the same, human nature, which is part of it, is constant and regular in its manifestations. It is not unchanging, though; it continuously changes and fluctuates. But in order to master this fluctuation, one must recognise the constancy and regularity of this change. Knowledge of this constancy, therefore, is necessary for learning how the world functions, because 'heaven, sun, elements, men [have not] varied in motion, order, and power from what they were in antiquity'.[23]

It is extremely important to stress that Machiavelli is not saying that one element – mutation or permanence, difference or repetition – is superior to the other. He is on the contrary drafting the chart of possibilities offered to men in interpreting and acting upon a nature that is constantly changing and fluctuating. It is the permanence of mutation, and the similarity of changes over time, that suggest the possibility of human action and that constitutes the ground of politics.

Here lies another similarity between nature and the human and political world. States are like living bodies. They consume their lives and run towards death. In the same way that medicine can sometimes slow this process for natural bodies, politics can affect the life of artificial bodies, by re-infusing *virtù* and strength into them. Different rules and principles, of course, apply to the two kinds of bodies: in this sense, politics is autonomous from nature. But the concept for interpreting the two movements is the same: 'bodies' can undergo changes within certain conditions, and these changes can bring them back to their original *virtù*. This is the meaning of Machiavelli's famous argument on 'drawing back toward the beginnings':

> It is a very true thing that all wordly things have a limit to their life; but generally those go the whole course that is ordered for them by heaven, that do not disorder their body but keep it ordered so that either it does not alter or, if it alters, it is for its safety and not to its harm. Because I am speaking

of mixed bodies, such as republics and sects, I say that those alterations are for safety that lead them back toward their beginnings. [...] And it is a thing clearer than light that these bodies do not last if they do not renew themselves.[24]

This is one of the most important philosophical and political assumptions Machiavelli makes: that the nature of political bodies makes it possible – or rather necessary – to act on them just as physicians act and produce effects on individual bodies.[25]

The necessity of drawing back to the beginnings also shows that Machiavelli's 'naturalism' does not imply an unconditionally positive judgement on nature itself. Nature is not a model, but rather a paradigm through which one can interpret the world and act upon it. Sometimes the natural course of events has to be favoured and helped.[26] Other times it has to be contrasted and opposed. Events are not necessarily positive just because they are natural – another bold philosophical assumption made by Machiavelli.

When Machiavelli moves from reflection on the common ground between the natural and the human world, and focuses more deeply on political action, his ideas are still led by the same principles.[27] One example occurs very early on, in the *Provision for Infantry*, a 1512 '*ordinanza*' (constitution) of a citizen army for Florence. In it, he boldly suggests to his fellow citizens (and political employer) that they should not assume that they can continue to maintain their independence without an army, as they have in the past century, because times ('*i tempi*') have changed and therefore manner must change accordingly.[28]

Interestingly, Machiavelli connects this position to his claim that republics are superior to principalities. Republics, he argues, can exploit the diversity and the multiplicity of their citizens when times change, but an individual prince, 'accustomed to proceeding in one mode' and therefore incapable of following the changing times, is likely to stick to his own individual nature and refuse to change his attitude, thus coming to ruin. A republic therefore has 'greater life [and] good fortune than a principality'.[29]

Machiavelli offers here twofold political advice: follow the changing times as much as possible, using the regularities of such changes to be able to interpret them and act accordingly. This is when Machiavelli develops his famous theory of *virtù* and *fortuna*, as well as his conception of necessity and occasion. It is also when he more openly reflects on the historical and cultural tradition, through an open dialogue with his philosophical sources, the most important of which are the Greek historian Polybius and the Latin poet Lucretius. They provide

Machiavelli with the intellectual tools he needs to develop his own original ontology and theory of history. After having analysed the question of naturalism and, more specifically, the place of man in nature, I will now explore, in the next section, Machiavelli's conception of time or, more specifically, the place of man in history. This will allow the reader to connect Machiavelli's natural philosophy with his historical and political thought.

THE NOTION OF HISTORICAL TIME

In his theory of nature and succession of the forms of government, presented in the first chapters of the *Discourses*, Machiavelli makes use of the Greek historian Polybius and his idea of *anacyclosis*.[30] Machiavelli is among the first, in the early modern world, to use the recently rediscovered Book VI of Polybius's *Histories*,[31] and certainly 'the first to appreciate Polybius as a political thinker'.[32] He accepts some of Polybius's ideas, and yet he deeply modifies them and ultimately rejects some of the most important consequences of his philosophy of history, especially on questions of predictability and chance.[33]

Polybius defines *anacyclosis* as the natural and necessary cycle that happens inside every state, where the different forms of government – monarchy, aristocracy and democracy, and their corrupted forms tyranny, oligarchy and ochlocracy – follow each other in an endless rhythm.[34] This endless cycle of birth, life and death of each form of government happens for natural causes (*kata physin*), following a biological law of development and corruption.[35] The concatenation of birth, development and death is in fact not only irreversible, but also predictable for the wiser observer of histories. The destiny of every political form is included in its very origin since the beginning, and forever determined according to this law.[36]

Machiavelli's use of Polybius's theory is remarkably original, insofar as he accepts the circular structure of historical time, but radically rejects the rigid necessity underlining the idea of a biological law. After having summarised Polybius's idea on the cycle of forms of government, Machiavelli ruins the certitude based on a narrow naturalistic ground, by maintaining that

> it is while revolving in this cycle that all republics are governed and govern themselves. But rarely do they return to the same governments, for almost no republic can have so long a life as to be able to pass many times through these changes and remain on its feet. But indeed it happens that in its travails, a republic always lacking counsel and forces becomes subject to a neighboring state that is ordered better than it; assuming that this were not

so, however, a republic would be capable of revolving for an infinite time in these governments.[37]

Machiavelli strongly attacks Polybius here.[38] There is not enough 'life' in republics for them to live through several cycles, and often not even a single one. In reality, other states exist, each one interacting with or opposing other states as each goes through its own cycle. If one of them has more force and more life, it will arrest the cycle, and therefore the life, of the 'neighbouring' one by conquering it.

Machiavelli's break with his authoritative source is carried out by using a powerful philosophical tool, with a long history and tradition: the notion of 'chance'. Within his description of the cycle of regimes, which is supposedly based on that of Polybius, Machiavelli in fact asserts that 'these variations of governments arise by chance among men'.[39] Although the degeneration of states follows a regular movement, the process that causes the variations is not – as it was for Polybius – *kata physin*. But why does Machiavelli precisely recur to the idea of chance in order to modify and ultimately oppose Polybius's theory?

Scholars have discovered, in recent years, that the young Machiavelli copied out Lucretius's poem *On the Nature of Things*. Certainly he did it with a strong intellectual curiosity and a certain empathy for the Latin atomist philosopher.[40] The meditation on the notions of necessity and chance is at the core of the atomistic philosophical tradition, since its inception in Leucippus and Democritus, then through Epicurus and Greek Epicureanism, up to the Latin atomism and Lucretius himself.[41] It is certainly through this tradition that Machiavelli becomes interested in his own notion of chance and its relationship with necessity.

Necessity already appears as a central theme in the few fragments of Democritus's thought that have survived. Democritus claims that a blind and mechanic necessity operates within the universe and determines the succession of events, forcing them within a causal chain totally predetermined. However, Democritus is also traditionally known as the philosopher 'who ascribes the world to chance'.[42] A certain contingency and randomness, a certain aleatory character of events still finds its place in this universe, characterising in particular some pre-cosmic movements. Contingency, however marginal and residual, exists in the world.

Although chance and necessity are normally considered in opposition, since at least Aristotle's criticism in Book II of his *Physics*,[43] they are certainly not mutually exclusive concepts in pre-Aristotelian philosophy. Democritus himself describes chance, or *automaton*, not as what happens in the absence of causes, but what happens by itself, spontaneously and yet necessarily. Chance is therefore only a different name for necessity itself.[44] Hence, it is not the same thing as lack of causality, as Aristotle and much of later Western philosophy suggest it is. Democritean chance suggests that the actors of a certain event assist in it and take part in it by partially or fully ignoring the causes of its production. Ultimately, chance is nothing more than the subjective manifestation of a necessity that, although ignored, is no less objective.[45]

However, this interpretation of chance and necessity was considered reductive, crude and even dangerous by many philosophers, and even by followers of Democritus himself, such as Epicurus. He, and eventually Lucretius after him, explicitly criticises this point of the early materialist philosophy. Necessity, for Epicurus, characterises the universe, but its power, far from being absolute, is definitely limited. By reworking Democritus's physics, Epicurus intends to reject rigid determinism and necessitarianism. Lucretius will follow the same pattern, trying to limit the absolute influence of necessity and actually subordinate it to a certain contingency. He does so by introducing the idea of a random deviation – a *clinamen* or 'swerve' – in what earlier materialists insisted was the straight-line motion of atoms.[46] This new and revolutionary hypothesis also has immediate consequences on the ethical dimension. Lucretius suggests, in fact, that the deviation provides a physical explanation of human free will, which would be impossible without it.[47]

Although the Lucretian *clinamen* represents the limitation of the crude Democritean determinism, it does not represent a wide fracture between two systems. Lucretius does not intend to eject causal necessity from the universe,[48] but rather to admit the possibility of human freedom and free actions into it.[49] Whereas necessity is the first and inflexible principle of the Democritean world, Epicurus and Lucretius open up a space – an 'occasion' – for the exercise of human freedom. Necessity is not an absolute determination any more, but rather a principle among other principles, existing within and not above nature.

Machiavelli naturally finds a powerful intellectual tool precisely in Lucretius's notion of chance, which he deeply twists toward the sense of 'occasion'.[50] Occasion becomes, in his philosophy, a real ethico-political *clinamen* that makes possible, and even necessary, human action. Echoing Lucretius, in fact, Machiavelli claims that if 'variations arise by chance among men' they certainly do not arise arbitrarily or without any cause. Chance never sets apart historical events from the causal necessity that rules the world.[51]

Chance, in fact, is not completely absent from Polybius's argument itself, and it already plays a role in his theory. Chance and fortune (*tyche*) are for him part of the development of historical events.[52] But the historian should not attribute to fortune what he is not able to grasp simply because of his ignorance of the causes of events. Hence, fortune can be intended in at least two different meanings: 1) as a final cause or providence that deliberately moves history without our being aware of its functioning; 2) as chance, or manifestation of unexpected and uncontrollable events that modify the course of events.

Machiavelli strongly rejects the first meaning of chance, excluding any outside providential or teleological control over the development of history. He also expands the second meaning of chance, that was only residual for Polybius, by establishing it as the ordinary dimension that men have to face in history. By rejecting teleology, Machiavelli focuses on the 'occasion' as the site where men can break the crude determinism and providentialism of the Polybian cycle.

Chance intended as occasion can also have two patterns. Either historical events occur without any necessary link between cause and effect; or else, because our mind is not strong enough to fully grasp the order of nature, events *appear to us* to lack causality, but in fact chance itself is one of the causes that contributes, necessarily, to the effect.

Machiavelli chooses the second and twofold pattern, by keeping intact a strong sense that events necessarily do have causes, which men sometimes grasp, but often ignore. Within the Polybian cycle of forms of government, for instance, the weakness of a state at a certain point of the cycle is certainly the result of necessary and specific causes, as much as a neighbouring state's power is. Their encounter is on the contrary by chance, in the sense of being spontaneous and belonging to unrelated chains of events. Once the chance encounter between the two states has happened, however, these causal chains melt together in a necessary way and produce a new course of events for both states.

Chance as a cause is conceived by Machiavelli as the ground of variations, as well as the result of several other causes that are not forecast and not reckoned in advance, and yet not less necessary in themselves. Machiavelli seeks a way out of a rigid deterministic logic of explanation of events, and away from an unavoidable fate, eternally decided and forever established. This would make *virtù* useless and pointless.

Chance as occasion is precisely the way out of this ethical cul-de-sac. Human freedom can be recovered via the possibility of imitating the ancients by understanding their history and comparing them with the possibilities offered by the necessary contingency of events. By using such understanding to challenge the opacity of the world, political *virtù* is therefore the constant attempt to interpret the elusive and yet determined and necessary character of chance and *fortuna*, whose character

Machiavelli finds in Lucretius's philosophy. Without renouncing the idea of causal necessity, both authors ground their idea of human freedom on this principle.[53] And this is when Machiavelli is also able to develop his dialectic between *virtù* and *fortuna*.

VIRTÙ, FORTUNA, NECESSITY, OCCASION

We have seen, in the previous sections, how Machiavelli connects nature and history, and how this connection, by appealing to an ancient and established set of philosophical ideas, enables Machiavelli to explain the possibilities for human action. Now, Machiavelli goes much further in this sense, coining a whole new set of ideas and concepts for concretely thinking and explaining *political* action in the human realm. In order to do so, he originally reworks traditional concepts *against* the tradition itself. In this section, I explain how he does this in his use of the categories of *virtù*, *fortuna*, necessity and occasion. These categories traditionally refer to the ontological structure of the universe. However, Machiavelli reworks them and transforms them into conceptual tools specifically adapted to understanding the *political* realm, and to successfully acting in it.

Machiavelli begins the *Discourses* by denouncing those men who honour antiquity without being able to learn anything from its study and knowledge. Men admire and pay a high price for a piece of an ancient statue, but then the histories of the ancients lie forgotten and buried in dust, although they would be of the highest utility for the present time.[54] A wise and attentive reading of these histories would allow men to detect the regularities and consistencies characterising the natural as well as the human world. With this knowledge men could imitate the ancients' enterprises, avoiding making the same mistakes, on the one hand, while being aware of the risks inherent in reproducing the ancients' actions, on the other. The dialectic between *virtù* and *fortuna* takes place between these two possible outcomes.[55]

The idea of *fortuna* rules out, for Machiavelli, the absolute contingency of history: although men usually perceive the opposite, it is not contingency – in the sense of absence of causality – that determines events. It is rather necessity, within which *fortuna*-occasion finds its place. This makes *virtù* possible. The virtuous action, however, is always determined by one's own force and potency, which, moreover, sometimes concur – sometimes clash – with other forces and potencies. They concur or clash, in other words, with *fortuna*, to determine a specific outcome. The field of *fortuna* is always crossed by *virtù* and, at the same time, the exercise of *virtù* is never absolutely independent from the occasions that *fortuna* can make available or take away.

One can clearly see this, for example, in *Discourses* II, 1, when Machiavelli discusses the old question of whether Rome was favoured more by *virtù* or rather by *fortuna* in building its empire. The opinions of Plutarch, 'a very grave writer', are here considered, together with those of Livy, Machiavelli's dearest author. Both Plutarch and Livy claim that *fortuna* has played the greatest role in making Rome prosperous. For example, *virtù* never appears alone in their accounts, but is always coupled with some fortunate event. To *fortuna*, moreover, Romans themselves devoted more temples than to any other god.[56] Yet Machiavelli dares to turn upside down the opinion of such illustrious historians. In order to claim his own position, he maintains that, rather than *fortuna*, the army's *virtù* has doubtless been the main ground of conquering peoples and lands, and the lawgiver's *virtù* has been the basis of maintaining them. Wherever *fortuna* appears to be in the foreground, one must observe more closely, and the *virtù* and the order of that glorious republic will always appear: 'All those princes who proceeded as did the Romans and were of the same *virtù* as they, would have the *fortuna* that the Romans had in this aspect.'[57]

This conclusion does not imply, however, that *fortuna* and even chance do not play any role in human affairs, or that they are only the pale shadow of *virtù*. It means, on the contrary, that *fortuna* materialises in the occasions offered to men to prove their *virtù*. Machiavelli had maintained that the study of history is the key to political action, but this claim now turns upside down the theories of his favourite historical sources. This is not a contradiction, though. It is rather the suggestion that, once again, no virtuous behaviour can be considered alone and independently from circumstances, not even the knowledge of history, which Plutarch and Livy certainly had. The knowledge of Roman *virtù* will not make the modern princes' *virtù* any stronger. Yet it is only through this knowledge that men can play their *virtù*'s power against *fortuna*'s power, when those two necessarily cross each other in the occasion.

Had Romans not grasped the right occasion, we would not remember their glory. Had they fought, for example, against more than one powerful enemy at a time rather than against only one at a time, and always less powerful than themselves, the course of their history would have been much different. One can find here a concrete application of Machiavelli's original reworking of Polybius's *anacyclosis*. Rome has always clashed with neighbouring peoples when its power (and hence *fortuna*) was higher than the rival's. Rome has managed to clash with them at a favourable point of the encountering cycles: this has been its *virtù and* its *fortuna.*

As it is in the case of chance, even *fortuna*, through Machiavelli's eyes, has to be reinterpreted in an original way. *Fortuna* cannot be an autonomous and independent power, without roots in the fabric of human relationships, free to direct its power according to its own will. On the contrary, Machiavelli's *fortuna* is the occasion that *virtù* can effectually grasp, and therefore dominate, or else ineffectually lose, and therefore be dominated by it. The Machiavellian prince is invited to learn this political lesson from the histories of ancient princes and statesmen. Those of Moses, Cyrus, Romulus and Theseus are the stories of occasions virtuously grasped and not of contingent *fortuna* disembodied from the effectual reality of their actions: 'As one examines their actions and lives, one does not see that they had anything else from *fortuna* than the opportunity, which gave them the matter enabling them to introduce any form they pleased. Without that opportunity their *virtù* of spirit would have been eliminated, and without that *virtù* the opportunity would have come in vain.'[58]

Grasping the occasion is therefore Machiavelli's advice: whenever possible, and with whatever means one has available. An erotic dimension colours this attitude in Machiavelli's famous images of *fortuna*/occasion, for example in Chapter XXV of *The Prince*:

> I judge this indeed, that it is better to be impetuous than cautious, because *fortuna* is a woman; and it is necessary, if one wants to hold her down, to beat her and strike her down. And one sees that she lets herself be won more by the impetuous than by those who proceed coldly. And so always, like a woman, she is the friend of the young, because they are less cautious, more ferocious, and command her with more audacity.[59]

One can find a more subtle, metaphysical and almost melancholic attitude in the personification of *fortuna* in the *Chapter of Occasion*:

> And I have wings around my feet, so that
> My never-ending speed may all men daze.
> I have in front all my disheveled hair,
> With which I cover both my face and breast,
> So that no one may know I am right there.
> The back of my head utterly is shorn:
> In vain, therefore, men try to grab me, when
> I pass them by, or if around I turn.[60]

Machiavelli's exhortation to grasp the occasion is one of the most important in his whole work, as here he precisely sets the stage for the dialectic between *fortuna* and *virtù*. The old question whether *fortuna* is more or less powerful than *virtù*, that many scholars keep asking, is in fact overcome by this new logic.[61] *Virtù* cannot express itself without the *fortuna*/occasion, and the occasion comes in vain if *virtù* is not ready to grasp it. Moreover, it can actually become dangerous and malignant where *virtù* is not ready for it. Events are produced, in Machiavelli's universe, only within the encounter – or within the missed encounter – between *virtù* and occasion, leaving behind the old image of *fortuna* as a blind force producing chaotic or malignant contingency and only causing apparently uncomprehensible disasters for men.[62]

Virtù as well needs to be reinterpreted in this light. It is not the actual exercise or the punctual application of force against another contrary force, in a sort of ultimate clash between the two principles guiding the human world. It is rather the patient and meticulous preparation and predisposition to face mutations and variations that are necessarily produced in the world. *Virtù* becomes the capacity of adapting oneself to the movement of times, and the possibility of following and exploiting the manifold nature of reality, by escaping its sometimes destructive effects. Here Machiavelli uses the image of the 'river', another powerful metaphor taken from nature – a nature, though, which man is a part of:

> I liken [*fortuna*] to one of these violent rivers which, when they become enraged, flood the plains, ruin the trees and the buildings, lift earth from this part, drop in another; each person flees before them, everyone yields to their impetus without being able to hinder them in any regard. And although they are like this, it is not as if men, when times are quiet, could not provide for them with dikes and dams so that when they rise later, either they go by a canal or their impetus is neither so wanton nor so damaging. It happens similarly with *fortuna*, which demonstrates her power where *virtù* has not been put in order to resist her and therefore turns her impetus where she knows that dams and dikes have not been made to contain her.[63]

Fortuna as occasion implies precisely the necessity of building 'dikes and dams' when times are quiet and calm, coupled with the awareness that, when the river grows, it is too late to undertake that kind of work. *Fortuna* as 'arbiter of half of our actions' means, in this context, that *no* action is in our power when *virtù* is not prepared and the occasion is wasted, while *all* actions are in our power when *virtù* is prepared and effectively grasps the occasion.

Men ignore the pattern of *fortuna*, as much as they ignore when the occasion will manifest itself. When it happens, therefore, it might seem the result of fate. Yet virtuous men, although unaware of the causal chain in all its details, are fully aware of the general principle and therefore must be always ready to grasp the occasion. Its origin might appear casual and driven by chance, because ignored, but nonetheless it is necessary.

Fortuna can produce unexpected and uncontrollable events. Yet it is not itself the product of 'contingency' (intended as 'the lack of causes'). Resisting its dangerous effects depends on human *virtù*. What does it mean from the point of view of human action? Should one think that only the wise experts and savants who know histories can resist the impetuous course of the river *'fortuna'*, while everyone else is condemned to suffer its devastating effects? It is not so, as Machiavelli abandons the old traditional opinion that only a particular class of learned men are fit for governing the masses. *Fortuna* as occasion becomes in this sense a tool against any elitist and aristocratic conception of politics. Machiavelli's work is not an ethics written for the wise elite. It is rather a practical principle of political action for whoever wants to and can grasp the occasion. As he boldly states:

> Men can second *fortuna* but not oppose it, that they can weave its warp but not break it. They should indeed never give up for, since they do not know its end and it proceeds by oblique and unknown ways, they have always to hope and, since they hope, not to give up in whatever *fortuna* and in whatever travail they might find themselves.[64]

Grasping history's teaching means therefore understanding when the occasion is favourable and when, on the contrary, times are not propitious. Machiavelli's call is not to despair of the apparent omnipotence of *fortuna*. Weaving its warp and not breaking it means, once again, that the action's result depends on the favourable encounter between *virtù* and occasion within the 'singular conjunction'.[65] Nobody, however, knows the end of *fortuna*.

Against the teleological tradition of providence and the concept of *telos* as 'end' or 'purpose' itself, the 'end' becomes here not the deadlock of fate and destiny, but rather the openness toward human freedom. The Aristotelian background of final causes, as much as the Polybian one of *tyche* as providence, is boldly turned upside down. Machiavelli steps into the atomistic and Lucretian ontological universe, ruled by the connection between freedom, necessity and chance as an autonomous cause.

This is why Machiavelli can suggest never giving up, but rather thinking that men's own *virtù* is part of the melting pot of different causes whose interaction produces history. *Virtù* is one of those causes, a cause that autonomously takes part in the conflict with other multiple causes. This conflict is closely reminiscent of the collision among atoms, due to the Lucretian *clinamen*, which is the physical explanation of the very ground of free will. The encounter between *virtù* and occasion is always possible, although never given in advance or taken for granted. This is, once again, the 'effectual reality'. Machiavelli's realism does not have anything to do with cynicism or pessimism. It is rather a pedagogic principle for learning fortitude and steadiness vis-à-vis the conflictual structure of reality. The knowledge of this structure, of its obscurity and malignity, becomes increasingly important for Machiavelli, as much as the firmness required when facing the horrible and amazing spectacle of the world:

> Great men are always the same in every *fortuna*; and if it varies – now by exalting them, now by crushing them – they do not vary but always keep their spirit firm and joined with their mode of life so that one easily knows for each that *fortuna* does not have power over them. Weak men govern themselves otherwise, because they grow vain and intoxicated in good *fortuna* by attributing all the good they have to the *virtù* they have never known. Hence it arises that they become unendurable and hateful to all those whom they have around them. On that depends the sudden variation of fate; as they see it in the face, they fall suddenly into the other defect and become cowardly and abject.[66]

Precisely because nothing is sheltered against *fortuna*, no *virtù* can be considered absolute. And yet, although not absolute, *virtù* is the only ground on which men should try to anchor their way of life. It is in fact the only weapon men possess, and the only attribute that ultimately belongs to them, whether or not it is sufficient to survive the challenge of the varying times. The variation and instability of time itself, therefore, can become an occasion and an opportunity to resist decadence.

Machiavelli maintains the necessity of drawing back toward the beginning, that is to say the starting place from which multiple outcomes are possible – a place where history is constantly reopened, and human action is offered a possibility to act within the contrasting forces of nature. Lucretius argued similarly, writing that the more the bodies are composed of multiple shapes and faculties, the more powerful and full of life they are.[67] Men should not fear the diversity and the apparently destructive variation of times. They should rather lean on it and consider it as the chance that times give them to prove their *virtù*.

When Machiavelli denounces his own time, this same teaching resonates in his pages. Italian princes had ruled undisturbed for decades. They did not think, in those quiet years, that times always change; they '[didn't] take account of the storm during the calm'.[68] They hoped that their people would eventually help them in fighting against their enemies:

> This course is good when others are lacking; but it is indeed bad to have put aside other remedies for this one. For one should never fall into the belief that you can find someone to pick you up. Whether it does not happen or happens, it is not security for you, because that defense was base and did

not depend on you. And those defenses alone are good, are certain, and are lasting, that depend on you yourself and on your *virtù*.[69]

It is necessary, therefore, to conduct one's life only following one's own *virtù* and knowing the favourable occasions. This is the teaching of Machiavellian realism and the core of Machiavelli's philosophy. Ethics, politics and philosophy are intertwined in its works, and follow a precise set of ontological ideas, on causality, determinism and freedom. This is also the core of the revolutionary call to observe and follow the 'effectual truth'. Machiavelli's different works represent converging attempts to explore this reality, tackling different matters – political, historical, philosophical, military – and trying to give them the virtuous shape that they require and they deserve in Machiavelli's mind. Machiavelli's philosophy crosses all of them and makes them intersect in a common aim: the transformation of reality and the political engagement in favour of freedom. After having synthesised the main philosophical ideas in Machiavelli's thought, it is now time to see how they specifically work in the different works written by Machiavelli during and after his political career. The next chapters will respectively be devoted to the *Discourses, The Prince*, the *Histories* and the *Art of War*.

3. *The* Discourses on Livy

A PUZZLING BOOK

When Antonio Blado and Bernardo Giunta, the first two publishers of the *Discourses*, prepared the text for its publication in 1531, they were certainly struck by its lack of coherence, the rhapsodic and unsystematic style, as well as the number of apparent inconsistencies it contained. The *Discourses* appear as a collection of texts on several different matters, often confusedly placed side by side. Sometimes a group of chapters presents a certain coherence, but then the flow of the argumentation is suddenly interrupted and the matters abruptly changed. Or else, after a conclusion on a certain topic has been reached, this same conclusion is reversed after a few pages and apparently disavowed. How was the sixteenth-century reader supposed to read the text, and how is the modern reader supposed to interpret it, as well as Machiavelli's own political thought? This is the first puzzling question surrounding this book.

Another puzzling question concerning the *Discourses* is the date of their composition. Machiavelli has left no information on it, and scholars have struggled in reconstructing the possible timing of the book's writing, trying to deduce it from the internal structure and relationship among the fragmented groups of chapters, as well as from the internal references to coeval or past events mentioned by Machiavelli. Some of the finest scholars in the field, such as Meinecke and Baron, Chabod and Martelli, Sasso and Inglese, have engaged in the difficult task of putting a date on the text, or at least on the different major layers composing it. Were the *Discourses* written in a limited period of time, very close to *The Prince*, or are they the fruit of several years of work and reflections, carried out in very different political and personal conditions of life?

These questions are not, of course, only of philological interest. They also involve the nature of Machiavelli's political engagement in the years he was employed in the second chancery of the Florentine Republic and immediately after. They also involve the nature of the *Discourses* as a book of practical political theory and historiography, as its author intended it to be, having an impact on the actual politics of his own city. The question of its composition, then, as well as the circumstances in which it was thought out and the form in which it was written are of great relevance to the understanding of its content. I will show that the apparent incoherence of the book's structure is not due to the author's lack of interest in the organisation and systematisation of the materials available to him. I will also identify some of the major theoretical kernels at the core of the book and show the great consistency both among them and, as it will become clear through this book, with the other major works of Machiavelli.

I have organised my reading of the *Discourses* in the next sections as follows: I will first analyse the question of the composition of the book, especially with regard to the *Orti Oricellari* (Rucellai Gardens), namely the intellectual and cultural environment where Machiavelli's reflection was conceived and discussed. I will then show how this genealogy influences Machiavelli's methodology, and the meaning of his unsystematic style. I will then analyse the book's content, focusing on the topics that, in my view, represent the most original and innovative contribution of Machiavelli to early modern political thought, namely the question of social conflict and the question of war and imperialism, in particular the political meaning of Machiavelli's choice for a citizen army. I will finally connect Machiavelli's conclusion on conflict and war to the role of religious ideology in governing people and inducing them to act in a certain way.

THE *ORTI ORICELLARI* AND THE COMPOSITION OF THE *DISCOURSES*

Two main theses have been maintained by scholars over the last decades concerning the chronology of the *Discourses'* composition. According to the first one, the early chapters of the book were drafted in the beginning of 1513. Then, the work was suddenly interrupted in order for Machiavelli to write *The Prince*, in a short period of time, and then it was resumed to complete the unfinished project.[1] However, in Chapter II of *The Prince* itself, Machiavelli refers to a previous work in which he deals with republics 'at length'. This passage might be a later interpolation, but still suggests that at least some part of the materials that eventually will flow in the *Discourses* – and this is the second thesis – already existed at a previous date, long before 1513.[2] The nature and extent of this material can not be clearly established, and scholars are far from agreeing on this matter. Yet the hypothesis of an earlier composition of a more or less extensive part of the book, dating back to the years of Machiavelli's employment in the chancery, has become widely accepted.[3]

This rough material was reworked and merged with new ideas that Machiavelli presented to his friends in the reunions taking place at the Rucellai family gardens – the *Orti Oricellari* – at least from 1515. These friends encouraged him to gather and systematise his reflections in a more coherent book, which eventually became the *Discourses on Livy*. Whatever the starting date of this enterprise and the amount of pre-existing material, the *Discourses* had a long period of gestation and testify first and foremost to a method of work consisting in the accumulation of examples and arguments around a theme and its commentary, with several references to sources and problems, both ancient and modern, in order to develop a multifaceted political discourse. The sources used and the way of dealing with them testify to a tumultuous reflection on critical political issues rather than to systematic planning, carefully thought out and clearly organised. Not only the rough and earlier pre-existing materials, then, but also the more accomplished and later reflections, following the *Orti*'s discussions, appear to be very unsystematic.

The environment of the *Orti Oricellari* itself, in fact, certainly had a huge impact on Machiavelli's writing.[4] Hosted by Bernardo Rucellai and characterised by a fierce opposition to the *gonfaloniere* Soderini (see Chapter 1), political gatherings had taken place in this garden, in the centre of the city, near the church of Santa Maria Novella, since the early sixteenth century. Machiavelli began participating in these reunions at a later stage, after the fall of the Soderini regime, under the aegis of Cosimo Rucellai. Some of the most prominent aristocrats of the city, like Cosimo himself and Zanobi Buondelmonti (to whom the *Discourses* are dedicated[5]), Luigi Alamanni, Antonio Brucioli and Donato Giannotti, regularly participated in these encounters.

The political environment of the *Orti* and its sharply aristocratic composition had deeply changed since the old days of Bernardo. In later years, supporters of the republican regime and popular ideas would find their place in these discussions, and Machiavelli – a man of the people who had always written in favour of the people – was very well accepted and encouraged to present his own ideas. The *Orti* became a melting pot not only for theoretical discussions, but also for political actions: the anti-Medicean conspiracy discovered and neutralised in 1522 was conceived here and led by some of those attending these discussions. Machiavelli did not take an active part in the conspiracy, but this is a sign of the character and nature of the place, and what it had become in those years. Machiavelli's teaching certainly played a role in this transformation. Forging one of his powerful metaphors, Francesco Guicciardini writes in his *Oratio accusatoria* that 'the Rucellai garden, like the Trojan horse, sparked the conspiracies, the reinstatement of the Medici, and the flame which burnt the city'.[6]

The *Orti* should also be considered as the theoretical and political counterpart to one of the most important cultural institutions of the European Renaissance, namely the Platonic Academy, which flourished under the Medici and was led by Marsilio Ficino until its closure in 1494. The Academy had an enormous influence on culture and the arts, in Italy and beyond. Set in the idyllic hills of Careggi, it represented the renewal and flourishing of the Platonic and neo-Platonic thought in Italian culture. When Bernardo Rucellai opened his gardens to the Florentine intellectuals, he was somehow continuing the Medicean tradition of patronising and supporting the cultural life of the city. Yet whereas art and literature were the most prominent themes discussed on the hills of Fiesole, politics and civic engagement slowly but steadily became the main interest of the urban discussions of the *Orti*. Whereas Plato and his utopian world were at the centre of the Academy's ideology, Aristotle and Livy attracted the more politically engaged discussions in the *Orti*. This opposition between the hills of Fiesole and the plain of Florence resonates in Machiavelli's dedicatory letter of *The Prince*, when he claims to write his revolutionary political 'map' for the new age like those who place themselves 'on low ground', in order to understand the 'character of the mountains and other high points' of politics.[7]

THE CHOICE OF AN UNSYSTEMATIC METHOD

The circumstances of composition of the *Discourses*, their original meaning as theoretical discussions among friends sharing a common political attitude and intellectual background, necessarily influence the methodology followed by Machiavelli to gather his thoughts on Livy. This methodology, though, as I will show in this section, is not only the result of these circumstances. This methodology also has a precise theoretical meaning that needs to be interpreted in light of Machiavelli's arguments and the political as well as theoretical message that he pursues through this book.

Machiavelli's praise for the people's political reason is striking and bold, and has to be taken as a fierce claim of his own popular status, distinct from and even opposite to that of the Medici and, more in general, of the *grandi*. This is clear in *The Prince*'s dedicatory letter, where Machiavelli claims his membership in the people, and it is even more evident all through the *Discourses*. Thus, inconsistencies and even contradictions that can be found in the three books on Livy should not be taken as hesitations, doubts or even theoretical weaknesses of the republican spirit of the *Discourses* and their author. Machiavelli was not a Medicean, he had never been such when he was in office, and would never be such even when he tried so desperately to be placed back into office after the fall of the Republic. He might have seen a valorous Medici as an extreme and necessary solution – actually the only one realistically possible – to the deep crisis of the Italian states after 1512. Even when he supported and advised the Medici in the later years of his life, then, he never lost his republican inclination.

More probably, then, the inconsistencies and contradictions of the *Discourses* result from the long period of their composition. Over the years, the author himself went through many different events and theoretical stimulations, and was forced to tackle a multitude of problems with different tools and approaches. The lack of coherency and revision in developing his *Discourses* over the years could therefore be one of the causes of their unsystematic character, given the historical and biographical circumstances of their composition. And yet further and more important elements must also be considered.

Machiavelli's lack of a systematic approach can be interpreted as a choice related to his philosophical approach to reality, and in particular to political reality. Given his strong naturalistic mentality and Lucretian philosophical background (discussed in Chapter 2), his anti-systematic approach can be considered a strong theoretical response to the problem of the ontological and political crisis of the early modern world. If bodies become stronger the more complex and composed they are, why should this not also be true of a philosophical thought? Seen in this light, the *Discourses* become the training field for the historical and anti-systematic method that Machiavelli claims as the necessary revolution in philosophy, and especially in political philosophy. To the threatening fractal character of political reality, made of continual crisis, of both regular and chaotic as well as chance recursions, a fractal thought is the best response.

It would have been contradictory if the confused and unsystematic thought had been presented under the veil of a coherent treatise and system, following the model of the traditional political literature of the previous decades. Yet this is not the case. Machiavelli himself recognises the apparent confusion and inconsistency of his analysis in key passages of his work. He thinks locally and punctually around one theme or problem, according to the data, information and possible solutions available at a particular time, and varying his responses following the necessity of demonstration and the multiplicity of points of view to be taken into account. As I will show in the following pages, this is not an inconsistency, but rather a theoretical and rhetorical choice following the philosophy that Machiavelli coherently and precisely chooses. Against the utopian dreams of Platonists and the empty rhetorics of humanists, but also against the sceptical pattern that Montaigne will polemically choose, Machiavelli opts for what he considers the most effectual way of grasping the truth.

This philosophical choice can be used, then, to interpret the structure of the *Discourses*. If the state has somehow to be seen as an organism, placed in a world in continual transformation, and if politics has somehow to be considered as the art of resisting corruption and embodying a virtuous resistance to it, then the three books on Livy can be regarded as the analysis of the origin, growth and maintenance of the state's life.[8] Following the powerful metaphor of the cycles of government borrowed – but deeply transformed – from Polybius, one could consider, for example, the three books as related to the beginning of those cycles, to their internal development, and to their external conflictual relationships with other political entities. Machiavelli himself implicitly suggests this organisation of the apparently scattered materials, insisting on the importance of Rome not as an abstract example or model, but rather on its origin and superiority over other republics, such as Venice, Sparta and Athens (Book I), on the causes of the Roman imperial power (Book II), and on the quality of Rome's actions, especially in the external wars (Book III).[9]

The analysis of the *Discourses* can thus focus on what Machiavelli considers the main topics related to any of these parts. The most important and original point developed by Machiavelli is certainly the relationship between violence and politics, and especially the nature of the social conflicts that characterise Rome's history and constitution vis-à-vis the other republics. The question of Rome's empire and imperialism needs to be read as a consequence of this first point, as well as the question of the nexus between war and politics. To this original core of his political philosophy, Machiavelli adds the fundamentally important corollaries concerning one's own arms, as well as the relationship between religion and politics.

SOCIAL CONFLICT

Right after having reworked the Polybian theory of *anacyclosis*, the life-cycle of states, in Chapter 4 of the first book of the *Discourses*, Machiavelli puts forward one of his strongest theses. This is not only one of the most striking and original theses of his political thought, but also one of the most controversial in the whole history of Western political thought, namely the assertion that 'the disunion of the plebs and the Roman Senate made that republic free and power-ful'.[10] Philosophers had 'damned' social conflict and praised union in the name of the common good for centuries before Machiavelli. And for centuries after him, most of them would keep blaming con-flicts and tumults as a degeneration of political life in every kind of regime.[11]

In addition to viewing conflict in a positive light, Machiavelli also directly contradicts the traditional view of history as tending (or being directed) towards a definite goal or end, and attributes positive results to historical 'accidents'. Machiavelli moves from the analysis of Roman history after the expulsion of the Tarquins and the quarrels that led to the creation of the tribunes of the plebs in 494 BC. He calls these events 'accidents', underlining the lack of any institutional planning or con-stitutional design: no wise legislator is involved in this process and yet the result is for him one of the most praiseworthy events in the politi-cal history of Rome. Because the established Platonic and Aristotelian political thought, both before and after its Christian reworking, espe-cially by Augustine of Hippo and Thomas Aquinas, taught that nothing good could be done without a wise political reason, supported by God's providence, Machiavelli's conclusion represents a harsh attack against the whole tradition. His invocation of 'accidents', moreover, strongly suggests that, once again, he is assuming a Lucretian vision of reality, and is stressing the good effects of aleatory events, autonomously hap-pening outside every teleological and providential pattern.

Machiavelli consciously claims the originality of his conclusion and is well aware of the controversial character of the theory that he is developing here, 'contrary to the opinion of many who say that Rome was a tumultuous republic and full of [. . .] confusion'.[12] Yet the truth is that

> those who damn the tumults between the nobles and the plebs blame those things that were the first cause of keeping Rome free, and that they consider the noises and the cries that would arise in such tumults more than the good effects that they engendered. They do not consider that in every republic are two diverse humours, that of the people and that of the great, and that all

the laws that are made in favour of freedom arise from their disunion, as can easily be seen to have occurred in Rome.[13]

Machiavelli employs here the language of medicine, evoking the 'humours' of the political body, and the analogy with the human body, which is constituted – according to traditional Hippocratic and especially Galenic medical science – by four different humours: blood, yellow bile, black bile and phlegm. Machiavelli's use of this concept drawn from classical medical science is extremely interesting. Once again, in fact, as was the case for the Polybian concept of *anacyclosis*, Machiavelli is not the first one to use this idea. Parallels between medical knowledge and political science were already common.[14] Marsilius of Padua, for example, borrows the Galenic notion of humours to illustrate the dynamics of the parties within the city. And he does so because, like Machiavelli, he is looking for an immanent principle of causality, rather than a transcendental or divine principle of explanation.[15]

However, Marsilius still shares the traditional view of the balance and right equilibrium of the humours that would represent both the healthy complexion of the human body and the harmonius concord of the political body. When Machiavelli decides to make use of the medical paradigm of the humours, on the contrary, he turns upside down its traditional meaning, by supporting the idea that not the union but rather the disunion, the disequilibrium and the conflictual dynamics of the humours represent the healthiest status for the political body. Machiavelli takes the concept of humours from medicine, but disentangles it from its original field and originally reworks it in order to maintain his radical conclusion.[16]

People are frightened by the clamours engendered by the disunion, and are therefore unable to perceive the good effects that they produce. Social conflict is the best way of reaching institutional effects that, like the tribunes, can defend and preserve the people's freedom. This conclusion, placed by Machiavelli at the beginning of Book I of the *Discourses*, influences all the subsequent reading of the Roman history. Machiavelli touches upon the idea of social conflicts in several other parts of the book, and then in *The Prince* and the *Florentine Histories*, in order to examine the differences between the conflicts of Rome and Florence. In all his works, he never changes his opinion and consistently refers to his theory on the positive nature of conflicts, even when history itself seems to contradict his conclusion, as at the time of the Agrarian law, namely the one that 'in the end was the cause of the destruction of the republic'.[17]

The Agrarian law was first promulgated in the fourth century BC, and it caused 'offenses of two sorts to the nobles': the limitation on the extension of lands legally possessed, and the redistribution of the fields conquered from the enemies to the plebs. The nobility, says Machiavelli following Livy's account, successfully temporised with this law. Eventually, though, when the law was reconsidered and 'aroused' again by the Gracchi, it brought the city to the civil war of Marius and Sulla, and then of Caesar and Pompey, finally causing the tragic end of Roman freedom.

The main reason for this shift in the results of social conflict and their embittered nature is clearly pointed out by Machiavelli by expanding on the characteristics of human nature in general. In fact, men always and irremediably struggle. They struggle 'through necessity' first, but when necessity is gone, they 'engage in combat through ambition, which is so powerful in human breasts that it never abandons them'.[18] The passage from necessity to ambition is essential in Machiavelli's analysis as it represents not only the modality of the struggle, but also its aim and target. 'Ambition' means for Machiavelli that the plebs starts struggling for possessions, belonging and richness, against the great and the nobles. Through necessity, the plebs is able to create the tribunes, one of the most praiseworthy Roman institutions. Through ambition, however, the plebs expands the combat toward 'substances' and 'belongings', eventually causing the struggle that led the city to the civil war.

It seems, therefore, that Machiavelli is distinguishing and opposing two sorts of social conflicts: those positive because grounded only on political honours, and those negative because aimed at goods and richness. The former seems moderate and brings good laws and freedom, while the latter seems extreme and violent, and brings harmful laws and the ruin of freedom. This is apparently another inconsistency in Machiavelli's argument: after having praised social conflicts for their virtuous institutional outcomes, he now seems to condemn them, at least some of them, namely those following the Agrarian law. And yet Machiavelli himself explicitly claims the consistency of his argument, by expanding it in two different directions: the critique of the common good, and the primacy of economic conflicts. In fact, he adds that

> such, thus, was the beginning and the end of the Agrarian law. And although we have shown elsewhere that the enmities in Rome between the Senate and the plebs kept Rome free by giving rise to laws in favor of freedom, and although the end of this Agrarian law appears not to conform to such a conclusion, I say that I do not, because of this, abandon such an opinion. For so great is the ambition of the great that it soon brings that city to its

ruin if it is not beaten down in a city by various ways and various modes. So, if the contention over the Agrarian law took three hundred years to make Rome servile, it would perhaps have been led into servitude much sooner if the plebs had not always checked the ambition of the nobles, both with this law and with its other appetites.[19]

The Gracchi, adds Machiavelli, are therefore to be praised more for their intention than for their prudence, as they failed to see that the disorder – namely the economic inequalities – had grown too much in the Republic, and the timing for such a conflict was not the best. Their law, in the end, 'accelerates the evil'. Yet Machiavelli is unambiguous: if the plebs had not resisted the greedines of the great, the great would have destroyed Roman freedom even earlier.

Machiavelli sharply opposes the two social groups, the people and the great. This is not original, once again: Aristotle himself, after having developed his threefold model of forms of government, realistically asserts that the real opposition within the state is always, in fact, the one between rich and poor.[20] The originality and strength of Machiavelli's position lies in his unambiguously taking the poor's side. Men in general, he had maintained, are ambitious and greedy. They all move towards struggling for belongings when they no longer need to fight out of necessity. And yet the judgement is clear. Machiavelli claims that the great are more harmful than the people in the Republic, because 'it does not appear to men that they possess securely what a man has unless he acquires something else new'.[21]

Therefore one has to meditate this principle when one must choose into whose hands the 'guard of freedom', one of the most necessary things to be ordered in a republic, has to be put. History, once again, provides different examples. In this case, the alternative is between Sparta and Venice on the one hand, and Rome on the other. The former cities put the guard of freedom in the hands of the nobles, while only Rome, among ancient and modern republics, decided to trust the people more than the nobles. Machiavelli is not naively praising the people over the nobles: arguments can be found in favour of both models. And yet it is not the cold logic of the statesman to speak here, but rather the passion of the republican, unambiguously ranking himself on the side of the people:

> I say that one should put on guard over a thing those who have less appetite for usurping it. Without doubt, if one considers the end of the nobles and of the ignobles, one will see great desire to dominate in the former, and in the latter only desire not to be dominated; and, in consequence, a greater will to live free, being less able to hope to usurp it than are the great. So when those who are popular are posted as the guard of freedom, it is reasonable

that they have more care for it, and since they are not able to seize it, they do not permit others to seize it.[22]

This conclusion, once again, dominates all the *Discourses* and is connected, as we shall see, to Machiavelli's considerations on Roman empire and imperialism. It also dialogues with ideas throughout the other major works of Machiavelli, especially *The Prince*, who is strongly advised to ground his power on the people rather than on the nobles, and the *Florentine Histories*, where the role and nature of both social groups is analysed in the historical reconstruction of his own city's history. One thing is clear, though: Machiavelli always thinks that the rich and nobles are a danger for the city, and inequalities are harmful to freedom. In fact, inequalities are synonymous with corruption and can only sustain a corrupted way of life:

> Those republics in which a political and uncorrupted way of life is maintained do not endure that any citizen of theirs either be or live in the usage of a gentleman; indeed, they maintain among themselves an even equality, and to the lords and gentlemen who are in that province they are very hostile. If by chance some fall into their hands, they kill them as the beginnings of corruption and the cause of every scandal. To clarify this name of gentlemen such as it may be, I say that those are called gentlemen who live idly in abundance from the returns of their possessions without having any care either for cultivation or for other necessary trouble in living.[23]

This is only another aspect of the analysis of social conflict and the partisan view that Machiavelli always maintains in favour of the people. The argument is not only theoretical, but has a very practical side: in his own time, Machiavelli argues, this uncorrupted way of life can be found only in some provinces of Germany, which he had already sharply analysed in the time of his employment in the chancery.[24] Italy, France and Spain are on the contrary deeply corrupted. Tuscany yet is still an exception, and this is why Machiavelli mainly develops his argument here: his country is and can only be free. The three Tuscan republics, Florence, Siena and Lucca, fiercely opposed to each other, embody the uncorrupted way of life, and therefore the hope for a proud resistance to the foreigner's invasions and the Italian crisis. In fact, 'in [Tuscany] there is no lord of a castle and no or very few gentlemen, but there is so much equality that a civil way of life would easily be introduced there by a prudent man having knowledge of the ancient civilizations'.[25]

Equality – both political and economic – and social conflict are strictly related.[26] Beginning with Book I of the *Discourses*, Machiavelli sets the framework of his theoretical reflection on ancient history and modern politics. Conflicts are not to be blamed, insofar as they produce good laws in favour of freedom and against corruption. Within this dynamic and conflictual notion of politics, a partisan stance has to be taken, and this is unequivocally on the side of the people or the plebs, because the people and the plebs are the only groups that can guard and defend freedom against the greedy and ambitious attitude of the great. Equality of honours and belongings is the best antidote against them to preserve republican freedom.

EMPIRE, IMPERIALISM AND ONE'S OWN ARMS

Machiavelli's praise for social conflict is the backbone of Book I of the *Discourses*, as well as, more generally, of his political theory and its radical character, played against the whole philosophical tradition. It also represents, in terms of the philosophical background of the Florentine, the core of his reworking of Polybius's theory of the cycles of the form of governments. The cycle, in fact, is no longer the naturalistic and inexorable movement of the political body. It is rather the political dimension of the struggle between social groups, within which one has to take a side. The inner dimension of the cycle, though, as I will show in this section, is inextricably connected with its external dimension, namely with the cycles – and therefore lives, conflicts, political dynamics – of neighbouring republics and states. Domestic policy cannot be considered, for Machiavelli, independently from the foreign policy. On this ground, the peculiar and revolutionary conclusion of Machiavelli on the positivity of social conflict touches upon his consideration on the topics of empire, imperialism and, more generally, war. In fact, war and politics can only be seen as two sides of the same coin.

After having praised social conflict, and explained its internal dynamics, Machiavelli repositions the question on the external dimension, asking whether Rome could have been ordered in a different way, removing its conflicts, while achieving at the same time the great enterprises that characterise its history. In other words, Machiavelli asks if Rome, without its social conflict, would have been the same powerful and virtuous republic that it has been. The question is not merely rhetorical because, as often happens, it opens up for him the possibility of the imitation of the ancients, and the opportunity to follow a certain model in the present times. Different paradigms from the past, therefore, have to be scrutinised once again, and once again Machiavelli evokes Sparta among the ancient republics, and Venice among the modern ones.

The choice of Sparta and Venice is both logical and meaningful, insofar as these republics were traditionally considered paradigms of successful politics and virtuous ways of life. It is even more striking, then, that after having recognised their qualities, Machiavelli does not hesitate to consider them as both exceptions and failures vis-à-vis the problem of resistance to corruption. They are exceptions, to the extent that their example cannot and must not be followed. They are also failures, insofar as when the critical time came, they were not able to resist the assaults of enemies, and the encounter with external forces resulted in their destruction.

Both Sparta and Venice were free for a long period of time and without conflicts and tumults, contrary to the case of Rome. Sparta was governed by a king and a small Senate. Thanks to Lycurgus's laws, the causes of struggles and conflicts were removed. Keeping the number of citizens low, and refusing to accept foreigners among them, Spartans were able to resist corruption and avoid expansion. In Venice, the original inhabitants governed the city in councils, and early on they closed access to the government to new inhabitants. They called themselves 'gentlemen', and the others 'people', removing, once again, the ground and the occasion for tumults and conflicts. Both republics were able, in this way, to live quietly.

Yet they organised their internal structure without considering that times change, and that the internal life of republics has to confront itself with external events. Hence, after having subjected almost all Greece, Sparta 'showed its weak foundation upon one slightest accident' and could not resist the uprisings of subjected cities, ignited by the rebellion of Thebes. Even more striking was Venice's ruin: 'After having seized a great part of Italy [. . .] when it had to put its forces to the proof, [it] lost everything in one day', at the battle of Agnadello, in 1509.[27]

The case of Rome is completely different, as its legislators followed a different pattern, both employing the plebs in war, contrary to the Venetian mode, and opening the way to foreigners, contrary to the Spartan mode. This, according to Machiavelli, 'gave the plebs strength and increase and infinite opportunities for tumult'. We find here the causes and the ground of the social conflict that Machiavelli has just praised in the preceding chapters. The link between the internal and the external dimension of the state's life is clearly explained: 'If Rome wished to remove the causes of tumults, it removed too the causes of expansion.'[28] Rome was pushed by its internal conflictual dynamics toward an aggressive politics of imperialism, which was also inclusive of the conquered populations. Rome was able to resist foreigners only by conquering them, and conquering other peoples and lands, on the contrary, gave it more strength and more causes of internal conflicts. The Empire is somehow both the result and the cause of internal conflict.

Machiavelli explores ancient history in order to develop a political discourse for his own time. He is resolved to defend his model of conflictual and expanding state. When it comes to the theoretical question, then, he clearly condemns the Spartan and Venetian model in favour of the Roman one. In principle, one could order a republic anew in both ways, either avoiding conflicts and therefore expansion, or allowing them, and producing the necessary conditions – mainly the use of the plebs in war – for imperialism. Yet as Machiavelli has already suggested, one can never think only about the internal dimension, preventing the external forces from affecting the inner dimension. In fact,

> to many things that reason does not bring you, necessity brings you. So when a republic that has been ordered so as to be capable of maintaining itself does not expand, and necessity leads it to expand, this would come to take away its foundations and make it come to ruin sooner. So, on the other hand, if heaven were so kind that it did not have to make war, from that would arise the idleness to make it either effeminate or divided; these two things together, or each by itself, would be the cause of its ruin. Therefore, since one cannot, as I believe, balance this thing, nor maintain this middle way exactly, in ordering a republic there is need to think of the more honorable part and to order it so that if indeed necessity brings it to expand, it can conserve what it has seized. To return to the first reasoning, I believe that it is necessary to follow the Roman order and not that of the other republics.[29]

Necessity, once again, rules the game. The Roman mode is not only an alternative among others any more.[30] It would be difficult to do better than Sparta and Venice, if one wanted to avoid conflict and refrain from expansion. But expansion – especially considering the sixteenth-century Italian and European reality – is not an option any more. Even if a state does not want to make war, the new scenario forces it to prepare for war coming from outside, as the Italian states learned all too well with the French invasion of 1494. Once again, Machiavelli is making use of ancient history's teaching for the sake of modern policy. He does so in order to strongly assert, as no one had made so clear before him, that war and politics are two aspects of the same reality that every state, with no exception, has to experience.

Machiavelli constantly and consistently asserts this truth using a binomial expression that recurs throughout his works, namely 'justice and arms'. The virtuous republic, for him, achieves justice through freedom inside the state, and power through conquest outside the state. The two elements, once again, are solidly joined together, and, according to Machiavelli, the armed force must be drawn from among the people.

Since the early years of his employment as a secretary of the Republic, as we have seen, Machiavelli had worked with the intent of reforming the military system and building an army composed of citizens and not of mercenaries. In 1506, Machiavelli wrote the *Cagione dell'ordinanza* to persuade his government of the necessity of the enterprise. Here, he boldly asserts that in order to resist the political and military storm of those years, the Republic should avoid passively enduring the change of times, but rather try to autonomously control them, as far as possible. A good political organisation is possible. Even more important, though, is the understanding that such an organisation will be good only insofar as it is matched with a strong army. The two elements can only go hand in hand, as he writes to the Republic's magistrates: 'Whoever speaks of empire, kingdom, principality, or republic, and whoever speaks of men who command, starting from the highest rank and descending to the captain of a brigantine, speaks of justice and arms. You have little justice, and no arms at all.'[31]

Machiavelli strongly maintains the necessity for a republic of having its own army – an army at once faithful, effective and powerful enough to resist the foreigner's invasions, thus avoiding the use of mercenary troops, which is one of the causes of the ruins of the Italian states. 'Present princes', says Machiavelli, 'and modern republics that lack their own soldiers for defense and offense ought to be ashamed of themselves.'[32] The ancient Roman king Tullus, according to Livy's accounts, had the great merit of recognising this aspect and avoiding the use of Samnites or Tuscans in war. Although Romans had been at peace for forty years, Tullus preferred to re-educate his fellow citizens, out of whom he was able to make excellent soldiers. Modern examples also show this reality, such as the virtuous Henry VIII, who decided to invade France taking no soldiers other than his own people.

The whole *Art of War* is developed around this theme, and *The Prince* itself confirms the preference for one's own army over mercenaries in the strongest possible way. Machiavelli's praise for the building of a powerful army should not be interpreted as an uncritical apology for warfare as such. Even if conflict is the core of politics, war is not its aim. On the contrary, a republic's having its own army is the expression of a healthy development between internal and external policy. The end of a virtuous army, Machiavelli claims, is fighting for its own glory and not for someone else's ambition. The affection for republican values is not empty rhetoric, but rather the active resistance to oppression and sincere love of freedom. A proof is once again in the history of Rome, when the armies always won under the consuls, but regularly lost under the decemvirs:

> From this example one can know in part the causes of the uselessness of mercenary soldiers, which do not have cause to hold them firm other than a

little stipend that you give them. That cause is not and cannot be enough to make them faithful and so much your friends that they wish to die for you. For in those armies in which there is no affection toward him for whom they engage in combat that makes them become his partisans, there can never be enough *virtù* to resist an enemy who is a little virtuous. Because neither this love nor this rivalry arises except from your subjects, it is necessary to arm one's subjects for oneself, if one wishes to hold a state – if one wishes to maintain a republic or a kingdom – as one sees those have done who have made great profit with armies.[33]

Only one's own subjects, virtuously educated in the love of their country, can defend it from both external and internal threats. The virtuous citizen is no match even for the most skilful mercenary, paid to fight and necessarily faithful to someone else.

Thus, the theme of one's own army invests both the external and military dimension and the internal and political one. The citizens' army is not only a weapon against foreign enemies, but also a tool for maintaining freedom. The Machiavellian concept of the army is strongly democratic in itself and, as such, it is opposed to other coeval projects of reform, such as the one of the Dominican friar Domenico Cecchi.[34] The army's power is based not on money but rather on *virtù*. 'Where strong defenders are lacking,' Machiavelli says, 'every mountain, every lake, every inaccessible place becomes a plain. Money also not only does not defend you but makes you into prey the sooner. Nor can the common opinion be more false that says that money is the sinew of war. [. . .] for gold is not sufficient to find good soldiers, but good soldiers are quite sufficient to find gold.'[35]

As much as the political culture, also the military culture of Machiavelli's time shows the sign of a deep crisis, especially in the widespread and shameful belief that armies could be bought with money, and war kept away by buying peace. Money, though, also played a huge role in the organisation of the army itself. Whereas an aristocratic conception of the army centres on the cavalry, more elitist and expensive to maintain, a democratic conception revolves around the centrality of the infantry, less expensive but most of all based on active popular participation. In Machiavelli's eyes, the armed people is the 'sinew' of a virtuous defence against both external and internal enemies of freedom:

Among the sins of the Italian princes that have made Italy servile toward foreigners, there is none greater than having taken little account of this order, and having turned all one's care to the military on horseback. This disorder has arisen from the malignity of the heads and from the ignorance of those who held states. For since the Italian military was transferred twenty-five years ago to men who did not hold states but were like captains of fortune, they at once thought of how they could maintain their reputation while staying armed themselves with the princes unarmed.[36]

This is, once again, Rome's teaching. The authority of the Romans has to be followed because it shows the virtuous way of joining internal and external policy, producing a culture of autonomy, independence and love for freedom, not in the rhetorical void of ideology, but in the concrete struggle for it, as the example of religion also demonstrates.

RELIGION

As I have shown in the previous sections, the inner and the external politics (and conflicts) can only be analysed together, according to Machiavelli. They have reciprocal influences, and are inextricably linked. In the last section of this chapter, I will show how this nexus between war and politics is enriched by Machiavelli by introducing the theme of religion. *Virtù*, in fact, which is the ground of a good army of citizen-soldiers, has to be learned. Men, one could say, are not born virtuous, but they become so, they are taught how to be so, and one of the main instruments to teach them *virtù* is, for Machiavelli, religion. As is the case for every other element we have seen so far, also in the case of religion the historical analysis provides different and opposed alternatives. This brings Machiavelli to the controversial domain of historical and political judgement on religions, and in particular the confrontation between paganism, the religion of the ancients, and Christianity, the religion of the moderns.

Machiavelli apparently disconnects his reflection on religion from his argument on social conflicts. Religion does not help the praiseworthy conflictual dynamics. On the contrary, going back to the source and the role it plays in Rome's ancient history, religion produces quite the contrary, namely obedient and fearful men. This, paradoxically, is the great merit of Numa Pompilius, who recognises the unfinished work of his predecessor Romulus and, in order to tame a 'ferocius' people and reduce it 'to civil obedience', decides to 'turn to religion'.[37] His successful enterprise, which consists in inspiring the fear of God into men's hearts, eventually makes everything easier for the Senate of Rome, which does not encounter resistance from the people for many centuries. As it happens at the time of the tribune Terentillus, who wanted to limit the power of the consuls, the Senate uses religion to put 'terror into the breasts of the plebs', and stop tumults.[38]

Machiavelli endorses here the traditional ideology of religion as *instrumentum regni*, as a tool for controlling and governing people.

Not only Numa Pompilius but other mythical legislators such as Lycurgus and Solon are praiseworthy for having 'invented' a political role for religion, and bent it toward their virtuous design: 'Whoever considers well the Roman histories sees how much religion served to command armies, to animate the plebs, to keep men good, to bring shame to the wicked.' Numa, therefore, deserves the highest recognition, because 'where there is religion, arms can easily be introduced, and where there are arms and not religion, the latter can be introduced only with difficulty'.[39]

The subtle irony underlying Machiavelli's argument, though, can not be missed here. Not because religion would not be a powerful tool, but precisely because being so powerful, it can in fact be shaped in any possible direction, and used to manipulate people for different reasons. Religion in itself does not have any higher or transcendent value. It is only a powerful pedagogic tool that can serve good causes in the same way it serves a bad one, as the case of Florence proves once again. Machiavelli stresses this with irony, saying that the Florentine people is not particularly superstitious or naive, and yet it was 'persuaded by Friar Girolamo Savonarola that he spoke with God'.[40] Even more striking is that 'an infinite number believed him without having seen anything extraordinary to make them believe him'.[41] Savonarola, the 'unarmed prophet', grounded his empty power on the authority of his voice and the superstitious and widespread belief that he was God's messenger.

Machiavelli, once again, is taking a traditional argument – religion as *instrumentum regni* – to both endorse it and turn it upside down. The traditional ideology maintained that there existed a true core of religion, for example within Christianity, and showed how it had been perverted for the sake of politics, for example by the Catholic Church, and transformed into an instrument to corrupt and influence naive people. Machiavelli actually shares the opinion that religion has a strong political motivation, but he also thinks that this is not the corruption of a supposedly true core of religion. When he says that every people, even the more sophisticated like the Florentines, can be fooled with no great effort, he is in fact maintaining that the true core of religion is nothing but its capacity to shape minds and sway behaviours in a particular direction. The very same concept of a *true* religion is here diminished, insofar as a religion is true only because and when it is *strong*. It does not mean that every religion is false, but rather that the 'effectual' truth of religion is nothing but its force.

Romans always used and interpreted religion politically and, as Machiavelli says, 'according to necessity'. It was always necessary, as the opposite cases of Papirius and Publius Pulcher demonstrate, to maintain an exterior agreement with religion's ceremonies, at the same time preventing it from disrupting what must be done according to political or military considerations.[42] Roman religion, therefore, is not strong in itself, but is rather made strong by the strength and *virtù* of men who understand the benefits that can derive from respecting it, and the damage that can stem from despising it. They always, for example, take the greatest care in respecting and keeping its institutions and customs alive.

These customs are also the basis for distinguishing the ancient religion from the Christian one, and opposing the two. The latter's condemnation is in fact one of the pillars of Machiavelli's analysis of religion as a pedagogic tool to instil *virtù* in men's heart. Let's begin, Machiavelli says, from 'the magnificence of [the pagan or 'Gentile'] sacrifices as against the humility of ours, where there is some pomp more delicate than magnificent but no ferocious or vigorous action'.[43] The ancient religion's blood and ferocity render men 'similar to itself', preparing them to act vigorously and virtuously in the fight and in the struggle for the defence of their country. On the contrary, Machiavelli adds with a bitter irony, 'our religion [has] shown us the truth and the true way. [. . .] It has glorified humble and contemplative more than active men. It has then placed the highest good in humility, abjectness, and contempt of things human.'[44] Christianity, in a word, has pushed men toward heaven, and made them forget the heart, thus rendering 'the world weak and [giving] it in prey to criminal men'.[45]

The exterior customs of religions, and the cruel or humble nature of their sacrifices, though, are not the only or even the main thing for Machiavelli. In fact, apparently retreating from the world is a political choice with striking political consequences – consequences that make the Roman Church *and* Christianity among the major factors of corruption of Italy, according to Machiavelli. This happens mainly for two reasons: 'because of the wicked examples of [the Roman] court, [. . .] which brings with it infinite inconveniences and infinite disorders', and, even more important, because 'the church has kept and keeps [Italy] divided'.[46] Whereas Spain and France have been united under a single sovereign, the Church is responsible for preventing the union of the Italian states:

> Thus, since the church has not been powerful enough to be able to seize Italy, nor permitted another to seize it, it has been the cause that [Italy] has not been able to come under one head but has been under many princes and lords, from whom so much disunion and so much weakness have arisen that it has been led to be the prey not only of barbarian powers but of whoever

assaults it. For this we other Italians have an obligation to the church and not to others.[47]

The Christian princes' fault is therefore twofold. They provoke the weakness and disunion of Italy, and they leave their religion sliding into the abyss of corruption, instead of holding on to it and its original and virtuous principles. Machiavelli's polemic is therefore both anti-Catholic and anti-Christian at the same time. The Roman Church, as an institution, has its own political responsibilities. The Christian religion, as a philosophy and a vision of the world, has its own cultural responsibilities.

Christianity, in fact, does not have any special *virtù* in its principles, or any privileged status vis-à-vis a supposedly higher truth. Every religion has something good in its foundation, even when it is false. Princes should 'favour and magnify' religions even though they judge them false, and 'so much the more as they are more prudent and more knowing of natural things'.[48] The knowledge of nature, presumably both the human and the worldly nature, should never push toward disrespect or contempt toward religion itself. It should, on the contrary, educate men to know how superstition and credulity shape human minds. Religion is a force among other forces, and as such it must be used. This is what Machiavelli is interested in. The virtuous and positive conjunction of religion and politics is still visible, for him, in the Swiss towns, where 'peoples [. . .] live according to the ancients as regards both religion and military orders'.[49]

This criticism of Christianity has a major importance for Machiavelli's political thought. It also has a major philosophical significance. In fact, by denying any special status to Christianity or to any other religion, and subordinating any pretence to a supposedly transcendent truth to the immanent dimension of politics, Machiavelli is able to develop a materialistic critique of religion, grounded on his Epicurean and Lucretian philosophical background, and connected, in an original way, with a long tradition of attack against the power of religious ideology and its secular consequences.

Machiavelli develops this critique at the beginning of Book II of the *Discourses*, by discussing the opinion of philosophers concerning the age of the world. History, once again, is the point of departure. Our collective memory does not have information older than five thousand years, as historians either did not leave any trace of older events, or are not reliable: for example Diodorus Siculus's history, which is generally reputed to be 'a mendacious thing'. It seems, therefore, that those philosophers, notably the Christian ones, who teach that the world was created hold the truth. Yet we also know that the world is in continual mutation, and these changes – real revolutions, in fact – are often violent and eradicate the collective memory. Moreover, these revolutions are caused both by nature and by men, and in particular by organised 'sects'. Echoing classic discussions on destruction caused by natural phenomena,[50] Machiavelli recalls the natural 'causes that come from heaven [. . .] either through plague, or through famine, or through an inundation of waters'.[51]

This naturalistic approach is also extended to human intervention. Men become part of nature, and by their action – a violent and destructive one – they cancel the memory of the past and build a new one. Organised religions act in this way, positioning themselves at the very origin of history, and therefore of the civilised world itself. Christianity has been particularly harsh in trying to destroy the memory of ancient religions, obstinately persecuting 'all the ancient memories, burning the works of the poets and the historians, ruining images, and spoiling every other thing that might convey some sign of antiquity'.[52] Notwithstanding this violent and consistent attack, its action is a complete failure, insofar as this 'sect' has been unable to couple its destructive attitude with the use of a new language, which is the necessary condition for the success of such enterprise. The failure, therefore, 'arose from having maintained the Latin language, which they were forced to do since they had to write [the] new law with it. For if they had been able to write with a new language, considering the other persecutions they made, we would not have any record of things past.'[53]

This is the core of Machiavelli's materialistic critique of religions as organised sects acting to destroy the memory of other competing religions. There is not any moralistic judgement in his critique.[54] Machiavelli is exclusively interested in seeing how ideas develop and clash against each other; how they can have perverse effects of corruption, as the Christians do, but also how they can be used as sources of education and *virtù*, as the Romans did. Again, religion is only a force among other forces. As Simone Weil, one of the most important twentieth-century Christian philosophers, suggests, certainly remembering Machiavelli's teaching: there is no other force than force itself.[55]

Against the apparently inconsistent development of the three books of the *Discourses*, a strong and coherent set of ideas underline Machiavelli's historical and political comments on Livy's masterpiece. The striking praise for social conflict, the considerations on the nature of war and its necessary relationship with politics, the political role played by the army, and the pedagogic role played by religion form the core of Machiavelli's republicanism. However, Machiavelli's coherence is not limited to this book. It is striking to see how, reworked, these ideas also find a place in *The Prince*, the handbook for individual political leaders and, as it has often been defined, one of the most dangerous books of the Western tradition. Dangerous, maybe, but, once again, dangerous for whom?

4. The Prince

A MAN OF THE PEOPLE SPEAKS TO A PRINCE

The puzzling question of the date of the composition of Machiavelli's masterpieces concerns not only the *Discourses*, but also *The Prince*, the most infamous political pamphlet of the modern age or, as King Frederick II of Prussia would say, 'the most dangerous'.[1] Lack of systemacity and apparent inconsistencies and contradictions also characterise this work, making it difficult, if not impossible, to determine precisely its layers and circumstances of composition. Thus, I will use in this chapter the same methodology applied to the *Discourses*: I will first discuss the circumstances of the book's composition, its place within Machiavelli's production and its meaning as a political pamphlet, intended this time not for intellectual reflection, but rather as a tool of direct political intervention in the Italian crisis. I will then guide the reader through the major theoretical themes that emerge from this striking book. I will first discuss the status of politics as a science, and in particular the way that historical awareness and political theory converge to produce not only a neutral knowledge, but also a political education intended to move men to action. In the following section, I will underline the question of the extraordinary circumstances within which men often have to act. This opens up the space for discussing the all-too-discussed question of evil and of the supposedly wicked nature of this book. This will of course link to Machiavelli's acute analysis of Cesare Borgia, the most wicked character of the period. My aim is to show – and this will be the matter of the final section of this chapter, on the 'civil principality' – that, even in *The Prince*, Machiavelli does not modify his stand in favour of the people and does not deny the striking theories that the reader can find in his other works.

The official story of this book and its author's intentions are, at least in part, clear. Published only posthumously in 1532, in Rome by Antonio Blado and in Florence by Bernardo Giunta, the book was finished by Machiavelli in 1513, according to Machiavelli's own declaration in the famous letter of 10 December to his friend Francesco Vettori, ambassador in Rome: a letter that is also one of the deepest and most moving testimonies of Machiavelli's own character and sensibility, as he faced the sad and tragic events of the Republic's fall and his forced retreat in the country, at Sant'Andrea in Percussina. Machiavelli recounts to his friend Vettori how he spends most of the day in the wood, in the company of woodcutters, or reading some poetry, and then at the village hostel, playing cards and cursing life and bad destiny. We see in this letter one of the greatest men of the century sincerely enjoying the simple life of the countryside, but secretly suffering for his fate. And then, suddenly, a different light is cast upon these dark days:

> When evening has come, I return to my house and go into my study. At the door I take off my clothes of the day, covered with mud and mire, and I put on my regal and courtly garments; and decently reclothed, I enter the ancient courts of ancient men, where, received by them lovingly, I feed on the food that alone is mine and that I was born for. There I am not ashamed to speak with them and to ask them the reason for their actions; and they in their humanity reply to me. And for the space of four hours I feel no boredom, I forget every pain, I do not fear poverty, death does not frighten me. I deliver myself entirely to them. And because Dante says that to have understood without retaining does not make knowledge, I have noted what capital I have made from their conversation and have composed a little work, *De Principatibus*, where I delve as deeply as I can into reflections on this subject, debating what a principality is, of what kinds they are, how they are acquired, how they are maintained, why they are lost. And if you have ever been pleased by any of my whimsies, this one should not displease you; and to a prince, and especially to a new prince, it should be welcome.[2]

Once again, the story of the composition of this pamphlet is not only an exercise in pure erudition, but also a necessary enterprise in order to understand the evolution – and somehow the sense itself – of Machiavelli's political thought, and in particular of some of his most intriguing and controversial theses. *The Prince* was originally dedicated to Giuliano de' Medici, brother of Giovanni, who became pope with the name of Leo X in 1513, consecrating the Medici as one of the most powerful families in Italy and establishing their power as one of the main outcomes of the first period of the Italian wars, which ends not only with the fall of the Florentine Republic and the sack of Prato, but also with France, Florence's historical ally, losing its recently acquired possessions in Lombardy. At some point, though, the dedication was changed, either because of Giuliano's death on 17 March 1516, or because Machiavelli had already seen Lorenzo di Piero as a better dedi-catee, even during Giuliano's lifetime. The book was then addressed to Lorenzo, the pope's young nephew, to whom power in Florence was given, and who became the pillar, in the pope's and the family's dreams, of a new large and stable state in central Italy.

In principle, by virtue of this appointment, the young Lorenzo embodied the prototype of what Machiavelli also dreamed about: a strong prince to whom the occasion is given, by history, to prove his *virtù* and thus reconstitute the power of Florence, resisting strangers' invasions on the peninsula. This might explain Machiavelli's decision to modify the dedication. In practice, the Medici were anything but keen to give any recognition, at this stage, to the former loyal servant of the Republic, openly associated by everybody with the past anti-Medicean regime of Soderini. It is not clear if the book was actually presented to the new dedicatee. And even if it was, Lorenzo probably would have not even been able to recognise the geniality of its author, so remote was the new Florentine Lord's *virtù* from the one that the Italian crisis needed: on being presented with *The Prince*, according to a famous anecdote, at the same time as a couple of dogs, he quickly dismisses the former, and pronounces praiseful words to glorify the latter![3]

Machiavelli, at this time, was still isolated on his estate in the coun-tryside of Florence, after having been implicated in the conspiracy of Pietro Paolo Boscoli and Agostino Capponi against the Medici, impris-oned and tortured. He had not yet started to attend the reunions at the Oricellari Gardens and, in his solitude, was already thinking about a way to be involved in the active politics of his city once again. What was at stake in the new political situation transcended his own per-sonal position vis-à-vis the new regime: higher and more urgent things pressed him to reflect and to act in order to save what was still saveable – if anything – in the Florentine and Italian situation. Moreover, the passion for politics was irresistible for him, and the letters of this period testify, once again, to his sincere and devoted dedication to the cause of the freedom and independence of his city, even if this had to happen under the government of the hated Medicis, because, as he wrote to Vettori on 9 April 1513, '*Fortuna* has seen to it that since I do not know how to talk about either the silk or the wool trade, or profits or losses, I have to talk about the state. I need either to take a vow of silence or to discuss this.'[4]

In these sad times, Machiavelli found the courage and the force to make the most out of his forced exile and solitude. He went toward his beloved classics, embraced them and carefully listened to their words, persuaded, as he had always been, that men can learn a lot from history and experience. Being forced into abstinence for what concerns the latter, he found a fruitful and sweet refuge in the former. And yet the two can only go hand in hand. The awareness of this principle is the first undeserved gift that Machiavelli dares to offer to *The Prince*'s dedicatee – an awareness 'learned – as he says – from long experience with modern things and a continuous reading of ancient ones'.[5] The long experience he claims for himself is of course what nobody denies to him, namely the primary role he played in the political, diplomatic and military life of the Florentine Republic between 1498 and 1512. Although this is what discredits him in the eyes of the new rulers, he dares to openly claim it, because the masters of the past, Livy and Cicero, Sallust and Tacitus, are of no use if they are not considered together with the protagonists of the present, Louis XII and Cesare Borgia, Ferdinando the Catholic and the Medici themselves.

If Machiavelli's aim was to be put back in office, if what mainly counted for him, besides or despite who is actually ruling Florence, was the contribution that he thought he would be able to make to his own city, a more prudent approach might have favoured him. Yet what could help more than showing his true face, as well as the highest degree of intellectual honesty vis-à-vis his own former enemies, in the time they were winning and he was losing? The modern scholars who have accused him of duplicity and opportunism for offering his services to the Medici, such as Leo Strauss and Mario Martelli, are clearly unable to grasp the true spirit of this offer to the new prince, an offer that is consistently republican and openly on the side of the people, in the time when the Republic is lost and the people has to suffer a new servitude and must acclaim its new prince. Machiavelli's claim of belonging to the people and his constitutive distance from the new prince – which should paradoxically testify to his honesty and the loyalty offered to the new rulers – is one of the strongest pages of the whole book, and the core of its political meaning:

> I [do not] want it to be reputed presumption if a man from a low and mean state dares to discuss and give rules for the governments of princes. For just as those who sketch landscapes place themselves down in the plain to consider the nature of mountains and high places and to consider the nature of low places place themselves high atop mountains, similarly, to know well the nature of peoples one needs to be prince, and to know well the nature of princes one needs to be of the people.[6]

Knowledge *and* politics: against a long and established tradition, Machiavelli dares to claim that political rationality belongs to a man of the people at least as much as it belongs to the prince. The latter, then, needs the former more than one usually believes. By accepting his republican experience, the new prince can certainly take advantage of this former enemy's knowledge.[7] By offering it, Machiavelli does not feel any inconsistency or embrace any opportunist attitude: his loyalty is offered to a prince and his faith is put in something higher than the person of the Medici himself.

Knowledge *is* politics: what Machiavelli submits to the young and inexperienced new ruler is a book talking of the ancients and the moderns, of war and politics, of people and princes. It is a book in which the interpenetration of theory and practice, of 'modern affairs' and 'ancient history', is explored in a new and revolutionary way. This is – or must have been, at least for the dedicatee – even more striking, insofar as Machiavelli consciously avoids the use of a new and unheard-of revolutionary form to present his reflections. On the contrary, he ambiguously follows the long and established tradition of the *specula principis*, or the mirror of the princes, the short books written by philosophers to advise princes, especially in the humanist tradition of the thirteenth and fourteenth centuries.

One of the many faults attributed by scholars to *The Prince* is that it is a 'utopian' book.[8] In this view, although *The Prince* appears to be radically realistic, it is, instead, utopian insofar as it calls for a virtuous prince and virtuous action to save Italy's destiny, even though by Machiavelli's time this had become impossible. These scholars see *The Prince* as a desperate appeal to an ideal force, grounded in the atemporal past of Roman glory rather than in the critical present of early modern Italy and Europe. They see its utopian character in both its historical and its theoretical content: historically, for its treatment of the economic and political circumstances that are producing the modern state abroad, vis-à-vis the old declining institutional structures in Italy; and theoretically, for the limits that Machiavelli himself has posited for the *virtù*, against the domain of *fortuna*. This desperate appeal is seen as resounding even more acutely in the short and striking pamphlet of *The Prince* than in any of Machiavelli's longer and more complex work, such as the *Discourses*. This opinion also underlies the idea that a deep gap and a profound fracture divide the two major works – the comments on Livy, fully republican in spirit, and the princely booklet, advocating a quasi-tyrannical and anti-moral attitude against republican values.

Both these conclusions derive more from the preoccupations of contemporary scholars, trying to frame Machiavelli's thought within theoretical and political schemes that do not belong to his own horizon, than from Machiavelli's text himself. Here, without overlooking the inconsistencies or the unsystematic attitude that I have already mentioned, which was often due to strategic or theoretical purposes, or to the evolution of a work spanning two of the most turbulent decades of Italian history, the attentive reader is able to ascertain both the deep realism and the anti-utopian character of *The Prince* as well as his profound consistency with the *Discourses*.

Machiavelli's thought developed as a reaction against the closed world of the Renaissance utopia, when princes used to believe that it was enough to think of a sharp response or to write a beautiful letter.[9] Machiavelli always shows the highest awareness of the necessity of waking up from that dream, before it becomes too late. *The Prince* is the highest point and the most striking appeal in favour of this radical realism. That is why, he writes, 'I have not ornamented this work, nor filled it with fulsome phrases nor with pompous and magnificent words, nor with any blandishment or superfluous ornament whatever, with which it is customary for many to describe and adorn their things.'[10] Machiavelli is not the creator of a utopia.[11] He neither proposes an abstract or utopian model to contrast the deep crisis of his political reality,[12] nor falls prey to a utopian illusion by trying to think about a model of a virtuous prince to act in that same reality.[13]

On the contrary, he recognises in *The Prince* that the situation has reached its extreme degree of corruption, and therefore only an extremely strong and resolute analysis can shake the minds of those who can still do something to resist the forces that are preparing to devour Italy, and sacrifice its political weakness on the altar of the new European balance of powers.[14] Everything, in Machiavelli's *The Prince*, depends on this awareness: the mind-blowing prose he employs, the shocking examples he makes use of, the radicality of the conclusions he reaches and proposes as a model to follow. Nothing is further from the peaceful morality of the contemporary utopian masterpiece of Thomas More,[15] or from any other utopian discourse.

The Prince, therefore, is not the powerless cry of a solitary genius thrown into the void of an epoch that has lost any link with reality. This is also why *The Prince* is coherently and consistently linked with all other works of Machiavelli, and especially the *Discourses*. Scholars have often attempted to save Machiavelli from himself, and separate his two major works: the republican and highly moral theory of the *Discourses*, advocating the glories of ancient Rome, would have to be distinguished from the tyrannical and highly immoral pages of *The Prince*. Machiavelli is able to maintain opinions so apparently different and even opposed, and he is able to counsel both the virtuous republic and the wicked prince, because he would in fact be interested in the possibilities offered by a rhetorical approach to the political matters rather than to politics itself.[16] The most shocking conclusions of *The Prince* should therefore be taken with a pinch of salt and should thereby be prevented from poisoning the highest moral conclusions of the *Discourses*.

Besides being methodologically dubious (one should always be suspicious of scholars trying to save an author from himself), this conclusion is also substantially weak: although the two books are addressed to different readers, and were written in different political circumstances, not a single page of *The Prince* obliterates the theoretical conclusions of the *Discourses* or displaces their political standing. This is true, in particular, for the superiority and the preference that Machiavelli grants to republics over principalities:[17] 'In republics there is greater life, greater hatred, more desire for revenge; the memory of their ancient liberty does not and cannot let them rest [. . .].'[18] The virtuous prince does not represent the crisis of the republican discourse, or the dusk of the popular attitude toward politics, in favour of the individual attitude and the tyrannical approach. The virtuous prince is on the contrary the embodiment of that same popular *virtù*, in the forms and modes that are still possible – and indeed necessary – at the time Machiavelli wrote the book.

THE PRINCE'S METHOD: POLITICS AS A SCIENCE?

The main purpose of *The Prince* is to present, in a concise way, an extreme character, whose exceptional *virtù* allows him to survive in the exceptionally tragic play that he is forced to act in, namely Italy as it is being transformed in the international scenario of the beginning of the sixteenth century. At the same time, to intensify the impact that his work must have, Machiavelli decides to present the exceptional historical situation as the new normality: not as a temporary crisis, to be overcome soon by reaching back to the old golden age of the earlier Italian Renaissance, but rather the beginning of a new age, which paradoxically reveals the permanent and inner character of politics itself. Only now, Machiavelli maintains, can politics overtly be seen for what it has always been: a tragic confrontation of forces, where violent conflict is ordinary and unavoidable.

Here lies the ground of Machiavelli's claim that the 'experience of modern affairs' and the 'study of ancient history' must converge in a meaningful knowledge that can be implemented into an actual praxis: a practical knowledge that remarkably anticipates the attitude of philosophy and science in the modern age. Machiavelli's 'scientific' approach, based on the convergence of experience and theory or, even better, on the elaboration of a theory that is necessarily grounded on experience, has soundly been compared to the attitude of Leonardo da Vinci, Galileo Galilei, and Lord Francis Bacon, some of the founding figures of the modern scientific method.[19] Machiavelli, it has been said, is the father of modern political science, as well as the forerunner of the modern scientific method. This claim certainly contains some grains of truth. Yet it must be clarified, or else it will remain a void formula without any anchorage in the reality of the history of thought, precisely one of those claims that Machiavelli himself despises so much, and for good reason.[20]

The Prince presents a theory that claims to be scientific insofar as it offers elements of explanation of political reality, as well as elements of prediction and effective action to take part in and influence such reality. The purpose of *The Prince*'s science, therefore, is not only to understand, but also to exhort to action, without which any understanding would be completely useless. The book was not written for political scientists, detached from political reality, or for every prince in every time regardless of their historical moment. It was written for the Florentine prince, in a very critical and peculiar moment of the city's history. In this sense, it is more practical and political than scientific. If, however, it can be called 'scientific', and can be deemed valid widely beyond its chronological and geographical boundaries, it is because in order to produce effects in that peculiar time and situation, the political mind must grasp, according to Machiavelli, precisely what goes beyond them, and more widely relates to the broader aspects of men and of politics in general. In order to be specifically effective, politics has to embody general and universal knowledge; in order to be generally valid, theory has to assimilate the specificity and peculiarity of the actual experiences from which it arises. The universal and the particular stem from each other and closely relate to each other. By recognising this truth, this brief pamphlet on sixteenth-century Florence, therefore, exceeds its own limits and becomes one of the grounding texts of the following centuries and of the whole Western history of political thought.

Chapter XXVI of *The Prince* testifies in a particularly effective way to this complex relationship between the particular and the universal. It is the famous *exhortatio ad capessendam Italiam*, the 'Exhortation to Seize Italy and to Free Her from the Barbarians', that closes the book. After one of the most tragic and striking pages of his whole works, in Chapter XXV, in which *fortuna* is described as a river and compared to a woman who must be treated roughly, Machiavelli decides to close the book, in Chapter XXVI, with an exhortation to the virtuous prince to defend Italy from the strangers' power and liberate it from the yoke it is forced to bear. The 'time' has never been 'more appropriate' for such a ruler to rise from the misery of the present condition to a new and eternal glory: 'more enslaved than the Hebrews, more servile than the Persians, more dispersed than the Athenians, without a head, without order, beaten, despoiled, torn, pillaged, and having endured ruin of every sort', Italy can and must embrace the new leader who will 'heal her wounds, and put an end to the sacking of Lombardy, to the taxes on the Kingdom and on Tuscany, and cure her of her sores that have festered now for a long time'.[21]

The abundant and extraordinary *virtù* required can rise only from within an excessively and extraordinarily corrupted situation. This is the 'occasion' that Machiavelli has been talking about for so long. And yet in vain the reader of this so-called Galileo of political science will look for any sign of 'scientific' demonstration or explanation of how this *virtù*, so sorely needed, is also both possible and necessary. The 'liberator', Machiavelli says, will be received with 'love', 'thirst for revenge', 'obstinate faith', 'piety' and 'tears'.[22] The more the appeal becomes heartfelt, the more Machiavelli abandons the scientific approach, with its balanced analysis, to enter the terrain of powerful rhetoric. Remarkably, the chapter ends with the quotation of Petrarch's verses of the *canzone 'Italia mia'*, one of the noblest examples of the tradition of appeal to Italian values, but also one of the furthest – even symbolically – from the actual current situation.

This chapter, it has been said, represents the crisis of Machiavelli's theory, facing the obstacle of a reality that can not be embraced by his conclusions. It represents the insuperable obstacles that *fortuna* constitutes for *virtù*.[23] It has also been interpreted as the proof that Machiavelli is not a 'scientist' and his intention is not 'scientific' at all, but purely rhetorical, and directed to incitement to action rather than to the comprehension of reality.[24] Machiavelli himself, though, had always been careful to write his works precisely so as to avoid dissociating the scientific and the rhetorical dimensions. In this respect, he is really modern, and modernly scientific, in the sense that the only meaningful function that knowledge can perform is precisely to influence actions and to move toward the transformation of reality and the political situation.

If *fortuna* seems sometimes almighty and sometimes tameable, if action appears sometimes deemed to failure and sometimes destined for success, this is due to the fundamentally mutable situation of men and nature. This is not an inconsistency in or a crisis of theory, but it rather reflects this same mutability. Theory's role is, in Machiavelli's view, to interpret it, raising human knowledge, and at the same time exhorting men to action. Knowledge and action, the scientific and the rhetorical approach, are in Machiavelli only two faces of the same reality and can not be disjoined. His rational calculus is not like a mathematical formula that can provide the one correct solution for every problem. Indeed, Machiavelli's approach, in this sense, is not scientific. If, on the contrary, one perceives Machiavelli's real modernity precisely in the necessary conjunction of scientific interpretation and rhetorical exhortation, of theory and practice, of intellectual study and practical experience, one will be able to see the differences, but also the resonances with the methods that will be developed by philosophers such as Galileo and Bacon, Descartes and Spinoza, as well as several other exponents of the modern scientific revolution, many of whom openly admire Machiavelli himself for his contribution to the development of a new method.

THE *STRAORDINARIO* AND THE QUESTION OF EVIL

It can be argued that the striking character of much of the contents of *The Prince* precisely depends on this relationship between the rhetorical and scientific approaches. The shocking nature of Machiavelli's attitude stems from the recognition of the necessity of action, elaborated and illustrated under the conditions of a new scientific knowledge. From the rhetorical perspective comes the energy of the proposal; from the scientific perspective comes the sharpness of his conclusions and the amorality of their contents; from both of them comes what readers have been finding so disturbing and subversive of the tradition. In extraordinary (*straordinarie*) conditions, only extraordinary solutions can be effective.

The *straordinario* is precisely the underlying dimension of the examples that Machiavelli employs in order to develop his arguments. *The Prince* has widely been accused of promoting evil to subvert the basis of civic coexistence and morality. But in fact, for Machiavelli, the question is not the choice between evil and good, 'for a man who wants to make a profession of good in all regards must come to ruin among so many who are not good'.[25] This is one of the effectual truths that the book sharply unveils. The question, for Machiavelli, becomes rather the relationship between ordinary and extraordinary means, as well as the actual nature of the extraordinary times that Machiavelli is living in. His conclusions are of course that extraordinary means are needed but also, and even more important, that what men consider 'extraordinary' has in fact become the ordinary and normal dimension of politics in the contemporary age.

Machiavelli's striking attitude, therefore, is to bring into the reflection on the present not the virtuous examples employed by more traditional discourses, but rather the examples that those discourses have always blamed as the most despicable and wicked. Chapter VIII of *The Prince* deals with princes who acquire their state *per scelera*, through wicked means. Machiavelli chooses the story of Agathocles the Sicilian in ancient times, and Oliverotto da Fermo in modern times: once again, the study of ancient history and the experience of modern affairs converge. Agathocles is a man of extraordinary energy who decides to hold the power in his city violently. 'One morning,' Machiavelli writes, 'he assembled the people and Senate of Syracuse as if he had to decide things pertinent to the republic. At a signal he had ordered, he had all the senators and the richest of the people killed by his soldiers. Once they were dead, he seized and held the principate of that city without any civil controversy.'[26] Oliverotto da Fermo is also strong in body and spirit. Conspiring with Vitellozzo Vitelli, he decides to seize his native town of Fermo, and attracts Giovanni Fogliani, his uncle and the legitimate ruler, together with the leading citizens to a banquet that he transforms into a deadly trap:

> When the food and all other entertainments customary at such banquets had been enjoyed, Liverotto, with cunning [ad arte], opened certain grave discussions, speaking of the greatness of Pope Alexander and of Cesare Borgia, his son, and of their undertakings. While Giovanni and the others were responding to these discussions, Liverotto at a stroke stood up, saying that these were things that should be spoken of in a more secret place; and he withdrew to a room into which Giovanni and all the other citizens came behind him. No sooner were they seated than soldiers came out of secret places and killed Giovanni and all the others.[27]

Machiavelli does not intend to propose such wicked actions merely as examples to follow. He does not condemn them either, though, as examples to avoid. This is not an opportunistic suspension of judgement, but rather the intention to present different contrasting aspects and outcomes characterising similar events and circumstances. Both Agathocles and Oliverotto successfully take power. Only the wicked Agathocles, though, is eventually able to live securely in his own country for a long period of time, defend himself against enemies, and never be plotted against by citizens. The seemingly wicked Oliverotto, on the contrary, falls prey to the fury and plot of Cesare Borgia, only one year after having seized power in Fermo. 'One cannot call it *virtù*', Machiavelli explains, 'to kill one's citizens, betray one's friends, to be without faith, without mercy, without religion' as Agathocles and Oliverotto did: 'these modes can enable one to acquire empire, but not glory'.[28] Yet the issue is precisely that glory can be defined as seizing power *and* being able to maintain it.

Machiavelli's explanation is therefore extreme: cruelties must be used, when necessary. Cruel deeds, though, can be committed well or badly. All at once in the former case, because they are done

> out of the necessity to secure oneself, and then are not persisted in but are turned to as much utility for the subjects as one can. Those cruelties are badly used which, though few in the beginning, rather grow with time than being eliminated. Those who observe the first mode can have some remedy for their state with God and with men, as had Agathocles; as for the others it is impossible for them to maintain themselves. Hence it should be noted that in taking hold of a state, he who seizes it should review all the offences necessary for him to commit, and do them all at a stroke, so as not to have to renew them every day and, by not renewing them, to secure men and gain them to himself with benefits.[29]

By condemning the immorality of Agathocles and Oliverotto, Machiavelli is able to transform the actions of the former in the powerfully amoral and yet necessary economy of evil that the situation requires, and distinguish them from the unredeemable and powerless actions of the latter. Having legitimised this new dimension of political action, based not only on success, as it has often been claimed, but on the success of the ruler posited at the service and in favour of his subjects, Machiavelli is able to develop his revolutionary theory of amoral *virtù*, largely based on the character of Cesare Borgia and his unscrupulous actions.

A SPECTRE IS HAUNTING ITALY – THE SPECTRE OF VALENTINO

Machiavelli's virtuous prince must embody the *straordinario*.[30] He must express, in a word, the exceptional features that an exceptionally challenging situation requires, in the present times, as the ordinary means to survive. *The Prince* is the book that illustrates this *straordinario*. And because a living example is the most powerful tool with which to persuade readers, Machiavelli builds such an example around the cursed character of Cesare Borgia, son of Pope Alexander VI and Duke of Valentinois (or 'the Valentino', as he was commonly called) since 1498. I will show in this section how Machiavelli puts to work, on the living example of Valentino, the conclusions he has reached on the extraordinary features needed to act virtuously in politics, and in particular in the middle of a deep crisis such as the one that Italy is going through at his time.

Valentino perfectly fits Machiavelli's need of such a model. In fact, he was traditionally considered the quintessence of wicked and treacherous behaviour. In his attempt to set up an independent state in central Italy, he had used extraordinary means, obliterating every consideration of morality, loyalty and faithfulness, and subordinating them to his scope. In the Italian mentality of the early sixteenth century, he became the paradigm of the evil prince and the treacherous tyrant, whose actions are to be feared and whose words are to be distrusted. Machiavelli's choice of Cesare as his exceptional example to be proposed sounds therefore like a bold provocation. As in the case of Agathocles, however, was Valentino really a tyrant? Was he particularly evil in a world that had generally become evil and where the distinction between evil and good tended to disappear, leaving space only for the distinction between effectiveness and ineffectiveness?

In Chapter VII of *The Prince*, discussing the principalities 'acquired through the power of others', Machiavelli introduces Cesare, comparing him to Francesco Sforza. While the latter became ruler through ability, and had no trouble in maintaining his position in Milan, Cesare became prince through 'favour and luck', and lost everything once his father's support came to an end with his premature death. The conclusion seems evident: 'Those who become princes as private individuals solely by *fortuna* become so with little trouble, but maintain themselves with much', unless they 'know immediately how to prepare to keep what *fortuna* has placed in their laps; and the foundations that others have laid before becoming princes they lay afterwards'.[31]

The Duke only approaches a stable success. When his father dies, however, he is about to die himself, and suddenly one element – and only one – becomes uncontrollable for him: the election of the new pope. He should have made a Spaniard pope, but he could not. Allowing his former enemy Giuliano della Rovere to become pope as Julius II, he causes his ruin and the destruction of what he had built with so much effort in central Italy. Cesare's vicissitudes testify to Machiavelli's conclusions on the relationship between *virtù* and *fortuna*. He was prepared to face almost everything, and having started from nothing, he did so with great effort and amazing *virtù*. But 'almost everything', in his case, is 'not enough'. The Duke's fall only confirms, once again, the possibilities as much as the limits of *virtù* against *fortuna*.

In Machiavelli's mind, however, the Duke represents the possibility of proposing an entirely new model of *virtù* that his contemporaries only despise in the name of morality and he, on the contrary, admires in the name of effectiveness and *virtù*. When he moves on to discuss the details and the actual moves of princes, notwithstanding Cesare's final failure, Machiavelli strikingly becomes favourably interested in his actions, and somehow turns upside down his first conclusion: it is true that he fell because he was not able to control the pope's election after his father's death, yet 'if I summed up all the actions of the Duke, I would not know how to reproach him; on the contrary, it seems to me he should be put forward, as I have done, to be imitated by all those who have risen to empire through *fortuna* and by the arms of others. For with his great spirit and high intention, he could not have conducted himself otherwise [. . .].'[32]

Valentino is a real 'son of *fortuna*'.[33] And yet he acts virtuously, in the given circumstances, to transform his condition, about which he is well aware. He has, for example, understood that he is dependent on the military support of the king of France and of the Roman enemy families, Colonna and Orsini. He interprets, then, his condition as an occasion, and tries to transform his powerlessness in a favourable situation to build a stable state. He is gifted with many *virtù*, both military and political. Most of all, he embodies the new values – better: the new features – necessary to survive in a violent and merciless political scenario. As Machiavelli had written a few years earlier to the Ten (Florence's military council), in his *Legazione* to Valentino, he was faster than his enemies, nobody knew his thought or intentions, nobody could anticipate his moves and stop him.[34]

Machiavelli is not only interested, though, in the formal character of this amazingly astute and canny prince. He is most of all interested in the nature of his actions and politics, which are for him the very grounds of his success. Cesare Borgia is not only extrinsically virtuous, because he moves faster than his enemies. He is intrinsically virtuous – at least in Machiavelli's interpretation – because 1) whereas the previous lords only exploited the subjects, he acts in favour of his people, and 2) realising how destructive it is to rely on someone else's arms, he builds his own army, as every other prince and republic, with no distinction, should do.

The territories over which Cesare intends to build his new state have been under the control of the factional families of the Roman nobility or local feudal lords, who have maintained them in misery and harshly exploited them. Valentino – and Machiavelli certainly agrees with this – realises that the ground of a solid power must be built on a relationship of trust and mutual support with one's own subjects. This might not be the first aim of the prince, but it is certainly a necessary condition to avoid revolts and rebellions in one's own territories. The Romagna 'had been commanded by impotent lords who had been readier to despoil their subjects than to correct them'.[35] Cesare does not hesitate to violently intervene against this situation, and precisely makes use of the cruelties 'well used' that Machiavelli had mentioned regarding Agathocles the Sicilian.

In the first place, he sends his envoy, the cruel Remirro de Orco, to restore order, using the same violent and unscrupulous methods employed by the local lords. He prepares, in such a way, the occasion to give to his subjects the example of cruelty's use in their favour. In fact,

> because he knew that past rigors had generated some hatred for Remirro, to purge the spirits of that people and to gain them entirely to himself, he wished to show that if any cruelty had been committed, this had not come from him but from the harsh nature of his minister. And having seized this opportunity, he had him placed one morning in the piazza at Cesena in two pieces, with a piece of wood and a bloody knife beside him. The ferocity of this spectacle left the people at once satisfied and stupefied.[36]

The same shameless attitude was used by Cesare in destroying his former unfaithful allies Vitellozzo Vitelli and Oliverotto da Fermo in 1502, as well as Paolo Orsini and the Duke of Gravina in 1503 when, having lured them into a trap, he had them ruthlessly strangled in Senigallia and the Castel della Pieve.[37] Yet once again Machiavelli is interested in the reasons and grounds for the Duke's decision. Cesare becomes the example and the model worthy to be followed not only because his methods are effective, but most of all because his intentions are consistently grounded in a virtuous politics.

Having experienced how unfaithful and useless mercenary armies are, 'the Duke decided to depend no longer on the arms and *fortuna* of others'.[38] He therefore disbands disloyal troops and puts together his own army, devoted and faithful only to him. Machiavelli had preached the necessity of such politics to the republics and actually worked for it when he was in charge. He now sees this evil model of treachery actually pursuing the same virtuous policies that he himself had always pursued.

Throughout *The Prince*, Machiavelli maintains the necessity of a citizens' army as one of the most important achievements for every prince and republic. Chapters XII to XIV deal in depth with this critical issue for the current Italian states. Along with very few other examples, Cesare Borgia stands out for his military policy and contrasts with the general misery of the Italian custom of using mercenary and auxiliary forces. After having experienced them, Cesare decides to become militarily self-sufficient. Thus, he also becomes greater and more esteemed than everyone else, being 'the total owner of his arms'.[39] Machiavelli does not hesitate to put him together with a mythical and biblical example drawn from the Old Testament:

When David offered Saul to go and fight Goliath, the Philistine challenger, Saul, to give him spirit, armed him with his own arms – which David, as soon as he had them on, refused, saying that with them he could not give a good account of himself, and so he would rather meet the enemy with his sling and his knife.[40]

Valentino thus grasps some of the necessary elements for grounding a new stable power. At the same time, being a son of *fortuna*, he is forced to use extraordinary means, and build his favourable occasions against fate and conflicting forces. He must quickly acquire, then, those *virtù* that make a ruler despicable according to the standards of morality, but that are indeed necessary if one wants to succeed.

Once again, however, Machiavelli is interested not only in the formal character of these skills, but also in their contents and political meaning. Asking, in Chapter XVII of *The Prince*, 'whether it is better to be loved than feared', Machiavelli dismantles the canonic and easiest assumption: 'The response – he maintains – is that one would want to be both the one and the other; but because it is difficult to put them together, it is much safer to be feared than loved, if one has to lack one of the two.'[41] The reason is that being loved largely depends on people's perception of the ruler's actions, while being feared depends on what the ruler actually does. Autonomy, once again, versus heteronomy: a wise ruler should rely on what is under his own control. Significantly, Valentino is one more time presented as a virtuous model, surpassing also – especially – Machiavelli's own beloved city:

Cesare Borgia was held to be cruel; nonetheless his cruelty restored the Romagna, united it, and reduced it to peace and to faith. If one considers this well, one will see that he was much more merciful than the Florentine people, who so as to escape a name for cruelty, allowed Pistoia to be destroyed. A prince, therefore, so as to keep his subjects united and faithful, should not care about the infamy of cruelty, because with very few examples he will be more merciful than those who for the sake of too much mercy allow disorders to continue, from which come killings or robberies; for these customarily hurt a whole community, but the executions that come from the prince hurt one particular person.[42]

Borgia acted cruelly, but for what purpose? To unite his domain and make it more powerful and capable of resisting the foreigner's attacks. Valentino the ruler is implicitly compared with the wise lawgiver of the *Discourses*, and, boldly, with Romulus himself, for whom 'it is very suitable that when the deed accuses him, the effect excuses him; and when the effect is good, as was that of Romulus, it will always excuse the deed; for he who is violent to spoil, not he who is violent to mend, should be reproved'.[43]

The shadow of Valentino is also projected on to Chapter XVIII of *The Prince*, one of the most controversial of the whole book, in which Machiavelli discusses 'in what mode faith should be kept by princes'. His father Alexander VI is mentioned here, but they both play the same theoretical function in this context. Once again, Machiavelli argues that it would be nice, for the ruler, to be able to 'keep his faith, and to live with honesty and not by astuteness [. . .]. Nonetheless one sees by experience in our times that the princes who have done great things are those who have taken little account of faith and have known how to get around men's brains with their astuteness; and in the end they have overcome those who have founded themselves on loyalty.'[44] Machiavelli is once again reverting the canonical assumptions on the gifts of the good prince.

Precisely as Pope Alexander,[45] and indeed Cesare his son, had been for their whole life, the prince who wants to survive in this world must be a great pretender and dissembler so that he appears to have all the canonical qualities, such as piety, trustworthiness, integrity, humanity and devotion. He does not actually need to have them, but he must seem to. Because the world continually changes, the prince must change accordingly, and be able to show all different faces to *fortuna*, so that he must 'not depart from good, when possible, but know how to enter into evil, when forced by necessity'.[46] Machiavelli illustrates this concept with one of his most powerful metaphors, openly directed against the classic teaching of Cicero:[47]

> Thus, you must know that there are two kinds of combat: one with laws, the other with force. The first is proper to man, the second to beasts; but because the first is often not enough, one must have recourse to the second. Therefore it is necessary for a prince to know well how to use the beast and the man. This role was taught covertly to princes by ancient writers, who wrote of how Achilles, and many other ancient princes, were given to Chiron the centaur to be raised, so that he would look after them with his discipline. To have as a teacher a half-beast, half-man means nothing other than that a prince needs to know how to use both natures; and one without the other is not lasting.[48]

Effectiveness, once again, is the only dimension that counts. Preserving the state is the task, it is the 'end' (if one wants to employ the term of the famous aphorism that 'the end justifies the means'), whose 'means' are always legitimate, because people judge only from results, and from what they see. They judge 'more by their eyes than by their hands', because 'the vulgar [*vulgo*] are taken in by the appearance and the outcome of a thing, and in the world there is no one but the vulgar; the few have no place there when the many have somewhere to lean on'.[49]

The few and the many here appear once again. These last words can be read merely as a criticism of the naivety of the common people, against the attitude of the few wise men, the 'discerning few, those who experience the realities of power, who do not only "see", who are not taken by appearances'. But I think that Machiavelli is suggesting something more profound here, namely the necessity of grounding the state's power on the many, and against the few. The many and the few may also be those who differently perceive appearance and reality. Nevertheless, they are also the political forces between which the prince must decide: either in favour of the people, or in favour of the few, as Machiavelli had made clear in Chapter IX of *The Prince*.

THE ONE, THE FEW AND THE MANY

Chapter IX can be considered the real core of *The Prince*, insofar as this book is not a handbook for tyrants,[50] but a theory of the 'civil principality'.[51] According to Machiavelli's quite generic taxonomy, a principality is 'civil' when 'a private citizen becomes ruler of his own country through the favour of his fellow citizens, not through villainy or intolerable violence'.[52] Although Machiavelli is not developing a discourse limited to the case of Florence, masking it under general language, one can recognise, with several nuances and even considerable differences, two cases that are of the utmost importance for him, the one of Soderini, *gonfaloniere* of Florence's Republic, and the one of the Medici, new rulers of the city after the restoration of 1512. Becoming ruler with the favour of one's own fellow citizens, in fact, does not mean without conflict. And conflictuality is precisely the dimension that Machiavelli is interested in and wants to discuss in this fundamental chapter.

Piero Soderini, a member of the Florentine aristocracy, was made *gonfaloniere* for life in 1502, following four years of turmoil and instability, with the favour of several aristocratic families. Once in office, though, he turned away from aristocratic support and largely favoured the people of Florence and a *governo largo*, a more inclusive government. Machiavelli himself profited from Soderini's popular turn. He also thought, however, that the *gonfaloniere* did not act strongly enough against the great, and especially against the Medici, head of the rival faction in exile, because, as he boldy writes in the *Discourses*, 'it is necessary to kill the sons of Brutus if one wishes to maintain a newly acquired freedom'.[53] Also the Medici, after the fall of the Republic in 1512, became de facto lords of the city with the favour of some families, and somehow represent the situation described by Machiavelli under the title of 'civil principality'. This will become even more clear in the *Discursus florentinarum rerum* (*A Discourse on Florentine Affairs*), addressed to the Medici in 1521 and devoted to a project of constitutional reform of the city. When he writes the chapter on 'civil principality', then, Machiavelli has in mind the concrete situation, past and present, of his city. He also has in mind, though, the political principle that he has always maintained, namely governing in favour of the many and against the few.

The 'civil' prince, Machiavelli maintains, generally faces a cardinal alternative: he has been brought to power either by the favour of the great or by the favour of the people. As in the case of Cesare Borgia, once again, he has been supported by an element that is not under his control. And, once again, the civil prince has to transform this situation in a favourable occasion, by grounding his power on the most stable political basis. Without any hesitation, and against the traditional discourse, Machiavelli strongly proposes that the prince rule in favour of the people. The reason is clear for him: 'The people desire neither to be commanded nor oppressed by the great, and the great desire to command and oppress the people.'[54] The people's aims are more honourable and, most of all, are more easily satisfied by the prince. The nobles are dangerous and untrustworthy, and the power that they might seem to offer to the prince is illusory and unstable, because he will never be able to control it. The people, on the contrary, are trustworthy and deserve the prince's reliance.

This is not only a simple preference, or an abstract alternative that is given to the new civil prince. It is rather a necessity that opens up a horizon of harsh conflictuality within the principality – a conflictuality that can be eliminated only in the utopian dreams of the golden age. The effectual truth is a different one:

> One who becomes prince through the support of the people should keep them friendly to him, which should be easy for him because they ask of him only that they not be oppressed. But one who becomes prince against the people with the support of the great must before everything else seek to gain the people to himself, which should be easy for him when he takes up their protection. And since men who receive good from someone from whom they believed they would receive evil are more obliged to their benefactor, the people immediately wish him well more than if he had been brought to the principality with their support. The prince can gain the people to himself in many modes, for which one cannot give certain rules because the modes vary according to circumstances, and so they will be left out. I will conclude only that for a prince it is necessary to have the people friendly; otherwise he has no remedy in adversity.[55]

This sounds, once again, more like a heartfelt appeal than like cold advice given to the wicked prince who aspires to become an absolute ruler.[56] This is not only the story of Soderini or the Medici, nor is it only Machiavelli's abstract preference for the people against the great. The civil principality is a theoretical core in which politics and the experience of modern affairs mingle with theory and the study of history. *The Prince* is here perfectly consistent with the popular attitude of the *Discourses*. Democracy is not at stake in this book devoted to the individual ruler. Yet if there is a 'democratic' attitude of Machiavelli, this is strongly expressed in this fundamental chapter on the civil principality. And, unlike many ancient and contemporary theorists, Machiavelli does not forget that the democratic foundation of the princely power is a conflictual one, where the *kratos* (power) is important at least as much as the *demos* (people). The civil principality does not open up the space for a peaceful coexistence of different forces. Like the *Discourses*, on the contrary, it opens up the tumultuous space of social and political conflictuality – a conflictuality that will be developed and investigated even further, by Machiavelli, in his main historical work, the *Florentine Histories*.

5. History as Politics

BACK TO THE GRIND

Between 1520 and 1525, Machiavelli produced some of the most important works of his whole career: the so-called historical works – the *Life of Castruccio Castracani* and the *Florentine Histories* – and the *Discursus florentinarum rerum*. The *Life of Castruccio*, dedicated to Zanobi Buondelmonti (also one of the dedicatees of the *Discourses*) and Luigi Alamanni, is the largely imaginary account of the mythical fourteenth-century *condottiere* from Lucca, who fiercely fought against Florence to enlarge his domain and unify Tuscany under his rule. This short piece of mythography was intended as an essay of historical reconstruction to be presented to the friends of the Oricellari Gardens, where it was read and commented on in 1520. It was also intended to be a preparatory essay for a larger and most important historical work that Machiavelli was about to be commissioned to write by Cardinal Giulio de' Medici and was eventually presented to him, now Pope Clement VII, in 1521. Within the same commission, Machiavelli was asked to offer his opinion on a potential constitutional reform for the city of Florence, which was submitted to Giulio and Giovanni de' Medici in the same year, with the title of *Discursus florentinarum rerum post mortem iunioris Laurentii Medices*. These works are coherently connected with each other and testify to a consistent attitude toward the new Medici regime and toward politics in general, in this last period of Machiavelli's intellectual life.

CASTRUCCIO

The main source for Machiavelli's reworking of his *Castruccio* is Niccolò Tegrimi's life of the *condottiere*, written in Latin and according to the humanist canon of celebration of this man who represents, to the people of Lucca, the last bite of glory for that Tuscan city.[1] Besides the irony of choosing to write about one of the fiercest enemies of Florence in preparation for his work on the history of Florence itself, however, Machiavelli transforms the mythographic materials to explore, once again, the figure of the new prince, this time in a rather fictional way. His Castruccio, who only shares some elements with the historical figure, reflects some of the most striking features of *The Prince*. Against the humanist model of biography, illustriously represented by works such as Petrarch's *De viris illustribus* (*On Illustrious Men*), Machiavelli's *Castruccio* also becomes a lively example of virtuous action against the background of a violent world dominated by factions, treasons and the treacherous and destructive power of *fortuna*. By reworking the classic models of Plutarch, Suetonius and Sallust, Machiavelli appropriates this historical material in order to write, with a different language and method, another chapter of his own political theory.

Like Cesare Borgia, Castruccio is, in Machiavelli's eyes, a son of *fortuna*. *Fortuna*, in fact, 'wishing to show the world that she – and not Prudence – makes men great, first shows her forces at a time when Prudence can have no share in the matter, but rather everything must be recognized as coming from herself'.[2] Castruccio enters the stage as a child found in a vineyard, brought up by a cleric first, and then adopted by Francesco Guinigi, one of the most prominent nobles in town, who by chance discovers his aptitude and skills. Although owing much to *fortuna*, in his tumultuous life Castruccio shows precisely those abilities that Machiavelli considers the necessary features of the virtuous prince. He becomes a strong military *condottiere* and the prominent figure of his town's life. He has military as well as diplomatic skills. In a treacherous world, he recognises his best allies, and he especially favours the people of Lucca while playing at the same time a smart game against the disloyal families of the great. Most of all, Machiavelli describes his enterprise of gathering an army of 20,000 citizens, in the territory of Lucca, to fight the war against Florence and in order not to depend on his allies' forces. What could a mythical *condottiere* do, more than this, to deserve Machiavelli's praise?

Castruccio's experience, therefore, evokes Valentino's life, but also Agathocles's and his virtuous example illustrated in *The Prince*.[3] Once again, though, *fortuna*, 'hostile to his fame', puts an end to Castruccio's life. After winning a fierce battle against the Florentines, he decides to wait for his soldiers and pay homage to them:

> All weary and soaked with sweat, he stood still near the gate of Fucecchio
> [. . .] judging it the duty of a good general to be the first to mount his horse
> and the last to dismount. Hence, standing exposed to a wind that generally

at midday rises from up the Arno and is almost always unhealthful, he grew cold as ice. This, not being regarded by him, as one who was used to such discomforts, was the cause of his death, because the next night he was attacked by a very severe fever.[4]

After having saved the emperor's power in Rome and having been nominated senator, after having put together one of the strongest territorial powers in Tuscany and Italy, and having represented the greatest danger for Florence, Castruccio is killed by a fortuitous fever. Machiavelli offers once again abundant material to reflect on the dialectic between *fortuna* and *virtù*, as well as on the necessity to consider history as the theatre where men can better learn it. The design of the *Florentine Histories* is thus clearly prepared: it represents precisely this theatre, where political and theoretical conceptions are once again tested by Machiavelli and offered to the wise reader.

THE *FLORENTINE HISTORIES*

Machiavelli started working on the *Histories* between 1520 and 1521. He would work on it for four years, mainly in his forced retirement at Sant'Andrea in Percussina. In the darkest period of his political isolation, he had written to his friend Vettori about his desire that the Medici would employ him, even if only at 'rolling a stone'.[5] And he now had a stone in his hands. He was far from occupying one of the most crucial positions in the government, as it was in the time of the chancery, but at least he was able to think about politics once again, and he had the prestige of being appointed the historian of his own city. This was a high recognition in the culture of the time. The city's chancellors traditionally performed this role and wrote histories of Florence that represented a political testament as much as a historical account. His illustrious predecessors are Poggio Bracciolini, Leonardo Bruni and Bartolomeo Scala, whose works constitute the political memory of Florence's struggle against the other Italian powers, as well as of the origin and development of its republican institutions.

The first set of problems that Machiavelli has to consider is therefore the relationship with this tradition, representing an important heritage of the humanist culture. The first choice that Machiavelli makes, being given complete freedom on this point, is to write his *Histories* in Italian and not in Latin. The use of the 'language of the people' had already been commended by Dante and by many other illustrious authors.[6] Yet the choice is not trivial and Machiavelli makes clear, in this way, that he will consider the *Histories* not as another work of celebration of Florence's status and nobility, but rather as a powerful tool of political analysis of the origin and causes of the present situation. He chooses, in short, the most difficult and potentially controversial pattern – the only one, though, that makes sense in his mind.

This pattern is made even more difficult, in Machiavelli's case, by the sensitive relationship with his patrons. While his predecessors had written in easier circumstances, Machiavelli has fallen into disgrace, and will now be carefully scrutinised by everyone on what he has to say about the city's history but, most of all, on the role played by the Medici family in this history. The risk is great of either flattering them or offending them, in both cases by saying too much or not enough. Machiavelli is of course well aware of this risk, as he testifies in a letter to his friend Francesco Guicciardini at a later stage of his work: 'I would pay ten soldi – I do not intend to say more – to have you by my side so that I could show you where I am, because, having to come to certain particulars, I need to learn from you if I give too much offence either by raising or by lowering these things. But I shall keep on taking counsel with myself and shall try to act in such a way that, since I tell the truth, nobody will be able to complain.'[7]

The truth he certainly says, as he has always done, to his fellow citizens as well as to his enemies. And because of the truth – a different truth – he decides to move away from the illustrious predecessors whose works he is forced to tackle. In the preface, he openly discusses two sensitive issues, strongly intertwined, and explains the grounds of his unconventional decisions. The first one concerns the periodisation and the choice of the point of departure of the reconstruction. Machiavelli explains that he first thought to begin with 1434, the year the Medici family 'gained more authority than anyone else in Florence',[8] as he thought that Bracciolini and Bruni had already told everything in their histories. Eventually, though, having better considered their works, he changes his mind and decides to begin the history 'from the beginning of [the] city', namely from its foundation. With an attitude that reveals the sensibility of the modern historian, Machiavelli feels that, since the inception, the city's history cannot be isolated and separated from those of other cities, of other peoples and external events. The city's history must be integrated into a wider dimension, in order that a present-day audience can better understand its development and its heritage. The theory of the republics' intertwined and conflictual cycles of life, described in the *Discourses* and representing the most original reworking of Polybius's theory, is put to work on the concrete domain of the historical account.

The second point discussed in the preface is even more delicate, and directly concerns the content and matter of the *Histories*. Machiavelli dares to openly criticise the 'two very excellent historians' who wrote before him, for the choice they made. In fact, Machiavelli writes,

> I found that in the descriptions of the wars waged by the Florentines with foreign princes and peoples they had been very diligent, but as regards civil discords and internal enmities, and the effects arising from them, they were altogether silent about the one and so brief about the other as to be of no use to readers or pleasure to anyone. I believe they did this either because these actions seemed to them so feeble that they judged them unworthy of being committed to memory by written word, or because they feared that they might offend the descendants of those they might have to slander in their narrations. These two causes (may it be said by their leave) appear to me altogether unworthy of great men, for if nothing else delights or instructs in history, it is that which is described in detail: if no other lesson is useful to the citizens who govern republics, it is that which shows the causes of the hatreds and divisions of the city, so that when they have become wise through the dangers of the others, they may be able to maintain themselves united. And if every example of a republic is moving, those which he reads concerning one's own are much more so and much more useful.[9]

A bolder exordium, for the city's history, is hard to imagine. Social and political conflict had been put at the centre of the stage in the *Discourses*, and had been the ground for maintaining seminal theses in other works, such as *The Prince* and its theory of the civil principality. Here, once again, Machiavelli states that the historian's account must focus mainly on civil discords, in order to produce a meaningful knowledge of the past as much as a useful ground for the present and the future politics needed to keep the city together and make it stronger and free.

THE CRISIS OF MACHIAVELLI'S POLITICAL THOUGHT?

Scholars have argued that the historical works, and especially the *Florentine Histories*, represent a crisis of Machiavelli's political thought: a crisis due to his personal experience, as well as to the material impossibility of maintaining his theoretical position in the new political scenario.[10] The strongest positions held in the *Discourses* and in *The Prince*, centred around *virtù*, lose, for those scholars, their strength, and leave space only for a horizon of crisis, fully deployed by Machiavelli in front of the reader's eyes, especially in the *Histories*: in the best case, 'there isn't anything politically new in the *Histories*'.[11]

I think that this judgement does not do justice to the complexity of Machiavelli's political positions. The *Florentine Histories* represent in fact the opposite, that is to say the boldest attempt, by Machiavelli, to reinterpret the conclusions reached in his previous works and put them to the test on the history of his city. As he maintains in his daring preface to the *Histories*, the analysis of the divisions and conflicts is not intended to support any moral condemnation or inflict any theoretical self-flagellation. It is, on the contrary, the necessary tool for better understanding the origin of the present day's divisions, and the intimate social structure of the city. This, and only this, can make history a powerful hermeneutical tool.

History, moreover, acquires a strategic importance precisely because it addresses the peculiarity of a city, and makes it possible to distinguish it from other similar cases and better understand it. This is what happens concerning Florence's conflicts which, being different from those of Rome, for example, not only tell another story, but also render another political outcome possible. Machiavelli adds in the preface that

> in Rome, as everyone knows, after the kings were driven out, disunion between the nobles and the plebs arose and Rome was maintained by it until its ruin. So it was in Athens, and so in all the other republics flourishing in those times. But in Florence the nobles were, first, divided among themselves; then the nobles and the people; and in the end the people and the plebs: and it happened many times that the winning party was divided in two. From such divisions came as many dead, as many exiles, and as many families destroyed as ever occurred in any city in memory. And truly, in my judgment no other instance appears to me to show so well the power of our city as the one derived from these divisions, which would have had the force to annihilate any great and very powerful city. Nonetheless ours, it appeared, became ever greater from them; so great was the *virtù* of those citizens and the power of their genius and their spirit to make themselves and their fatherland great that as many as remained free from so many evils were more able by their *virtù* to exalt it, than could the malice of those accidents that had diminished it overwhelm it.[12]

Notwithstanding the violence of the Florentine conflicts, the city has survived and maintained its independence and internal freedom. It is certainly not the time for celebration, though, as Machiavelli knows all too well. The independence from foreign powers is precarious, and the internal freedom is in the hands of the Medici family. Scholars who maintain that the *Florentine Histories* represent the crisis of Machiavelli's political thought tend to read this last passage as an ironic account through which Machiavelli would hide, under the name of freedom, what he in fact sees as the misery of the ultimate decadence of his own time.

Machiavelli's text, though, does not seem to be ironic at all. He describes the series of conflicts that progressively destroy the feudal powers – the nobles – and bring to the forefront the new bourgeois families – the people – that keep dividing and struggling among themselves. He also describes the entrance of the *popolo minuto* (the poorer class) and the plebs on to the political scene, as actors playing significant roles. He carries on, in short, the complex meditation that he had started in the previous works, by being faithful to the principles that have always guided his thought: the pre-eminence of the people over the great, and the positive evaluation of social conflict for the internal and external dynamics of a republic. As it was in the case of Rome after the Gracchi, these conflicts seem to cause destruction rather than freedom and power. However, as Machiavelli keeps repeating, the historian must be able to develop a deeper sight and go beyond the surface of events, deep into the past of a political body, in order to better comprehend its present.

The general preface is closely related to the prefatory chapters of the eight books of the *Florentine Histories*. These chapters roughly anticipate the content but, most of all, give directions on the theoretical dimension of what follows and connect it with the general design of the work. The introductory chapters of Books I to V were probably written together,[13] and can be read together as a summary of Machiavelli's theory of history, as well as the explanation of the main philosophical themes developed in the *Histories* and connected with the previous works: the importance of peoples' migrations to open and characterise new historical periods, the corruption of *virtù* and the emperors' responsibility in the decline and fall of the Roman Empire, the rise of new cities and powers – Florence among them – from the Roman ashes, the originary conflicts that tear apart Florence from its earliest times, the relationship between conflicts and laws and its meaning for freedom, the blame for the mercenary armies and the misery of Italy's military history, the financial and economic roots of politics and war. Formally, then, the prefatory chapters might resemble those of some medieval source, such as Giovanni Villani's *Cronica*.[14] Yet Machiavelli consciously deviates from their formal and rhetorical use, to present, on the contrary, a powerfully modern and original pattern of the theory of history in which he reworks his main political conclusions, sometimes giving them a twist that is even more radical than in previous works.[15] One of these conclusions, which underlines the whole *Florentine Histories*, is the critique of the common good.

THE IMPOSTURE OF THE COMMON GOOD

The common good has had a long and noble tradition in the history of political thought since its inception in the Greek and Roman world.

It traditionally represents the higher end that a community can aim at, and the strongest ground of its peace and stability. Through the Christian Middle Ages, it reached the Renaissance, and the humanist world was deeply informed by this ethical and political principle. Ethics is in fact its very origin, in the Aristotelian seminal theory concerning the natural division of roles, within society, between father and son, husband and wife, as well as master and slave, who must all embrace their diversity and accept the respective role assigned in the society, because they ultimately have 'the same interests'.[16] The friendship underlining these relationships guarantees that they will be governed with justice and reciprocity. The good of the whole community thus depends on the concord or *omonoia* that rules out any ground for conflictuality or rebellion.[17]

Humanist thought is deeply concerned by the issue of common good, as it stands as the natural antidote against the spirit of despotism and tyranny. Over the decades and in the deep crisis of the late Renaissance, however, which brings the 'effectual truth' of politics to light, the common good progressively becomes nothing more than a formula, rhetorically empty and incapable of both explaining political reality and offering effectual tools to resist its violence. In Machiavelli's time, for example, the rhetoric of the common good was alternatively used, together with inflaming denunciations, by a key figure of Florentine politics, the Dominican friar Girolamo Savonarola. The Thomist tradition recommending harmony and concord and the revolutionary tradition threatening apocalyptic condemnation converge in Savonarola, whom Machiavelli blames in the *Discourses* as a typical example of an 'unarmed prophet'.[18] In his *Treatise on the Rule and Government of Florence*, as well as in his sermons, Savonarola asserts the need for 'unity', strongly maintaining that 'where unity is greatest, there is greatest force, but whoever lives in grace and charity has greater union and therefore greater force'.[19]

In Florence, the 'name' of freedom has always been employed against the one of tyranny. In Florentine minds, the tyrant has always represented the negation of the spirit of freedom, corresponding to the common good opposed to private interest.[20] Savonarola pursues this humanist tradition of thought, describing the tyrant, whose aim is to usurp the city's freedom, as an almost inhuman or bestial force, who introduces discord and conflict within the city.[21] His claim, however, also grasps an aspect that is crucially important in the violently partisan life of Medicean Florence, namely the economic dimension of politics and political clientelism. He addresses the Florentines in this way:

I would like you to have one heart and a single soul and for each and every one of you to be occupied with the common good: and with the good you receive from the city, and I would like you to be grateful to the city and to the public rather than to some private citizen. [. . .] If you do as I say, two types of good will result: one relating to your lack of turmoil and freedom, and the other to temporal goods, which increase whenever there is peace and quiet, and you will always have a better name and reputation with your neighbours, and all shall stand in awe of you.[22]

The common good becomes in his eyes the antidote to clientelism and the private administration of the public good, an attitude that Machiavelli shares, but not, however, through the same vague rhetoric and empty message employed by Savonarola. Machiavelli's sarcasm is directed precisely against those generic formulae, intended to capture an agreement as universal as it is impossible to obtain.

Machiavelli, who is well aware of the tradition of the common good and the role it plays in Florentine political thought, brings into play a powerful rhetorical strategy. He makes use of the concept of 'common good', yet reworking it, transforming it and essentially emptying it of its original meaning. One of the main aims of the *Florentine Histories*, throughout its most conflictual books, is precisely to show the emptiness and vagueness of the common good, upon which traditional politics was based, revealing at the same time the necessity to step out of that rhetoric and fully grasp the necessary partial and conflictual nature of politics. In order to make this concept clear to his city for the present, Machiavelli goes back to its past, and reads Florentine history in a completely different light, attacking the concept of concord and common good.

Machiavelli recounts, for example, the story of Walter of Brienne, Duke of Athens, invited to Florence to pacify the struggle between the people and the great. The Duke shows his most human side, secretly preparing to seize power and crush both factions, as well as the Florentine liberty, under his yoke. To the late protests of some citizens, he responds that 'it was not his intention to take freedom away from the city but to restore it; for only disunited cities were enslaved and united ones free. And if Florence, by his ordering, should rid itself of sects, ambition, and enmities, he would be giving it liberty, not taking that away. It was not his ambition but the prayers of many citizens that led him to take on this charge; so they would do well to content themselves with what contented others.'[23] The tyrant, in Machiavelli's eyes, marches over the city's freedom holding high the standard of union and the common good.

By dismantling the traditional praise for the common good,

Machiavelli introduces a new paradigm for the interpretation of politics. History makes now visible, for him and for the alerted reader of the *Histories*, that war, and not concord, is the key phenomenon to interpret and act on in politics. Machiavelli goes back once again to the time of the war against Castruccio Castracani, in the early fourteenth century. This time, though, Machiavelli illustrates the Florentines' side of the struggle and the divisions that lacerate the city, not in order to morally blame them, but rather to show how one single point of view has become impossible to obtain. External war makes clear the irredeemably partial character of internal politics. The Florentine parties, in Machiavelli's account, reach a temporary agreement to resist the invader. As soon as the assault is stopped, though,

> this gave rise to dispute in the Florentine camp between the nobles and the people: the people wanted to follow [Castruccio], while the nobles wanted to return, saying that it was enough to have put Florence in peril in order to free Prato. It had been well when they were compelled by necessity, but now that necessity was absent, when they could acquire little and lose much, it was no time to tempt fortune. As they were unable to agree, the judgment was put to the Signori, who found the same dispute between the people and the great in the councils. When this was heard through the city, it brought many people together in the piazza uttering words full of menace against the great: so the great yielded out of fear.[24]

The story of Castruccio's pursuit clarifies the extension of war into the domestic situation: war and politics are two aspects of the same reality, because conflict is the essence of both. Machiavelli claims, in the prefatory chapter of Book VI, that 'it has always been the end of those who start a war – and it is reasonable that it should be so – to enrich themselves and impoverish the enemy. For no other cause is victory sought, nor for anyone else are acquisitions desired than to make oneself powerful and the adversary weak.'[25] This seems an apparently self-evident statement. Yet if it is considered within Machiavelli's introduction of war as the paradigm for understanding politics, it becomes a bold and powerfully modern assertion. 'Enrich oneself and impoverish the enemy', in fact, is true not only for the outside, but also for the inside, for the different and opposed parties of the city. The people and the great might appear to be engaged in the same war against the foreign enemy, but in fact they are, at the same time, inevitably taken in the internal struggle against each other.

Thus, in the *Florentine Histories*, Machiavelli's aim becomes more and more not only recounting past events, but also reconstructing this conflictual memory as a political tool for the present. The more the description approaches the present time, the more his criticism of the common good becomes a positive evaluation of social conflict in the city's life. In the fourth book, for example, Machiavelli engages with the story of the war against the Visconti of Milan. The city is again divided into two parts, one more prudent and favourable to peace and one desiring a more aggressive policy. New taxes are imposed to support the war, but this makes clear, once again, the different positions of the actors involved in the struggle. In fact, 'since the taxes weighed more on the lesser citizens than the greater, they filled the city with complaints, and everyone condemned the ambition and greed of the powerful, accusing them of wishing to start an unnecessary war so as to indulge their appetites and to oppress the people so as to dominate them'.[26] The war is a double-sided event, necessarily producing effects on the foreign as well as on the home battlefield. When the Florentine army is defeated at Zagonara, in 1424, the counterposed humours explode:

> At the news of this defeat, the whole city of Florence grieved, but especially the great citizens who had advised the war, because they saw the enemy vigorous and themselves disarmed, without friends, and the people against them. Through all the piazzas the people stung them with abusive words, complaining of the taxes they had borne, of a war begun without a cause, and saying: 'Now, did they create the Ten [Florence's military council] to bring terror to the enemy? Now, have they rescued Forlì and taken it from the hands of the duke? Look at how their advice has been exposed and to what end they were moving: not to defend freedom, which is their enemy, but to increase their own power, which God has justly diminished. They have burdened the city not only with this campaign but with many, because the one against King Ladislas was like this one. To whom will they now turn for help?'[27]

Machiavelli unveils the logic that binds together domestic and foreign politics, as well as war and social conflict. The medieval and humanist horizon of the common good seems definitely to have been overcome, in the direction of a new, more modern approach to the tragic reality of politics.

Machiavelli's modernity is represented also by the attention devoted to the economic aspects operating within the new paradigm and characterising this new logic. Economy and the economic background of social struggle already play an important role in *The Prince* and the *Discourses*, such as in the nature and outcomes of the Gracchi's Agrarian law. Yet Machiavelli's considerations remain quite superficial in those works, while in the *Florentine Histories* a much larger space and a much deeper importance is assigned to them in the political reconstruction of the city's life. One of the main aspects of this new attitude of Machiavelli is illustrated by the discussion of the *catasto*, a tax system based on property valuation rather than income, introduced in the 1420s.

A proposal is advanced to introduce a new tax to finance the military effort and continue the war against Milan. Once again, through fictional discourses, Machiavelli illustrates the two counterposed positions:

> [Great men] condemned it ceaselessly, declaring that it was most unjust because it was imposed also on movable goods, which might be possessed today and lost tomorrow; and that beyond this, many persons had hidden money that the catasto could not find. To which they added that those who had left their business in order to govern the republic ought to be less burdened by it, as it ought to be enough that they had labored in person; and it was not just that the city should enjoy their belongings and their industry and only the money of others. Others who were pleased with the catasto answered that if movable goods vary, the taxes could also vary, and frequent variation of them could remedy that inconvenience. And as for those who had hidden money, it was not necessary to take account of it, as it is not reasonable to pay for money that bears no fruit; when it does bear fruit, it must be discovered; and if to take trouble for the republic did not please them, let them put it aside and not try themselves over it, because the republic would find more loving citizens to whom it would not appear difficult to help it with money and advice; and so many are the advantages and honors that go with governing that these ought to be enough for them without wishing not to share the burdens.[28]

Here, Machiavelli approaches more and more the essence of the conflict, and reveals with lucidity what is at stake, namely the very nature of the parties involved in the struggle. A common good, a common solution to the city's problem, is materially impossible, because the city 'matter' itself is made up of conflicting parties with conflicting interests. War becomes the paradigm to interpret this new revealed reality. War describes not only Florence's foreign relations, but the relation of parties and factions within the city. The great complain because 'it pained them not to be able to carry on a war without loss to themselves, having to share in the expenses like others'.[29] They want the benefit of a possible victory at war, but they want the people to pay the full price of it. If Florentines are divided on the modality of organising and making this war, it is because they are not all fighting the same war or, in other words, they are also fighting each other, through the same war. There is no 'common' good.

This process of unmasking the ideology of the common good is even more tragic, in Machiavelli's eyes, because he is well aware that the truth is not made stronger by its own evidence and by being fully revealed. The political reality, which is one of factionalism and partisanship, disguises itself as promoting the common good. The ideology of the common good, in this sense, is particularly resistant to the 'effectual truth'.

Machiavelli demonstrates this with the example of the Medici family and in particular of Cosimo, the *pater patriae*, whom he overtly accuses of 'buying' the liberty of Florence. Once again, Machiavelli puts his truth in the words of the old and wise citizen Niccolò da Uzzano, whom the nobles want to put at the forefront and make lead the resistance to the Medici. Niccolò Barbadori[30] implores him to accept the burden, but he tragically and realistically frustrates the great's expectation: 'It would be better for you,' he responds to Niccolò, 'for your house, and for your republic if you and the others who follow you in this opinion had beards of silver rather than gold, as they say you have; for their counsels, coming from a grey head full of experience, would be wiser and more useful to everyone.'[31] After having unmasked the functioning of the ideology of the common good, Machiavelli reveals now its powerful ground, and how difficult and dangerous it is to fight against it:

> The deeds of Cosimo that make us suspect him are these: because he helps everyone with his money, and not only private individuals but the public, and not only Florentines but the condottieri; because he favors this or that citizen who has need of the magistrates; because by the good will that he has in the generality of the people he pulls this or that friend to higher ranks of honor. Thus one would have to allege as the causes for driving him out that he is merciful, helpful, liberal, and loved by everyone. So tell me: what law is it that forbids or that blames and condemns in men mercy, liberality, and love? And although these are all modes that send men flying to a princedom, nonetheless they are not believed to be so, nor are we adequate to the task of making them be so understood, because our modes have destroyed their faith in us, and the city, which is naturally partisan and, since it has always lived with parties, is corrupt, cannot give a hearing to such accusations.[32]

Behind the veil of his liberality, Cosimo is literally buying the city, piece after piece, building on his reputation. A private citizen is becoming prince of Florence, not suffocating the common good, but rather using it as the banner behind which he helps tyranny come forward.

Machiavelli's theory of conflict resonates in this page. In the *Discourses* he maintains that conflict had kept Rome free and that, notwithstanding the catastrophic outcomes of the Agrarian law, without those conflicts, the city 'would perhaps have been led into servitude much sooner'. The most tragic reality that the wise Niccolò da Uzzano reveals, from the standpoint of the great and against the new alliance between the Medici family and the people, is that it is too late to resist, and it is useless to even think about any kind of struggle against them. At this stage of corruption, there is no space for conflict any more, only for peace, tyranny and . . . the common good.

ROME AND FLORENCE: THE CRISIS AS OCCASION

The city of Florence is 'naturally partisan'. Its history is a continual development of factional struggles that shows its past and present state of corruption but also, paradoxically, the opportunities – and occasions – offered to whoever would and could reorder it in a new form of government. Scholars have maintained that the crisis of Machiavelli's political thought is clearly represented by the different nature of conflicts characterising Rome and Florence, and thus they have claimed the necessity of setting apart the *Discourses* and the *Florentine Histories*. They have tended to read Machiavelli's praise for social conflict through the opposition between parties and factions, as well as the related opposition between political and economic conflicts. Whereas the former are supposedly moderate, can be institutionalised, and can produce good laws for the sake of the common good, the latter are supposedly violent and extreme, cannot be institutionalised, and lead to the corruption and decadence of the republic. Within the former, only political honours are at stake, while the latter are mainly focused around wealth. This opposition, already present in the *Discourses*, becomes particularly evident in the *Florentine Histories*, where Machiavelli supposedly condemns the factional spirit of the Florentine politics, opposing it to the *virtù* of Rome.[33]

Although sketched in the first chapters of the *Discourses*, the contrast between moderate and political conflicts on the one hand and violent and economic conflicts on the other is in fact dismissed by Machiavelli himself in the *Florentine Histories*. Machiavelli is more and more interested in showing how politics and economics cannot be separated, and that Florence actually is the paradigm of the concrete possibility of transformation, precisely for the very nature and intensity of its own conflicts. In order to present this inconvenient and unconventional position, Machiavelli develops an original and powerful analysis of the most conflictual period of the history of Florence, in the fourteenth century, long before the establishment of the corrupted and apparently unshakeable power of the Medici. The central book of the *Florentine Histories*, in this sense, is Book III, and the central event of the city's history is the Revolt of the *ciompi*, the powerful wool workers, in 1378.[34]

In Machiavelli's eyes, the *ciompi* uprising is not just one conflict among others. Staging the struggle between this powerful but underrepresented guild of new plebeians and the citizens of higher status, Machiavelli is aware of touching a chord. The city is torn apart and, once again, Machiavelli makes use of his favourite rhetorical device, counterposing two fictional speeches, the one of the *gonfaloniere* Luigi Guicciardini, trying to calm spirits before the explosion of violence, and the other of an anonymous *ciompo*, trying on the contrary to animate his comrades to action and violent resistance. Guicciardini's words represent the point of view of the great, who consider themselves men of a higher rank, deserving the lowest's recognition for their role in leading the city. Thus, he blames the vile plebeians for both the nature and the mode of their claiming:

> What end will these demands of yours have, or how long will you abuse our liberality? Do you not see that we tolerate being conquered with more patience than you tolerate victory? To what will your disunions lead this city of yours? Do you not remember that when it was disunited Castruccio, a vile citizen of Lucca, defeated it? That a duke of Athens, one of your private condottieri, subjugated it? But when it was united, neither an archbishop of Milan nor a pope could defeat it, and after many years of war, they were left in shame. Why, then, do you want your discords to make a slave of a city in peace that so many powerful enemies left free in war? What do you get out of your disunion other than servitude? Or of the goods that you have stolen or would steal from us other than poverty? For those are the things that, with our industry, nourish the whole city; and if it is despoiled of them, they cannot nourish it; and those who will seize them, as things ill acquired, will not know how to preserve them: from this, hunger and poverty will come to the city.[35]

The mantra of social peace, concord and harmony within diversity resonates in Guicciardini's words. What also resonates, though, is the empty ideology of the common good. The *gonfaloniere* is not able to go beyond the surface of the struggle in order to grasp the fact that it is not the level of violence that makes this tumult different from many others, but it is rather its economic ground and reason. This new ground speaks about an institutional balance that no longer reflects the economic structure of the city.

The political institutions' ignoring of this new reality causes the *ciompi* to suffer from the distance between their fundamentally important role in the economy of the city and their almost completely unrecognised status in its politics. From this ground, the anonymous *ciompo* is able to lucidly express radical ideas that closely reflect many of Machiavelli's own conclusions. First of all, the *ciompo* recognises the role of necessity in the struggle, and the absence of any space of mediation, when things have arrived at such a level of gravity and radicality:

> Certainly I believe that if others do not teach us, necessity does. [. . .] We must therefore seek two things [. . .]: one is to make it impossible for us to be punished for the things we have done in recent days, and the other is to

be able to live with more freedom and more satisfaction than we have in the past. It is to our advantage, therefore, as it appears to me, if we wish that our old errors be forgiven us, to make new ones, redoubling the evils, multiplying the arson and robbery – and to contrive to have many companions in this, because when many err, no one is punished, and though small faults are punished, great and grave ones are rewarded; [. . .] it appears to me that we are on the way to a sure acquisition, because those who could hinder us are disunited and rich: their disunion will therefore give us victory, and their riches, when they have become ours, will maintain it for us.[36]

The strategy proposed by the *ciompo* may sound rough and naive, and yet one cannot help thinking that such naivety contains a deep truth. The 'effectual truth' of politics is, in this sense, quite crude compared to the sophistication and elaboration of the great's supposedly wiser vision. The *ciompo* appears to embody a plebeian version of the reckless prince, acting effectually and faster than his own enemies, as Machiavelli had learnt from the wicked and yet virtuous Valentino.

Even more striking, though, is the egalitarian content of the *ciompo*'s speech, which this reckless strategy is intended to support. To the pretentious assertion of the *gonfaloniere* Guicciardini, claiming superiority for the great over the people, the *ciompo* responds on the same anthropological terrain, developing a radically egalitarian point of view on humankind: 'Strip us all naked, you will see that we are alike; dress us in their clothes and them in ours, and without a doubt we shall appear noble and they ignoble, for only poverty and riches make us unequal.'[37] The *ciompo* dares to wipe away the boundaries of nobility, stating that they are built only on material circumstances deriving from the difference in possessions: the rich and the poor are 'men alike'. This might seem, again, a naive claim, and yet it is one of the boldest of the whole work, directed by Machiavelli against a centuries-old tradition of aristocratic thinking.

The field is finally open for the *ciompo* to address his plebeian audience with some maxims directly drawn from Machiavelli's theoretical arsenal:

Neither conscience nor infamy should dismay you, because those who win, in whatever mode they win, never receive shame from it. And we ought not to take conscience into account, for where there is, as with us, fear of hunger and prison, there cannot and should not be fear of hell. But if you will take note of the mode of proceeding of men, you will see that all those who come to great riches and great power have obtained them either by fraud or by force; and afterwards, to hide the ugliness of acquisition, they make it decent by applying the false title of earnings to things they have usurped by deceit or by violence. And those who, out of either little prudence or too much foolishness, shun these modes always suffocate in servitude and poverty. For faithful servants are always servants and good men are always poor; nor do they ever rise out of servitude unless they are unfaithful and bold, nor out of poverty unless they are rapacious and fraudulent. For God and nature have put all the fortunes of men in their midst, where they are exposed more to rapine than to industry and more to wicked than to good arts, from which it arises that men devour one another and that those who can do less are always the worst off.[38]

Machiavelli's political programme in the 1520s cannot be the same as the *ciompi*'s in the fourteenth century. This is not a sign of inconsistency in Machiavelli's argument though. It is even more significant, on the contrary, that Machiavelli puts many of his powerful ideas into the *ciompo*'s mouth. The orator's speech offers an unveiled explanation of the mechanisms of domination and exploitation that always characterise the great's attitude toward the people and the plebs. It also offers the call for a violent and necessary resistance, restating some of the most striking conclusions of the previous works: power can be and often is obtained by fraud and force, usurpations are passed off as honest earnings, good and honest men are prey of the wicked ones, government is a matter of force, and the pair formed by politics and economics has more to do with war than with peaceful and just administration. There is no such thing as an honest earning: Guicciardini's faction had previously usurped with force and violence, from the past nobility, those goods and riches that the *ciompi* are now claiming for themselves with a similar force and violence.

The city has reached its extreme degree of conflictual violence. Yet, against a widespread interpretation, one can hardly say that it has also reached the highest degree of corruption. This is Machiavelli's conclusion, apparently paradoxical but in fact in line with the praise for social conflict developed in the past works. The prefatory chapter of Book III is probably one of the richest passages in the text. Machiavelli compares the conflict of Florence to those of Rome. He seems to condemn the Florentine people for its 'injurious and unjust' desire, which led it to fight 'to be alone in the government', while the Roman people's desire, always 'more reasonable', was pursued to the satisfaction of both parties.[39] Yet the outcome of such different conflicts, with no irony, appears to testify in favour of Florence rather than Rome. In fact,

> in the victories of the people the city of Rome became more virtuous, for as men of the people could be placed in the administration of the magistracies, the armies, and the posts of empire together with the nobles, they were filled with the same *virtù* as the nobles, and that city, by growing in *virtù*, grew in power. But in Florence, when the people conquered, the nobles were left deprived of the magistracies, and if they wanted to regain them, it was necessary for them not only to be but to appear similar to men of the people in their conduct, spirit, and mode of living. [. . .] And whereas Rome, when

its *virtù* was converted into arrogance, was reduced to such straits that it could not maintain itself without a prince, Florence arrived at the point that it could easily have been reordered in any form of government by a wise lawgiver.[40]

The sudden reversal is apparently shocking, but certainly not ironical: it is true that Florence is the homeland of corruption, while Rome rose as a great power. Yet this power could be maintained only by selling republican freedom to a prince, and transforming the Republic into an empire. In Florence, on the contrary, the violent struggle progressively destroyed the nobility, bringing the great closer and closer to the people, and preparing the 'matter' for a virtuous lawgiver to reorder it. For its social and economic structure, due to its conflictual history, as Machiavelli has always repeated, Florence is apt only to receive the form of a republican government. This major conclusion echoes Chapter I, 55 of the *Discourses*, where Machiavelli discusses the difference between corrupted and virtuous cities. Rome, once again, is the example of *virtù*. And yet, the example of Tuscany is once again clarifying:

> One sees [here] three republics – Florence, Siena, and Lucca – [that] have long been in a small space of territory; and the other cities of that province are seen to be servile in such a mode that one sees that with spirit and with order they would maintain or would like to maintain their freedom. All has risen because in that province there is no lord of the castle and no or very few gentlemen, but there is so much equality that a civil way of life would easily be introduced there by a prudent man having knowledge of the ancient civilizations. But its misfortune has been so great that up to these times it has not run into any man who has been able or known how to do it.[41]

The occasion, thus, is there, in the very matter of the Tuscan social and political world. It has not been seized in the past, but could it be seized in the present? This is the key of Machiavelli's last political statement, delivered by the *Discursus florentinarum rerum*.

THE *DISCURSUS*

Between 1519 and 1520, the cardinal Giulio de' Medici began to consult some of the most skilled citizens in Florence on the future of the city. After the death of Duke Lorenzo, in fact, the family did not have a successor who could lead the city. Machiavelli was commissioned to write his reflections under the same 'condotta' that contracted him to write the *Histories*. Thus, between 1520 and 1521, Machiavelli wrote the *Discursus florentinarum rerum post mortem iunioris Laurentii Medices*, a text fundamentally important not only for understanding

Machiavelli's attitude in this critical period of his life, but also for interpreting the relationship and the very nature of all the works composed
in this period.[42] Even the *Discursus*, in fact, has been considered as representing the 'crisis' of Machiavelli's political thought. On the contrary,
in its apparently cautious pages, we can read the echoes of the most
provocative positions that we can find in the *Histories*.

After briefly reconstructing the city's history, Machiavelli offers his
plan for a reform of the state. His project is interesting not insofar
as it is a form of 'mixed' government, but rather because giving an
important role to each group within the city (the Medici, the great
and the people) at different times, it constructs a movement from
the quasi-monarchical Medici regime to a republican status, the only
one, once again, apt for the city of Florence: 'In all cities where the
citizens are accustomed to equality, a princedom cannot be set up
except with the utmost difficulty, and in those cities where the citizens
are accustomed to inequality, a republic cannot be set up except with
the utmost difficulty.' In the beginning, in fact, he preserves the whole
power of choosing the magistrates and assigns the powerful positions
in the government to the Medici themselves: 'If it is considered while
Your Holiness and the Most Reverend Monsignor are still living, it is a
monarchy, because you have authority over the armed forces, you have
authority over the criminal judges, you keep the laws in your bosom. I
do not know anything more to be wished for in a city.'

One of the most interesting innovations that Machiavelli seeks to
implement in the *Discursus* is an institutional role similar to that of
the plebeian tribunes in Rome, the *preposti*, or provosts, who directly
represent the people.[43] Their function would be to block any action that
is suspicious or is directed against the people itself. They would be able
to impose a veto on any decision of a smaller council, and bring the
discussion back to the more representative body of the whole people,
the 'Great Council'.

The re-establishment of the Council is the strongest point of the
project. This body had been created under the Savonarolan Republic,
and was revealed as a powerful instrument against the great. When the
Soderini regime fell in 1512, the violence of the aristocrats broke out
against the Council, and the 'Sala' – the hall where it used to gather –
was physically destroyed. Almost as a provocation, but not ironically,
Machiavelli proposes that Cardinal Giulio 'reopen' the hall and rein-
state the people in the government of Florence:

> Without satisfying the generality of the citizens, to set up a stable govern-
> ment [*repubblica*] is always impossible. Never will the generality of the
> Florentine citizens be satisfied if the Hall is not reopened. Therefore, if one

is to set up a republic in Florence, this Hall must be reopened and this allot-
ment made to the generality of the citizens. Your Holiness should realize
that whoever plans to take the government from you will plan before everything else on reopening it; therefore it is a good scheme to open it with conditions and methods that are secure, and to take away from anybody who
may be your enemy opportunity for reopening it to your indignation and
with the destruction and ruin of your friends.[44]

Machiavelli evokes here, once again, the necessity of putting the guard
of freedom in the hands of the people, as 'a few citizens do not have
the courage to punish important men, and therefore it is necessary that
for such a result many citizens should join, that their judgment may be
secret, and since it is secret, each man may excuse himself'.

This project was not seriously considered. Within the Machiavellian
circles, it was judged as 'strange' and 'eccentric'.[45] And it could not
be otherwise, as it is the last and final proof of Machiavelli's sincere
spirit and bold attitude, employed to serve his Republic, even under
the Medici, and notwithstanding them. The history of Florence, of its
struggles, of its economic and social fabric serves Machiavelli's political
purposes. History, theory and politics converge, in his mind, to support
the love of freedom and of the free Republic.

6. War as an Art

THE PRACTICE OF THEORY

Matteo Bandello, one of the most famous sixteenth-century Italian writers of novellas, recounts an amusing and almost certainly false anecdote, set at the siege of Milan in 1526. Machiavelli, the legendary Medicean general Giovanni delle Bande Nere and Bandello himself are spending time together, discussing literature and war. Because Machiavelli's book on the art of war is already famous, Giovanni challenges the former secretary to give a practical demonstration of his knowledge and skills, and asks him to order three thousand soldiers following the principles illustrated in his book. For about two hours, under a scorching sun, Machiavelli tries to organise the movement of the troops, dazzled and confused by his eccentric orders, while his two friends ironically smile and make fun of him. When the situation seems hopeless, Giovanni cuts it short: 'Let me take care of it,' he says, 'so that we can finally have lunch.' In a few minutes, with the help of drums, he orders his soldiers in the proper way, and ironically invites Machiavelli to step back into his role and think about literature and politics, instead of trying to be a man of war.[1]

The technical and practical limitation of Machiavelli's military theory, as it is illustrated in the *Art of War*, was recognised very early and has become a byword among historians.[2] Composed between 1519 and 1520, and published the following year by Giunta in Florence, the *Art* has appeared to many as the inappropriate intervention of a political writer in a field he does not belong to: a utopia, in the best case, revealing once again the nostalgic character of the author's unconditional praise for Rome and its ancient glory; an illusion, in the worst case, manifesting the theoretical weakness of its author, for example in his criteria for the choice of the soldiers, or in diminishing the importance of the firearms. Although scholars, more recently, have reassessed those conclusions, the extraordinary importance of the *Art of War* has to be considered not only on technical grounds, but also – and perhaps most of all – on political grounds, or, even better, in its capacity to renegotiate the boundaries and redefine the relationships between politics and the military in early modernity.

The *Art of War* is a book about the *virtù* of the Roman way of waging war, and the necessity of re-establishing it in the present times, in order to resist the current state of corruption of the Italian military situation, which mirrors the corruption of the political situation. Like Machiavelli's other works, and the *Discourses* in particular, the *Art* is strongly connected with the classical past, and profoundly indebted to ancient sources on the military way of life, and the techniques of fighting and of maintaining an army in peacetime. Laurence Arthur Burd has done an impressive job of reconstructing the ancient sources that Machiavelli certainly had in mind when he conceived and wrote his book[3] – Livy and Polybius, of course, but also Frontinus, Caesar, Sallust, Thucydides, Flavius Josephus and, most of all, Vegetius and his *Epitome of Military Science*, from which Machiavelli copies long technical passages. The importance of humanist sources has also been pointed out, in particular the influence of Matteo Palmieri, Francesco Patrizi and Leonardo Bruni.[4] Yet Machiavelli's *Art* is neither the simple revival of classic military ideology, nor a traditional reworking of humanist military thought. It is, on the contrary, a passionate and thoughtful continuation of the intellectual enterprise of his previous work, as well as an original attempt at proposing a direct intervention in the situation of his own time, connecting together military and political considerations.

Before being a political theory, though, the 'art' of war has been for Machiavelli a matter of practical experience, and a 'school' of realism and political life. In his own lifetime, Machiavelli has experienced the disaster of relying on mercenary troops, especially in the long and exhausting war against Pisa, the important seaport once under Florence's dominion. Unfaithful, treacherous, disloyal, the *condottieri* employed by the Republic have been only a source of deception and huge expense for the public treasury. Machiavelli will keep denouncing mercenary troops in later years, and especially in the *Art of War*, when he writes that

> those who take war for their art must be feared even by the king because the sinew of armies without any doubt is the infantry. So if a king does not order himself so that his infantrymen may be content in time of peace to return home and to live from their arts, of necessity he must come to ruin, for a

more dangerous infantry is not found than that which is composed of those who make war as their art. For you are forced either to make war always or to pay them always or to bear the danger that they may take the kingdom from you. To make war always is not possible and to pay them always one cannot do; thus of necessity one incurs the danger of losing one's state.[5]

This aversion to mercenaries, deriving from his practical political experience, is also supported by the classical ideology concerning the citizen militia, derived both from ancient history and from humanist sources. History and practice converge in Machiavelli's reflection from the very beginning of his career, when he supports, both in writings and with tireless work, the creation of a Florentine army.

The two main writings of the early period are the *Cagione dell'ordinanza* (*The Reason for the Militia*) and the *Ordinanza dei cavalli* (*On Cavalry*). The first text was written in 1506 as a report supporting the creation of a Florentine militia, recruiting peasants in the Florentine territories subjected to the city. Whereas the preoccupation, here, is to reassure the citizens that this infantry and this army will not be dangerous for the city itself and will not become a private army in the hands of the *gonfaloniere*, the later *Ordinanza dei cavalli*, written at the end of 1510, is more concerned with a positive spirit of involvement of the subjects in the active defence of the Republic. The war between Louis XII and Julius II is imminent, and therefore the already existing militia, created in the last few years by enrolling mainly peasants in the countryside, needs to be reinforced by a light cavalry to support its action. This new armed body might scare the citizens of Florence even more, but Machiavelli suggests that it is a necessary step in order to accomplish the project he has been working on since 1506. Moreover, in the *Art*, he reassures the citizens, by explaining that

As to the fear that such an order may take away your state by means of the individual who is made its head, I respond that arms, given by the laws and by order, on the back of one's own citizens or subjects never do harm; rather, they are always useful, and cities more often maintain themselves immaculate by means of these arms than without them. [. . .] for cities need arms; and when they do not have their own arms they hire foreigners. And foreign arms can do damage to the public good more quickly than one's own, because they become corrupt more easily and can be used more quickly by a citizen who has become powerful. And, in part, he has material that is easier to manage, since he has to oppress unarmed men.[6]

From the very beginning of his theoretical reflection and practical action for the constitution of a militia, Machiavelli stresses the importance of linking together politics and war because, in the new national and international scenario, separating them would simply mean failing to understand the necessary basis of governing states, precisely what Italian princes have been doing in the last decades:

> Whoever speaks of empire, kingdom, principality, or republic and whoever speaks of men who command, starting from the highest rank and descending to the captain of a brigantine, speaks of justice and arms. You have little justice, and no arms at all. And the only way to recover the one and the other is to order arms through public deliberation, and to maintain them with good orders.[7]

Machiavelli remains faithful to this conclusion and keeps repeating it as an unshakeable truth, enriched by his reflections on the ancients and his experience of modern affairs, as he repeats in the *Art of War*:

> Many have held and hold this opinion [. . .] that there are no things less in agreement with one another or so dissimilar as the civilian and the military lives. [. . .] But if ancient orders were considered, nothing would be found more united, more in conformity, and, of necessity, as much inclined toward one another as these. [. . .] good orders without military help are disordered no differently than the rooms of a proud and regal palace when, by being uncovered, they have nothing that might defend them against the rain, even though [they are] ornamented with gems and gold.[8]

This is also the reason for the crisis of the present times. Machiavelli is aware of living in a time of dramatic changes, when the balance of power in Europe is shifting toward the new national states. Italy has experienced this with the invasion of Charles VIII in 1494. Unless a serious remedy is found, freedom and independence, already threatened, will be lost forever. Nothing is more important than this awareness and, although the enterprise appears difficult, it is nonetheless necessary and urgent:

> Before they tasted the blows of the ultramontane wars, our Italian princes used to believe that it was enough for a prince to know how to think of a sharp response in his studies, to write a beautiful letter, to show wit and quickness in his deeds and words, to know how to weave a fraud, to be ornamented by gems and gold, to sleep and eat with greater splendor than others, to keep many lascivious ones around, to govern subjects avariciously and proudly, to rot in idleness, to give promotions in the military by favor, to despise anyone who may have shown them any praiseworthy way, to want their speeches to be responses of oracles. Nor did these wretches perceive that they were preparing themselves to be the prey of whoever assaulted them. From here arose in 1494 great terrors, sudden flights, and miraculous losses.[9]

By the time he started working on the *Ordinanza*, then, the militia had already become a political as much as a military problem for him. The aristocrats feared it, as they thought that the *gonfaloniere*, appointed for life, would use it as an instrument to increase his own personal power and use it against them. Although it is quite unlikely that the timid *gonfaloniere* Soderini would ever have attempted such a bold move, the concern was justified. Advised by the group supporting the new militia, the *gonfaloniere* also undertook the creation of a new institutional office, the *Nove* (the Nine): an important reform to prevent the *grandi* from influencing and sabotaging Machiavelli's project.

Within the existing constitutional framework, two of the main political domains – the diplomatic function and the administration of justice – are in the hands of two magistracies, the *Dieci di Balìa* (Ten of War) and the *Otto di Guardia* (Eight of Ward). Especially after the fall of Savonarola, the great have managed to expand and consolidate their influence on these two magistracies, and therefore to control two key aspects of Florentine politics.[10] Together with the formation of the new militia, Machiavelli and Soderini promote the creation of the new magistracy, the *Nove*, holding jurisdictional power over the members of the new militia, removing it, in this way, from the traditional competence of the *Dieci*.[11] This may appear a minor detail in the institutional development of Florence in these years, but it is in fact a reform of enormous importance, as it is intended to undermine the factual power of the great on the Florentine territories where the soldiers are recruited, as well as to question their role and influence in matters traditionally ascribed to their competences.[12] The introduction of the *Nove* represents a real break in the previous balance of power, in favour of Machiavelli's group, and his project of militia is fundamentally important for this attempt to limit the influence of the *grandi*.

The very nature of the reform clearly reveals this anti-oligarchic stand. The organisation of the new militia followed two major steps: the recruitment of the infantry since 1506, and the organisation of a cavalry to support it, around 1510. Now, infantry and cavalry have to be considered two mutually supporting parts of the same army. They must also be considered, though, as expressing different political principles, insofar as they are constituted by citizens or subjects with very different social backgrounds and economic possibilities. One *Lancia* ('lance') was composed of three, or six, or even eight persons, with different functions, all serving the main horseman or *uomo d'arme*. It was therefore a huge and expensive thing to organise and maintain. Hence, given the fact that the cost of the horse and its maintenance, the armoury and the weapons was met by the individual fighter at the time, only people with considerable wealth could afford to be part of this body. The infantry, on the contrary, was more naturally made up of the middle class or even of the lower class, especially if the cost of the weapons had to be met by the public, as happens in Machiavelli's project.[13]

One of the most interesting and important militia projects in Machiavelli's time is the *Riforma sancta et pretiosa* (*Holy and Precious Reform*), written by Domenico Cecchi to support Savonarola and his regime. Cecchi, like Machiavelli a few years later, is confronted with the question of who can be armed with the new reform. The mercenaries are excluded, being dishonest and treacherous. The nobles are also excluded, being utterly hostile to the populist regime of Savonarola. The people is left, but Cecchi introduces a highly significant distinction between the plebs and the middle class. Only the latter must be involved in the army, while the former has to be kept aside. This is done by imposing on the individual the cost of the weapons, and the duty to maintain them and keep them ready and efficient for training and for actual use in war. By doing so, Cecchi reveals his true intention to divide the people and ground the regime's power only on the middle class.

Machiavelli, on the contrary, insists on the opportunity of also involving the poor in the army. It is true that he only starts the recruitment in the country and not among the city's poor. And this is understandable for the extreme wariness necessary to reassure the oligarchy and have the project itself approved and realised in the first place. By completely financing the project and making the weapons available at the Republic's expense, however, Machiavelli clearly shows his openness toward the lower strata of the population. In this, he follows the ancient Roman and modern Swiss example – and makes a political as well as a military choice.

Machiavelli starts recruiting infantrymen for the new republican army. They successfully operate in the war against Pisa, but prove to be utterly inadequate to face the Spanish infantry at the siege and the taking of Prato in 1512. Notwithstanding this defeat, Machiavelli does not change his mind. No doubt, in Machiavelli's words, the choice between infantry and cavalry is political as much as it is military:

> This mode of arming was discovered by the German peoples, especially the Swiss. Since they were poor and wanted to live freely, they were and are necessitated to fight against the ambition of the princes of Germany; because [the latter] were rich, they were able to raise horses, which these peoples were not able to do because of poverty. From this it arises that, since they were on foot and wished to defend themselves from their enemy who was on horseback, they had to search the ancient orders again and find arms that might defend them from the fury of horse. This necessity has made them either maintain or rediscover ancient orders, without which, as every prudent [man] affirms, infantry is altogether useless.[14]

The Swiss certainly represent a model of military and civic *virtù*, first and foremost for their love of freedom and the equality their civil and political life is based on. All this is reflected in their military organisation. Yet the Swiss are also a military tool employed to conquer Italy and threaten the independence of Italian states and the freedom of Florence itself. Hence, Machiavelli compares their way of fighting to that of the Greek phalanx, and, in the same way that the Roman legion had defeated the Greek phalanx, so the new militia should follow the Roman example in order to defeat the Swiss *carré*, or 'pike square'.

This military formation, which had proved extremely efficient on the Italian battlefield, was the main problem that Italian armies had to face in the early sixteenth century. Because it recalled the ancient Spartan phalanx, Machiavelli chose to oppose it with something resembling the ancient Roman legion – the military (but also social and political) instrument that had triumphed over the Spartan machine of war.[15]

Machiavelli's preference for the Roman legion is also interesting from the point of view of the nature of warfare that he has in mind, which is eminently defensive. Notwithstanding the remarks and accusations that have often been made about Machiavelli's imperialism, his legion is technically more a defensive tool than an offensive one.[16] The cavalry is supposed to help and support the infantry, arranged on a relatively long horizontal front, made of three different lines. These lines have to move consistently, and progressively merge into two and finally into one single mass of men, more dense and better organised for resisting the assaults of the enemy. This one mass of men testifies again to the equality and the solidarity that has to inspire union in the army. Piero Pieri maintains that this theoretical construction, which was never realised, would never have resisted the impact of the huge and powerful Swiss squares. This might be technically true. But what Pieri misses here is the political point that underlies Machiavelli's construction: an army of citizens and subjects, united in the defence of the city and affirming the pre-eminence of the lower strata of the population in this key role.

The same thing can be said for firearms. One of the biggest limitations of Machiavelli's discourse in the *Art of War* is that he does not ascribe much importance to firearms and is not able to forecast the decisive role that they will have on the whole warfare scenario of the late Renaissance. The evolution of guns, lighter and more powerful year after year, is also a sign of the shift in the hegemony on the battleground. Rough peasants and highlanders, properly trained and armed, will soon be able to wipe away, with a few gunshots, the most noble and refined examples of old-fashioned fighters, with their beautiful armour and elegant horses.[17] This, once again, has been considered one of the most significant limitations of Machiavelli's *Art*. If Machiavelli underestimates gunfire, however, it is less because of his shortsightedness than because of their slow evolution in those years. The technical revolution going on on the Renaissance battlefield will only be clear a few years after the *Art of War*. Nevertheless, the class character of Machiavelli's military position, coupled with a sharp and consistent stand on the primacy of the people over the great, is to be recognised as the main feature of his own enterprise. 'The unarmed rich man', he writes in the *Art of War*, 'is the reward of the poor soldier':[18] the political stance could not be more clear.

Besides the technical aspects of the reform that Machiavelli has in mind, one has to recognise that the function of the army, in the long run, is also to educate the citizen to a *virtù* that is not only military, but also civic. Scholars have pointed out the limitation of Machiavelli's project in recruiting soldiers among the subjects of the country rather than among the citizens of the city. Yet it is clear, in the *Art*, that being a soldier actively engaged in the defence of republican freedom is a virtuous act, and an act that truly elevates every subject not only to the status of citizen, but also to that of virtuous man. A utopian accent seems to resonate, once again, in Machiavelli's words. Yet the necessity of reforming the customs, and not only the laws, following the ancient Roman model, in order to contrast the corrupted situation of his own time, sounds rather realistic in these pages of the *Art*. Training, discipline, love of freedom, and involvement in its defence is the basis for the new image of the citizen-soldier, with which Machiavelli intends to wipe away, once and for all, the power of the mercenaries over the life of his free republic:

> When could I make one of the soldiers who practice today carry more arms than they are accustomed to, and, besides the arms, food for two or three days, and a hoe? When could I make him dig and keep him every day for many hours under arms in fake drills, so as later to be able to avail myself of him in true ones? When would they abstain from games, from acts of lasciviousness, from curses, from acts of insolence that they do everyday? When would they be reduced to so much discipline and to so much obedience and reverence that one tree full of apples in the middle of their encampments may be found there and left intact as one reads happened many times in the ancient armies? What thing can I promise them, by means of which they might hold me in reverence with love or fear, when, the war having finished, they no longer have anything to connect them to me? With what would I make ashamed those who have been born and raised without shame? Why would those who do not know me have to observe me? By what God, or by what saints would I make them swear? By those that they adore, or by those that they curse? I do not know any that they adore, but I know well that they curse them all. How would I believe that they would observe their

promises to those whom every hour they disparage? How can they who disparage God revere men? What good form, then, could there be that one could impress on this matter?[19]

The people, in Machiavelli's eyes, can be an active force to support the freedom of the Republic. The poor, the peasants, the citizens must be involved, trained and educated to this project, which is at once ethical, political and military. In the *Discourses*, Machiavelli had maintained the same position, writing that 'present princes and modern republics that lack their own soldiers for defense and offense ought to be ashamed of themselves and to think [that] such a defect is not through a lack of men apt for the military but through their own fault, that they have not known how to make their men military'.[20] In this light, even the harshest attack that has been directed at Machiavelli's morality, because of his defence of Cesare Borgia's example, has to be reconsidered. Alongside the traditional use of mercenary forces, didn't Cesare put together his own army in order to wipe away the riotous power of the unfaithful *condottieri*? Was not Cesare trying precisely to ground a new state and resist the old power with a new army? Machiavelli makes it clear in the *Legation to Duke Valentino* in 1502.[21] Borgia responds to the defection of Orsini and Vitelli by raising an army in his own territories. The example strikes Machiavelli, who insists upon it with the Florentine government, suggesting how important it is to ground any power on one's own army. This is the message, at the same time military and political, that must be retained from the reading of the *Art of War*. And the early acute readers in Machiavelli's own time, including the mocking Matteo Bandello, did not misunderstand him.

PART III: LEGACY, RECEPTION AND INFLUENCE

Introduction to Part III

If history is, as Benedetto Croce writes, always 'contemporary history',[1] one should not be surprised by the complexity and multiplicity of interpretations of Machiavelli across the centuries. During the 'short twentieth century' (from World War One to the fall of the USSR), for example, the richness of these readings corresponds with the immense challenges that the Western world had to face and the ideologies that marked the period, among which at least fascism-nazism, liberalism, socialism and communism must be mentioned. It is perhaps because of this complexity, characteristic of the modern era, combined with the complexity of Machiavelli's thought, that Croce himself could only synthesise his thoughts on the Florentine by stating that 'the question' of Machiavelli 'will never be resolved'.[2] Nor will I attempt to do so in the remaining pages of this book. Once again I will confine myself to analysing the interpretations that I find to be most significant – those in which the comment on Machiavelli is not just incidental, but the result of a deep reflection that influences the author's thought profoundly, going well beyond superficial and explicit references to Machiavelli.

With this in mind, once again, it will not be difficult to understand the selection of authors discussed in the next two chapters. I will engage with those authors who have contributed to the interpretation and transmission of Machiavelli's thought, sometimes faithfully rendering it, sometimes doing violence to his ideas. I will not necessarily focus on the interpretations that are more faithful to Machiavelli's text, but rather on the interpretations that, by virtue of their force and sharpness, contribute, over the centuries, to making Machiavelli's thought what it is for us today. Once again, the reader expecting an uncritical survey of Machiavelli's legacy might sometimes find this selection odd.[3] Although some of the authors discussed in the following pages, such as Harrington, or Rousseau, or Gramsci, regularly appear in discussions of

Machiavelli's reception, other authors, such as Campanella, or Hobbes, or Spinoza, are less explored by scholars dealing with Machiavelli's influence. However, I think that *all* authors discussed below give striking interpretations of the themes that have influenced my interpretation of Machiavelli's philosophy. Thus, my choice falls on the authors whose interpretation is crucial for the understanding of topics that have guided my reading in the previous chapters.

My methodology is to organise this history of Machiavelli's influence around what I consider the pivotal cores of his thought. Once again, such a reconstruction is not only necessarily short, but also necessarily partial. I will not summarise each author's interpretation of Machiavelli in its entirety. On the contrary, I will explicitly question authors and theories on specific theoretical, philosophical and political points, avoiding the impression of producing an exhaustive reconstruction of their individual philosophies. For this reason, the reader will not find general references to the whole philosophy or political thought of the authors discussed below. I will deal only with their reading of Machiavelli, on and around specific themes. The aim is to test my reading of Machiavelli in the previous chapters, as well as my interpretation of what makes Machiavelli's thought so crucial for our understanding of modernity. The aim is also to follow the evolution of the interpretation of such themes across the centuries. Authors read Machiavelli in light of their own philosophical and political questions. If, however, they keep going back to certain themes in Machiavelli's thought, this means that Machiavelli keeps producing effects, directly or indirectly influencing those questions and ideas.

My concern with consistency, and with a selective reading of Machiavelli's influence, does not mean, however, that I will try to homogenise his reception across the centuries. As explained, on the contrary, authors focus on different themes in different epochs. Around such a diversity of themes I have organised my reconstruction of Machiavelli's reception in the next two chapters. In Chapter 7, I discuss Machiavelli's interpretations between the sixteenth and the eighteenth centuries: the invention of sovereignty as the main attribute of the rising nation-state, the questions of authority and obligation to the sovereign, the origin of civil society and the philosophical anthropology, both in nature and within the state, and the theologico-political question are the core arguments characterising the discussions of Machiavelli's thought in the early modern period. I then devote Chapter 8 to Machiavelli's reception between the nineteenth and twentieth centuries. Other philosophical themes and political concerns become prevalent in this period, such as nationalism and internationalism, class struggle and revolution, the nature of power, and in particular absolute power, the question of violence and its relationship with politics, and the question of empire and imperialism. The authors I discuss below mainly focus on these topics. My aim is to show the specific way these authors read Machiavelli, to explain why they are interested in certain aspects of his thought, but also to question them on what I have considered the central themes in Machiavelli's philosophy in the previous chapters, and to test my interpretation against the history of his reception and influence.

7. *Authority, Conflict and the Origin of the State (Sixteenth to Eighteenth Centuries)*

FRANCESCO VETTORI AND FRANCESCO GUICCIARDINI

Machiavelli's work became the subject of discussion and analysis very soon after his death, especially among those who knew him personally, such as his friends Francesco Guicciardini and Francesco Vettori. Both of them belonged to the Florentine nobility and thus were naturally connected with the ideological front that opposed the partisans of the Republic with whom Machiavelli identified and for whom he had worked. Both of them were keen observers of political issues – it is in their writings that we find clues about the issues closest to their hearts that Machiavelli had raised, not only with words but also with actions.

Francesco Vettori, for example, opens the tale of his *Viaggio in Alamagna (German Journey)*, which he had started writing in 1507 and revised several times, with a vivid description of the parade of the civilian militia that had been created following the advice of Machiavelli. Vettori imagines watching the military parade from inside a tavern in Mugello, in the Florentine countryside, where Machiavelli had begun to recruit his troops. Vettori naively declares this to be an act 'honourable and useful to our city'. The owner, however, a native of Florence and not of the countryside, responds with the same words as did the former detractors of the Machiavellian project:

> I do not doubt that these battalions, when they are armed and trained, will form a good infantry. But I do not know how Florentines will be secure; nor do I know for what reason armed and trained men would want to obey the unarmed and inexperienced ones. And I fear that, having been subjects in the past, they will now want to become rulers. Believe me, as I meet them every day: they do not love us, and have no reason to do so, because we are not merely their rulers but also their tyrants. And if we fear attacks by foreign

enemies, it is better to think of defending ourselves by paying money to the army, because this happens every four or six years, rather than defending ourselves with these troops, which could attack us every day. And if we can assemble them quickly, they could do the same for themselves to come and attack us. And if we frighten the neighbouring states with these troops, we also not only frighten ourselves, but damage ourselves.[1]

Vettori, as a good representative of the nobility, can see very clearly the problem inherent in a citizen militia. It is certainly an effective force of defence against external enemies but also a powerful potential instrument that a people's government might use to fight the nobles. The owner of the tavern speaks of the armed and trained peasants, comparing them to the Florentines, unarmed and untrained. The reference to the possibility of 'buying' peace every four or six years is clear: the nobles prefer mercenary troops and diplomacy to giving weapons to the people at the risk of seeing them rise up against their rule.

Vettori has learned a lot from Machiavelli, and his reference to tyranny is not accidental. In the *Sommario*, he repeats the lesson given by the author of *The Prince*, who argued with acute realism that there are no good or bad governments, but that each state is, by definition, a tyranny exercised by the ruling class over the oppressed one. Social and political conflict are thus situated at the centre of politics, reversing the classical tradition of good governance, which can be seen as a mere utopian fiction:

> If I am to speak of the things of this world sincerely and following the truth, I will say that those who make reference to republics such as the one imagined and described by Plato, or the one that the Englishman Thomas More says he found in Utopia, perhaps about these states one might say that they were not tyrannical governments. But in my opinion all those republics or principalities whose history I know and that I have seen myself, stink of tyranny.[2]

Francesco Guicciardini, who also witnessed the crisis of the Florentine Republic and its slow drift towards the Medici principality, does not go so far in his statements. In his *Considerations on the Discourses of Machiavelli*, he stresses the inconstancy and ignorance of the multitude – an argument traditionally put forward by aristocratic authors. To Machiavelli, who had contested the traditional view that 'he who builds on the people builds on the mud', Guicciardini replies that

> where there is multitude, there is confusion; in such disharmony of minds where there are differing judgements, differing ideas, and differing ends, there can be no rational discussion, no sound resolve, and no firm action. Men act frivolously on any vain suspicion or any vain rumour; they do not discern, they do not distinguish, and they revert with the same frivolousness

to decisions that they had previously condemned: to hating those they loved, to loving those they hated. Hence it is not without reason that the multitude is compared to the waves of the sea which, depending upon which way the winds blow, roll now this way, now that way, without any rule, without any firmness.[3]

And yet, in the pages of the *Considerations* we can also find the strong denunciation of the nobility that acts to manipulate the people for its own interests and uses them as an instrument of subversion of the republican order. Ambitious and seditious men are constantly working to deceive the people and to subvert institutions, while pursuing their own particular interest, which is contrary to the common good. Guicciardini points to the example of Tiberius and Gaius Gracchus – the authors of the Agrarian law that opened the way for conflicts between the plebeians and the Senate (I, 7).

Guicciardini thus supports the cause of harmony against the arguments of Machiavelli, who believed that social relations are and should be based on conflict. Against Machiavelli's historical analysis, Guicciardini goes so far as to say that the cause of the greatness of Rome was precisely 'harmony', coupled with the '*virtù* of arms' (I, 1). He recognises the centrality of the political conflict in Machiavelli's thought but then he immediately neutralises it:

> So it was not the discord between the Plebeians and the Senate that made Rome free and powerful, because it would have been better had there not been any causes for discord. Nor were the rebellions useful, though they certainly did less harm than in other cities, and it would have been very useful for Rome's greatness had the Patricians yielded sooner to the will of the Plebeians rather than thinking up ways to avoid needing the Plebeians. But praising discord is like praising a sick man's illness because the remedy that has been used on him is the right one.[4]

Guicciardini does not hesitate to express his preference for a mixed government based on the central role of an aristocracy of merit and *virtù*. And yet, as for Vettori, the lesson of Machiavellian realism left deep traces and indelible signs in his thought. For example, in the conclusion of his *Considerations*, by denying the superiority of people above princes, Guicciardini ultimately agrees with his friend and author of *The Prince*. Even if it is true that a long succession of virtuous princes would reinforce the state to a bigger extent than a long series of popular governments, the reality is that the successions of princes are aleatory and inconsistent. Ultimately, then, this is the only reason for which popular governments are stronger and more powerful (I, 58).

ALBERICO GENTILI

The debate on the theoretical status and the significance of Machiavelli's political thought soon extended beyond the narrow boundaries of Medicean Florence and Italy. It spread mainly thanks to Italian exiles and migrants, as in the case of Alberico Gentili, a law professor at Oxford, who is recognised, together with Grotius, as one of the fathers of modern international law. In his *De legationibus libri tres* (*Three Books on Embassies*), Gentili paints the image of a republican Machiavelli, whose aim was not 'to instruct the tyrant, but by revealing his secret counsels to strip him bare, and expose him to the suffering nations'.[5] This image would persist for a long time, influencing in various ways the republican interpretations of later centuries. Gentili is a perceptive reader and does not limit himself to the political significance of the life and writings of Machiavelli. For him, one of the major merits of the author of the *Discourses* is the method of historical investigation. Making history means to Machiavelli doing politics in a field pervaded both by empirical method and by philosophical-scientific generalisation.

Gentili is also sensitive to Machiavellian realism, but he does not deny the need for an ethical approach to the political and legal study of history. In his next book, entitled *The Wars of the Romans* (1599), in which he discusses the *virtù* and justification of Roman imperialism, Gentili does not neglect Machiavelli's teaching – for example, he highlights the relationship between necessity and legitimacy at the international level: 'That which is not allowable according to the law necessity makes allowable. Necessity has no law, but it itself makes law.'[6]

LOUIS LE ROY AND INNOCENT GENTILLET

In France, too, Machiavelli soon took centre stage in both political and philosophical debates. He is described as the wicked counsellor of tyrants and inspirer of the Catholic policies against the Huguenots, and in particular of the bloody massacre of St Bartholomew's Day in 1572. Machiavelli, in this context, is more often quoted than actually read, more often named than actually studied. Louis Le Roy – one of the sharpest writers of the period – focuses, however, on Machiavelli's method. An erudite humanist, and professor of Greek at the Collège Royal, Le Roy was interested in subjects from Platonism to philosophy of history and theory of politics. Living in the troubled period of the French wars of religion, he was also greatly concerned with the theologico-political question, and the problem of peace and social harmony.

In his *Les politiques d'Aristote* (*Aristotle's Politics*) of 1568, Le Roy attempts to neutralise the attacks against Machiavelli by showing that the Florentine does in fact develop some teachings of Aristotle's *Politics*. Discussing the causes of sedition, Le Roy quotes Chapter I, 4 of the *Discourses* on the conflict between the plebs and the Senate, together with other recognised and not so controversial authors, such as Plato, Sallust and Horace.[7] In a different work, Le Roy had noted how politics is backward compared to other sciences, and how important it would be, in politics, to apply a method that keeps together nature, doctrine and experience.[8] And if Aristotle is superior to Plato, on this point, Machiavelli is also to be considered a master, precisely because he developed a historiographical method that is not limited to a mere collection of historical facts, but is rather a selection and comprehension of their 'reasons'.

The most ferocious and systematic attack on Machiavelli in France is in the work of the Huguenot Innocent Gentillet. A refugee in Geneva after the St Bartholomew's Day massacre, Gentillet develops in his *Anti-Machiavel* (1576) a method that will remain very influential in later centuries; it consists in attacking Machiavelli indiscriminately without seriously addressing any topic raised by him. *The Prince* is defined by Gentillet as the 'Koran of the courtiers'.[9] The best way to fight it would be to erase it from memory and forget it forever. Gentillet, however, does the exact opposite: he writes a long and wordy text in which he attacks Machiavelli, highlighting his profound malice.

Gentillet guesses correctly and shows clearly the Epicurean and materialistic inspiration of Machiavelli. For him everything in the world of nature and of men happens at random and according to the haphazard encounter of atoms, hence his atheism with which he wants to overthrow the philosophies of Plato and Aristotle, who believed on the contrary in a supreme cause governing the world.[10] Gentillet claims that a republic should be harmoniously regulated just like the human body. The Machiavellian doctrine, in contrast, is quite opposite to belief in divine providence. Though Gentillet is among the first to clearly thematise the connection between Machiavelli and Epicurean atomism, he does not develop his criticism in a more extensive manner. He limits himself to trivially associating two cursed names of philosophy and establishing an uncritical equation between Machiavellianism and Epicureanism.

Gentillet is also interested in the subject of social conflicts and sedition. He acknowledges that sedition can sometimes be the backdrop to good changes in states, but denies that it can ever be their cause.[11] The Agrarian law of Tiberius and Gaius Gracchus, which, according to

Gentillet, was praised by Machiavelli, is in any case unfair, since it is unjust to cause damage to the property and to take from the rich to give to the poor. Rebellions are always stirred up by tyrants who use them as means to divide their subjects and maintain their power.[12] Gentillet misses, however, the point made by Machiavelli – tyrants often point to union and the common good as their public goals. He is in favour of the classical doctrine that points to the harmony of the various parties within the state and social peace as a synonym for freedom. There is some insight, however poorly developed, in the work of Gentillet. There is, however, probably some truth in what we read in the preface to the *Discourses* published by the London printer John Wolf in Italian in 1584 – that *Anti-Machiavel* was a book 'suited for sellers of sausages and sardines' for wrapping up their goods.

TOMMASO CAMPANELLA

Among the detractors of Machiavelli, however, apart from hasty judgements and distracted readings, we also encounter deep and thoughtful, though not less fierce, criticism. The work of Tommaso Campanella falls into this category. A Dominican friar, Campanella became interested in natural philosophy and Kabbalah. He was repeatedly put on trial for heresy and forced to retire to the Calabrian convent of Stilo. Rather than devoting himself to prayer and repentance, though, Campanella spent his time secretly organising an anti-monarchical plot to set his land free from Spanish domination and establish a free republic based on equality and theocracy. The plot was discovered in 1599 and Campanella was condemned to prison, where he spent twenty-seven years before being liberated in 1626. He kept fighting for freedom, for example supporting Galileo in his trial against the Church.

In his *Atheismus triumphatus* (*Atheism Conquered*, written in 1605 and published in 1631), the author condemns Machiavelli, at the same time developing a reading that will provide valuable arguments to the supporters and defenders of the Florentine throughout the seventeenth century. Campanella gradually moves away from the dogmas and 'non-sincere truth, or rather falsehood' of the philosophy of Aristotle and Aquinas to become more inspired by Plato but also by ancient materialism. In his criticism of Aristotelianism, he includes Machiavelli because, as he writes, 'Machiavellianism derives from Peripateticism [the school of Aristotle's followers]'. Campanella has in mind the Aristotelianism influenced by the twelfth-century Muslim philosopher Averroes, as developed by some authors of the Italian Renaissance, especially thinkers such as Gerolamo Cardano and Pietro Pomponazzi. For him it is only from this matrix that one could derive the idea of chance and *fortuna* as causes of natural and human events. It is this model that gave way to all the atheists and the sects that have corrupted the world, such as the Lutherans and Calvinists.

Campanella greatly simplifies the Machiavellian conception of *fortuna*, reducing it to chance, understood as the absence of causes. Thanks to this simplification, however, he is able to raise an important issue, namely that of the relationship between Machiavelli's philosophy and his politics. And most importantly, unlike Gentillet, Campanella takes seriously Machiavelli's thought to argue that philosophy and politics, as well as the method and the content, can not be separated and may only be refuted together. They both date back to the pernicious philosophical matrix of Aristotelianism and both lead to the worst atheism and anti-Christianity.

Campanella is an eclectic author and he often masks his true thoughts under fake arguments. After he was arrested, tortured and imprisoned for twenty-seven years, he wrote not only the *Atheismus* but also his most famous works, such as *The City of the Sun* (1602). From the trial's record we can see clearly the Machiavellian inspiration of Campanella. The military leader of the conspirators, Mauritio de Rinaldis, states that 'Brother Thomas convinced us by pointing to many examples of men who had built up their position from nothing, quoting Machiavelli [. . .] and pushing me in this way to take up arms at that very moment'.[13] Whatever the real position of Campanella was, his interpretation, unlike the ordinary anti-Machiavellianisms of the sixteenth century, not only takes Machiavelli's thought seriously, but also offers a modern image of the Florentine, critiquing his philosophy and his concept of politics at the same time: an image that will be developed and further clarified during the emerging scientific revolution of the seventeenth century.

Tommaso Campanella's hostile interpretation, though with a hint of ambiguity, intends to close this debate once and for all: if to sixteenth-century readers it seems theoretically possible – and politically sensible – to separate the philosophy of Machiavelli from his politics, this is in fact impossible for Campanella. Associating Machiavelli with the tradition of Renaissance Averroistic Aristotelianism, he supports the view that philosophy and politics in the work of the impious Florentine must be considered together, and condemned together. With this severe judgement, political and philosophical at the same time, Campanella consigns Machiavelli to the next century. But will this actually be the Machiavelli of the seventeenth century? Will his works be commented on in the light of an inseparable union of philosophy and politics?

FRANCIS BACON

Francis Bacon is one among the early modern philosophers who better embodies the conjunction, within modernity, of a new scientific consciousness and a new political awareness. Making his first political steps as an ambassador, he quickly scaled the social ladder under James I, becoming Attorney General and Lord Chancellor of England. His political conceptions revolved around the idea of a strong, stable and anti-feudal state. Because of his support for a strong monarchy, he had several enemies in the Parliament, who did not hesitate to destroy his political career by accusing him of corruption. Paralleling his political career, his studies on natural philosophy make him one of the strongest personalities of the early seventeenth century and one of the protagonists of the modern scientific revolution. Intertwining of political and philosophical thought is probably most evident in his late utopian work *New Atlantis* (1624).

Bacon reads Machiavelli through the lens of the relationship between philosophy and politics. And yet it will be precisely his new and revolutionary theoretical sensitivity that directs the interpretation of Machiavelli in a sense opposite to the one presented by Campanella. His analysis does not go towards an inseparable union between philosophy and politics, between method and content, but towards the possibility of separating them in a definitive manner. This leads inevitably not to the passionate disapproval of the politician, but to the cold recognition of the scientist and historian. The exponents of the scientific revolution do not focus their attention on the cruelty of Machiavelli's moral and political theory, but on the novelty of his scientific method, applied for the first time to history and politics.

Of all the judgements on Machiavelli, that of Francis Bacon is undoubtedly one of the most sympathetic. It is valid in terms of autonomy and independence as it emerges from a specific era, namely the Elizabethan one, during which, with the exception of Raleigh and the complicated judgement of Shakespeare,[14] it was common to defame the name of Machiavelli without any serious knowledge of his texts. Bacon became interested in Machiavelli quite early, beginning to study his works at around the age of twenty. His judgement would be influential and respected – and would play an important role in future attempts to re-establish the name of Machiavelli.

Machiavelli's influence on Bacon is mainly in methods of investigation and the scientific approach to human reality and politics. In *The Advancement of Learning* (1605), and later in *De augmentis scientiarum* (1623), Bacon recognises the merit of Machiavelli in establishing – and not just illustrating – scientific reasoning based on a historical example. Following a suggestion already put forward by Alberico Gentili, Bacon sees in Machiavelli nothing less than a forerunner of the inductive method, necessary for the study of both social life and natural science. It is not surprising, therefore, to find in the writings of the utopian author of *New Atlantis* explicit praise of the anthropological realism of Machiavelli:

> We are much beholden to Machiavelli and other writers of that class, who openly and unfeignedly declare or describe what men do, and not what they ought to do. For it is not possible to join the wisdom of the serpent with the innocence of the dove, except men be perfectly acquainted with the nature of evil itself; for without this, *virtù* is open and unfenced; nay, a virtuous and honest man can do no good upon those that are wicked, to correct and reclaim them, without first exploring all the depths and recesses of their malice.[15]

Machiavelli, therefore, dares to look into the abyss of evil for the benefit of honest and virtuous men. He teaches the necessity of being good (or not) in situations that require it, as the tendency to do good is no more natural than the tendency to do bad.[16] The Florentine discovers and reveals that a policy fully consistent with Christian morality can lead to ruin. The sacred scripture is not the best guide to the world of human affairs, and it is time to replace it with science and experience based on examples from history.

It is inevitable that the role of human action will become a point of focus in this framework, and that the constant ups and downs and challenges which man has to face will be perceived as something within the reach of an adequately prepared man. Just as, in Machiavelli's view, the river of *fortuna* can be controlled only if one builds 'embankments and shelters' in advance, so for Bacon every navigation beyond the Pillars of Hercules of ignorance and the limits of contemporary science shall be possible only for those who board a boat which has been equipped for the challenges of the journey. In the essay 'Of Fortune', Bacon presents the very Machiavellian concept of *fortuna* as opportunity: 'It cannot be denied but Outward Accidents conduce much to Fortune [. . .]. But chiefly the Mould of Man's Fortune is in his owne hands. *Faber quisque Fortunae suae* [each person is the maker of his own fortune], saith the Poet.'[17] The experience in question concerns primarily the method. Even if the world is constantly changing, still this mutation proceeds according to laws. If in the past luck was just the name of human ignorance, following Machiavelli, it now becomes an opportunity to measure people's skills: 'therefore, if a man looke sharply and attentively, he shall see fortune: for though shee be blinde, yet shee is not invisible'.[18]

As a supporter of monarchy, Bacon depended for his political support and career on the monarch and his minions. For this reason, his confrontation with the openly republican worldview of Machiavelli was eventually inevitable. In fact, Bacon goes a long way in his praise of the political position of Machiavelli. For example, in his essay 'Of the True Greatness of Kingdoms and Estates', later included in *De augmentis*, Bacon openly refers to the military and political theories of the *Discourses*. Bacon focuses especially on Chapter 10 of the second volume of the *Discourses*, which describes the controversial opinion that 'money [is not] the sinews of war (as it is trivially said), where the sinews of Men's arms, in base and effeminate people, are failing'.[19] Bacon, similarly to Machiavelli, advises the prince to maintain a 'militia of natives' built up of 'good and valiant soldiers' and, drawing from historical experience, he openly condemns mercenary armies. Bacon presents these arguments in the context of a praise of the organisation and distribution of lands by Henry VII, in which he highlights the differences between England and France. He seems to refer to the position of Machiavelli maintaining that when nobility is too strong, it corrupts society, and that, on the contrary, the 'commons' should be supported in order to form the class of citizen-soldiers of which virtuous armies are built up. That is why for both Bacon and Machiavelli the infantry is 'the nerve of an army'.

Though modern scholars have noticed this republican convergence, they have not paid enough attention to another essay written by Bacon, which is crucial for the aim of carrying out a comparison with Machiavelli. It is 'Of Seditions and Troubles', in which the name of Machiavelli is mentioned once again, but his theory that the greatness of Rome was grounded on conflicts is carefully avoided. In this essay, Bacon develops an argument which is at the same time bland and trivially Machiavellian, in the most overused sense of the term. Machiavelli has shown, according to Bacon, that it is better for the prince not to take the side of either of the competing factions, and that the prince can be endangered both by the aristocracy and by the people. But instead of favouring the people over the aristocracy, as Machiavelli did, Bacon argues that the people lack reason and that 'the rebellions of the belly are the worst'.

There are many reasons for sedition, and it would certainly be a good solution for the prince to avoid 'whatsoever in offending people ioyneth and knitteth them in a common cause', preventing first of all economic misery. But at this point, when Bacon could explain his judgement in more detail, his aversion to the popular element evolves into a preference for monarchy which leaves no space for the republican thought of

Machiavelli. Bacon turns into the most trivial 'Machiavellian', advising to the prince 'artificial nourishing and entertaining of hopes, and carrying men from hopes to hopes', as 'the best antidotes against the poyson of discontentment'.[20] The popular basis of the government of the prince is dissolved in a dull tale about manipulation of the people by the prince, a subject that is closer to 'reason of state' than to Chapter XVIII of Machiavelli's *Prince*:

> For removing discontentments, or at least the danger of them, there is in every state (as we know) two portions of subjects. The noblesse and the commonaltie. When one of these is discontent, the danger is not great; for common people are of slow motion, if they be not excited by the greater sort; and the greater sort are of small strength, except the multitude be apt and ready to move of themselves. Then is the danger, when the greater sort doe but wait for the troubling of the waters amongst the meaner, that then they may declare themselves. The poets faigne that the rest of the gods would have bound Iupiter; which he hearing of, by the counsell of Pallas sent for Briareus, with his hundred hands, to come in to his aid: an embleme, no doubt, to shew how safe it is for the monarchs to make sure of the good will of common people.[21]

The multitude, therefore, becomes the many-headed monster that the prince can instigate and manipulate whenever he wants to suppress the ambition of the factions and neutralise conflicts. In this passage, Bacon makes reference to a metaphor that will often appear in his works, namely that of monstrosity associated with the people and rebellion. However, he does not mention this topic in the context of the Machiavellian claim in favour of the positive and constituent role of the people, but on the contrary by evoking the need to crush the rebel monster. In 'Typhon, or a Rebel', the second image in the *Wisdom of the Ancients* (1619), the crowd is represented as 'a huge and dreadful monster' rising against the sovereign:

> Such designs are generally set on foot by the secret motion and instigation of the peers and nobles, under whose connivance the common sort are prepared for rising. [. . .] This growing posture of affairs is fed by the natural depravity and malignant dispositions of the vulgar, which to kings is an envenomed serpent. And now the disaffected, uniting their force, at length break out into open rebellion, which, producing infinite mischiefs, both to prince and people, is represented by the horrid and multiplied deformity of Typhon.[22]

The sovereign has no alternative but to adopt a moderate and affable attitude, to divide the rebels and push them into powerlessness, so that he can crush them easily 'as it were by the weight of a mountain'.

Bacon therefore understands at least in part the novelty of Machiavelli's analysis of human nature and its application to society.

But he also understands its political consequences and Machiavelli's choice in favour of a democratic foundation of the government, and of a tumultuous republic. Just like Campanella, Bacon clearly identifies two separate aspects: the method – that is the science – and politics. But unlike Campanella, he praises the scientific aspect and condemns the political one at the same time.

THOMAS HOBBES

During the first English revolution, in the mid-seventeenth century, Thomas Hobbes developed a groundbreaking version of the relatively new natural law theories. He develops his original and radical version of the state of nature, the social contract and the transition to civil society throughout his works, including *The Elements of Law, Natural and Politic* (1640), *De Cive* (1642) and *Leviathan* (1651). Mainly concerned with the problem of the generation of power, the absolute nature of the sovereign's power and the question of stability in one of the most troubled periods of English history, he inevitably comes across many of the problems raised by Machiavelli in his works. It would seem that Hobbes deserves his own place in the history of the reception of Machiavelli.[23] In fact, although the name of the Florentine never appears in Hobbes's work, his *Leviathan* can be considered in many ways an implicit response to some of the theoretical difficulties exposed by Machiavelli.

The theoretical and cultural context of Hobbes is completely different from that of the previous century. Hobbes tries to respond directly to fundamental issues raised in the thought of Machiavelli, showing the relevance of his own thought within this new context: the relationship between order and conflict,[24] the legal basis of the state and the theory of duty, the concept of man and of his affections,[25] and the role of experience in gathering knowledge and in the construction of a science of politics. Hence it is even more important to reflect on this author who, in an astonishing silence surrounding the name of Machiavelli, chooses him as his main opponent. He himself takes a strong anti-Machiavellian stance that will become a point of reference for countless future authors.

Hobbes seeks to establish a circular relationship between knowledge and power – he denies that the people can have any form of political wisdom, and based on that he authorises and justifies the concept according to which the point of view of the sovereign is right 'by definition': 'Common people know nothing of right or wrong by their own meditation; they must therefore be taught the grounds of their duty, and the reasons why calamities ever follow disobedience to their lawful sovereigns.'[26] Philosophy meets politics, or rather power. The power consists in the knowledge of One, which is opposed to the knowledge of many, in a theoretical conclusion in which Hobbes refers to Plato's view against the scandalous view of Machiavelli concerning popular wisdom.

The connection between the knowledge of One and the knowledge of many is therefore conflicting and mutually exclusive. But Hobbes – unlike Machiavelli – goes beyond the ideological dimension of the struggle for hegemony in the field of political knowledge. The sovereign, in fact, not only 'represents' the truth, but produces it with his own words. This leads the scientific premises of Hobbes's nominalism to extreme consequences, extending it from the field of physics to the area of ethics and politics. If it is a fact that mathematical knowledge is superior to dogma, as it is free from controversies, not subject to disputes and therefore self-evident,[27] Hobbes extends this model to the field of politics, where the action of the sovereign, like that of God,[28] is right by definition. This criterion does not apply only to the sphere of politics, but also to the whole of human knowledge, including the scientific: 'For example when upon occasion of some strange and deformed birth, it shall not be decided by Aristotle, or the philosophers, whether the same be a man, or no, but by the laws; the civil law containing in it the ecclesiastical, as a part thereof, proceeding from the power of ecclesiastical government, given by our Saviour to all Christian sovereigns, as his immediate vicars [. . .].'[29]

The superiority of the link between knowledge and power in the person of the sovereign needs a metaphysical foundation. Hobbes believes in a complete separation between the concepts of justice and success. Men are wrong when they think that 'unjust actions' are justified 'by the force, and victories'. He seems to paraphrase and reverse Machiavelli by denying that 'justice is but a vain word: that whatsoever a man can get by his own industry, and hazard, is his own: that the practice of all nations can not be unjust', because '[this] being granted, no act in itself [could] be a crime, but must be made so (not by the law, but) by the success of them that commit it; and the same fact be virtuous, or vicious, fortune pleaseth'.[30] The couple *virtù/fortuna* immediately evokes the thought of Machiavelli, who, however, remains unnamed. It is in the context of the concept of justice, which for Hobbes means respect for the 'covenant' (or contract), that we find one of the most anti-Machiavellian pages:

> The fool hath said in his heart, there is no such thing as justice; and some-
> times also with his tongue; seriously alleging, that every man's conservation,

and contentment, being committed to his own care, there could be no reason, why every man might not do what he thought conduced thereunto: and therefore also to make, or not make; keep, or not keep covenants, was not against reason, when it conduced to one's benefit.[31]

In this passage, Hobbes evokes the figure of Machiavelli through the symbol of the 'fool'. In other passages, however, the echo of Machiavelli sounds on the pages of Hobbes in a completely different way. For example, in the context of respect for the covenants we encounter a well-known Hobbesian statement about the necessity of respecting promises, including those extorted by threat or fear. It is not the free will that matters, but the conditions in which the promise is made. For instance, 'prisoners of war, if trusted with the payment of their ransom, are obliged to pay it'. Hobbes proceeds to add, however, that 'if a weaker prince, make a disadvantageous peace with a stronger, for fear; he is bound to keep it; unless, as hath been said before, there ariseth some new, and just cause of fear, to renew the war'.[32] This is a very Machiavellian clause because Hobbes knows all too well that it will always be possible for a sovereign to state that only fear drove him to establish peace and subsequently find a new and just cause of war.

Hobbes concludes with an even more Machiavellian statement according to which, in the end, 'it is man, and arms, not words and promises, that make the force and power of the laws',[33] which makes reference to one of the theoretical pillars of the entire Hobbesian philosophy, summed up in the famous maxim that 'covenants, without the sword, are but words, and of no strength to secure a man at all'.[34]

The cultural context in which Hobbes writes differs completely from that of Machiavelli. The establishment of a new scientific worldview and the constitution of great national states, as well as the political and religious struggles which were to tear apart societies – all of these factors induce Hobbes to abandon Machiavellian realism in favour of an entirely different approach. In the context of political conflicts and of the construction of the internal order of the state, Hobbes rejects Machiavelli's view of conflict and criticises what he sees as the ruinous philosophy of Greek and Latin classics: 'There is nothing so absurd, that the old philosophers [. . .] have not some of them maintained', and the most absurd of them would be Aristotle's *Metaphysics*.[35] This is not just a philosophical aversion, common to many representatives of the new era. Hobbes was the first to formulate such a refusal based on an ethical and political point of view – he quite succinctly sums up the entire classical philosophy as a 'school of sedition':

> And as to rebellion in particular against monarchy; one of the most frequent causes of it, is the reading of the books of policy, and histories of the ancient Greeks, and Romans; from which, young men, and all others that are unprovided of the antidote of solid reason, receiving a strong, and delightful impression, of the great exploits of war, achieved by the conductors of their armies, receive withal a pleasing idea, of all they have done besides; and imagine their great prosperity, not to have proceeded from the emulation of particular men, but from the *virtù* of their popular form of government: not considering the frequent seditions, and civil wars, produced by the imperfection of their policy.[36]

Therefore, science and politics converge also in Hobbes's philosophy, but in a completely different manner to what we have seen in Bacon's praise of Machiavelli as the initiator of the inductive method. Because the tales told by the classics are primarily stories of sedition and rebellion, according to Hobbes it is necessary to expel them from the cultural education of citizens.

Machiavelli developed knowledge based on experience and legacy of the past, assuming that human nature, though constantly changing, changes according to natural laws that cannot be changed by reason. For Hobbes, on the contrary, reason itself produces general, eternal, immutable truth. Experience, he says, is not part of philosophy because we do not reach it through reasoning, but consists only in recalling events and their sequence in time, and it can be found both in men and in lower animals.[37] It would not be fair, though, to state that Hobbes condemns altogether the role of experience in developing correct reasoning. If it is true that 'when [. . .] there be infallible rules, (as in engines, and edifices, the rules of geometry) all the experience of the world cannot equal his counsel, that has learnt, or found out the rule', it is also true that 'when there is no such rule, he that hath most experience in that particular kind of business, has therein the best judgement, and is the best counsellor'.[38] Machiavelli believes that because men vary (and even if they do not vary, the events that surround them do), such stability and certainty of the rules of politics is merely a chimera. On the contrary, Hobbes sets for himself the goal of laying a base for this certainty and building a system according to the rules. Whereas, based on the example of the inductive method, Bacon sees in Machiavelli the founder of a new scientific knowledge, Hobbes perceives him merely as a bad adviser and a teacher of disobedience.

What does Hobbes's new science suggest in this situation? Because where there is conflict cohabitation is impossible, and because every conflict is synonymous with war, Hobbesian politics condemns conflict and ascribes it to the state of nature. The state of nature is not part of a historical past but of a theoretical one, which should be seen only as a conceptual basis which enables conceiving the state's sphere as a completely pacified and neutralised one. From this point of view, the origin is for Hobbes a place from which we should stay away as far as possible for the healthiness and safety of the state. Whereas for Machiavelli the return to the principles, as we have seen, means opposing the corruption by returning to the roots of the original conflict (because, as it was also stated by Hobbes, all sources are of a conflictual type – not only in the theoretical sense, but also in the historical one),[39] for Hobbes such an approach will necessarily lead to a final catastrophe.

The theoretical hypothesis of a destructive and hyper-confrontational state of nature goes against the Aristotelian concept of man as a political animal. Hobbes adopts, and brings to its logical extreme, a Machiavellian, radically egalitarian anthropology based on conflict, in opposition to the social and fundamentally inegalitarian nature as described by Aristotle. As has already been clearly pointed out by Carl Schmitt, Hobbes denies the possibility of a natural turn towards the common good which could occur under the sign of harmony and moderation.[40] And in this aspect, willingly or not, he is fully Machiavellian. For Machiavelli, however, the theoretical nature of the original conflict is articulated in a variety of real conflicts (hence the need to study them in their historical development) becoming the basis of the power of the republic in its expansive movement. In Hobbes's view, on the contrary, this conflict is neutralised in the artificial body of the state and institutionalised in the form of the modern mechanism in which the individuals are represented by the ruler.

JAMES HARRINGTON

It has been stated all too often that James Harrington, perhaps the most important exponent of seventeenth-century English republicanism, is an opponent of Hobbesian absolutism. Harrington openly declares his admiration and fondness for Machiavelli. His interpretation, however, is quite selective, and he is certainly not inclined to accept many of the conclusions which, as we have seen, are at the centre of the Florentine's thought. In addition, Harrington explicitly follows the reasoning of the author of *Leviathan* in many aspects (with the exception – undoubtedly fundamental – of his preference for the republican form of government rather than monarchy). His goal is 'to go [his] own way', thus producing an original synthesis of the thought of Hobbes and Machiavelli.[41]

Harrington highlights especially the difference between the method of Machiavelli and that of Hobbes. He himself is clearly in favour of the former, and of historiography understood as political theory, taking a stand against the claims of a pure theory that intends to dispense with history. Before offering any advice on politics or government, '[it is] necessary that the archives of ancient prudence should be ransacked'.[42] Following Bacon and, above all, the medical researcher William Harvey, whom Hobbes had listed among the fathers of modern science, Harrington argues that the inclusion of history is a truly scientific method. Harrington thus opposes the animosity towards the empirical and experiential knowledge of Greeks and Romans, whom Hobbes accuses of drawing their knowledge not from the principles of nature, but from the very system of their states. This, Harrington replies, is 'as if a man should tell famous Harvey that he transcribed his circulation of the blood not out of the principles of nature, but out of the anatomy of this or that body'.[43]

The method embraced by Harrington, therefore, draws from the experience of the ancients and from modern science. Indeed, the foundations of his theory seem quite modern. For example, against the excessive 'politicism' of Hobbes, who reduced almost everything to the legal foundations of the state, Harrington argues that, apart from politics, economy and the balance of wealth are the secret of a prosperous and virtuous republic: 'An equal commonwealth is such an one as is equal both in the balance or foundation and in the superstructures, that is to say in her agrarian law and in her rotation.'[44] 'Balance of dominion' and rotation of offices, that is 'succession unto magistracy [...] succeeding others through the free election or suffrage of the people', constitute fundamental elements of republicanism in the spirit of Harrington.

The introduction of economy into the theoretical framework is an achievement of paramount importance, and Harrington is glad to make his stand against Hobbes with genuine Machiavellian realism, arguing that

> as he said of the law that without this sword is but paper, so he might have thought of this sword that without an hand it is but cold iron. The hand which holdeth this sword is the militia of a nation [...]. But an army is a beast that hath a great belly and must be fed; wherefore this will come unto what pastures you have, and what pastures you have will come unto the balance of property, without which the public sword is but a name or mere spitfrog.[45]

Above all, however, Harrington adds economics to the entirely political solution that Hobbes had given to the problem of order and peace. Machiavelli had clearly pointed out the question of the economic nature of the political conflict, arguing that 'it has always been the end of those who start a war – and it is reasonable that it should be so – to enrich themselves and impoverish the enemy'.[46] Harrington, unlike Machiavelli, believes that it is in the field of economy that one can find a solution to the conflict which, according to Machiavelli, pertains to the very nature of republics and that he himself considered to be an incentive for their development. The sedition that occurs in republics must be seen as an exception and not as a rule – it is so in the thought of both Hobbes, who condemns it entirely, and Machiavelli, who believes in its favourable effects.[47] In the life of republics and political bodies, conflict is not a part of the normal function, but rather of pathology and disease. Such a disease can be prevented through proper distribution of economic resources and a wise organisation of institutions.

The originality of Harrington is also evident in the way in which he uses and effortlessly modifies the theories of Machiavelli. Against Hobbes, for example, he repeats the statement of Machiavelli according to which 'great *virtù*' cannot appear without 'best education', 'best education' cannot exist without 'best laws', and these without 'the excellency of [the best] policy',[48] which are precisely the mechanisms that remove the 'infirmity' of the 'seditions'. But on this topic Machiavelli expresses the exact opposite opinion, writing that 'striking examples of *virtù* [...] proceed from good education, good education from good laws, and good laws from those very tumults which many so inconsiderately condemn'.[49] Harrington, therefore, consciously takes a stance which is between these two opponents in an attempt to develop a theory of republicanism which, based on order and internal peace, will be able to thwart the absolutist outcomes of Hobbes's philosophy.

Another aspect which enables us to recognise the difference between Harrington and Machiavelli is the question of the common good. Denying the Aristotelian theory of the inherent social nature of the human animal, Hobbes rejects any possibility of a natural unification of individuals around a common good. Machiavelli reaches the same conclusion – for him common good is nothing but ideology used by the ones who dominate to mask their dominance. Harrington's standpoint is different from both. He returns to the Aristotelian idea of natural sociality which has been corrupted by a long history of injustice and abuse of power, but can and must ultimately be recovered and restored in present conditions.

First of all, Harrington explicitly rejects the radically egalitarian anthropology of Machiavelli and Hobbes. Men, for him, are not equal in terms of intellectual capacity and political *virtù*, which, in turn, is dependent on reason. In a congregation of men, no more than one-third will be wiser, 'or at least less foolish', than the others. And while the third, 'discoursing and arguing one with another, show the eminence of their parts', the others 'discover things that they never thought on' and 'hang upon their lips as children upon their fathers'.[50] This is the 'natural aristocracy' which deserves to sit in the elected Senate, that in the mixed government of Harrington would have the function of counselling and not of commanding. This is the point in which, attempting to justify the concept of the natural inequality of men, Harrington develops some of his most powerful metaphors. Similarly to an army which needs both officers and soldiers, the commonwealth requires people and gentry: 'Let the people embrace the gentry, in peace as the light of their eyes, and in war as the trophy of their arms. [. . .] Let the nobility love and cherish the people that afford them a throne so much higher in a commonwealth, and in the acknowledgement of their *virtù*, than the crowns of monarchs.'[51]

The idea of common good is expressed even more forcefully in a metaphor that has rightly caught the attention of careful interpreters, especially the ones closer to the liberal matrix of Harrington's republicanism.[52] The popular government is certainly the closest to the interest of mankind and thus also to right reason. But how to prevent private interests from overriding common interest? Even two 'silly girls' have the answer, which comes – notwithstanding Hobbes's opinion – from the mundane experience of everyday life rather than from the highest principles of political science: 'Two of them have a cake yet undivided, which was given between them. That each of them therefore may have that which is due, "Divide" says one unto the other, "and I will choose; or let me divide, and you shall choose".'[53]

The problem of the stability of republics is reduced by Harrington to the equal division of resources (economic aspect) and their distribution (political aspect). As Machiavelli had already clearly seen and extensively criticised, however, this pacific and pacificating solution of the economic and political problem assumes the common good not so much as a point of arrival, but rather as a starting point. In essence, the common good to which even the two 'silly girls' have the key is a premise more than a promise and a result. This premise, which Machiavelli had so boldly revealed and which Harrington hastily buried under its euphoric simplification, actually hides the original violence. The one who divides and the one who distributes must beforehand agree to the rules of the game and share common aims and objectives.

According to Harrington, only the Senate has to discuss, and only the people – through their representatives – have to decide. The former divides the cake, while the latter distributes it. But the whole process is presented as choosing the best solution to a problem that is common to all and that affects everyone *in the same way*: 'To debate is to discern, or put a difference between things that being alike are not the same, or it is separating and weighing this reason against that and that reason against this, which is dividing.'[54] This common ground is exposed by Machiavelli (and also, in a different way, by Hobbes) as an impossible premise. An anticipative and universal acceptance of the rules of the game is a solution that can appeal to the theoreticians of contemporary liberalism (the dominant doctrine today) but it is quite unlikely in the political conditions of Harrington's era (and probably of all time). Harrington's *Oceana* may not be a utopian text, as it is claimed by Pocock,[55] if read in the context of the immediate political purposes that the author sets for himself. But it is certainly utopian in assuming that the conflicting parties of the political arena will actually share the same means and ends.

In his interpretation of the history of republicanism Harrington is an extraordinarily original and modern author. His attempt to establish the importance of the economic dimension on the same level as politics is of considerable interest and its Machiavellian inspiration is evident. Christopher Hill, however, writes that 'Harrington has been called a precursor of Marx, but he never even approached that conception of class struggle as the motive force in history which Marx held to be his chief contribution: one object of Harrington's theory, on the contrary, was to explain the English Revolution as a natural phenomenon, and so to *exclude* the political activity of the masses of the population'.[56] Not only is Harrington not a precursor of Marx (and this has little or no interest for the historian of ideas, given the ambiguity of the category of precursor), but he also cannot be considered a follower of Machiavelli, as his whole theoretical effort – through the harmony of the common good and the institutional representation – is aimed precisely at overcoming the conflictual aspect which was the basis of the Florentine's scandalous version of republicanism.[57]

BARUCH SPINOZA

Not all early modern republican thought, however, took the anti-conflictualist stance of Harrington. If we move to the Netherlands, we shall find in the writings of Baruch Spinoza one of the most interesting readings of Machiavelli in the seventeenth century and, probably, in the entire history of Western political philosophy.[58]

Raised in the Sephardic Jewish community in Amsterdam, Spinoza was excommunicated after clashing with the religious authorities over the most fundamental beliefs concerning God and the world. He quickly became one of the leading figures in the seventeenth-century European philosophical landscape, yet always lived at the margins, earning his living as a lens grinder and working on his philosophical masterpieces, including the *Theologico-Political Treatise* (published in 1670 and condemned by the authorities in 1674, together with Hobbes's *Leviathan*), the *Ethics* (published posthumously in 1677) and the *Political Treatise* (unfinished, and also published by his friends in the *Opera Posthuma*).

Spinoza is always reluctant to point out his sources. However, this is not the case when he evokes the name of Machiavelli in two places in his *Political Treatise*. In the first of these he argues:

> In the case of a prince whose sole motive is lust for power, the means he must employ to strengthen and preserve his state have been described at some length by that keen observer, Machiavelli, but with what purpose appears uncertain. If he did have some good purpose in mind, as one should believe of so wise a man, it must have been to show how foolish are the attempts so often made to get rid of a tyrant while yet the causes that have made the prince a tyrant cannot be removed; on the contrary, they become more firmly established as the prince is given more grounds for fear.[59]

Spinoza is referring to the long chapter of the *Discourses* in which Machiavelli expounds on the removal of the tyrant, useless and harmful, without at the same time removing the material and moral causes that led the tyrant to power. In this context we immediately think of Spinoza's criticism of 'English people, who sought to remove their monarch only to recognize another one under a different name, and restore, with great bloodshed, the primitive state'.[60] With this statement, Spinoza takes the part of those who had already begun to reassess the intellectual honesty and political position of Machiavelli, against the prevailing anti-Machiavellianism.

It is reasonable, for Spinoza, to draw from Machiavelli in order to construct his own vision of the best conditions for a republican regime. The civilian militia, also for the Dutch philosopher, is one of the essential elements necessary for the freedom and independence of peoples. This was a well-known fact among the citizens of the free cities of the United Provinces who, during the crisis of 1672, opposed William III of Orange, Stadtholder of Holland and Zeeland, as well as, eventually, the other provinces. Taking up explicitly Machiavellian themes, Spinoza argues that when the army is composed only of citizens, men desire peace more than war, because 'the soldier in the camp was a citizen in the forum, the officer in the camp was a judge in the law-court, and the commander-in-chief in the camp was a ruler in civil life'. War is necessary only 'for the sake of peace and the defence of freedom',[61] and for Spinoza one cannot exist without the other. In fact, it is quite clear – as it was for Machiavelli – that the aim of the existence of national militia was more political than military. In the Hebrew state, for example,

> among other considerations that restrained the unbridled licence of the captains was one of considerable importance, in that the armed forces were recruited from the whole citizen body with no exception between the ages of twenty and sixty, and that the captains were not allowed to hire foreign mercenaries. This, I repeat, was of considerable importance, for it is a fact that rulers can subjugate a people simply by means of hired mercenaries, while there is nothing they fear more than the independence of a citizen soldiery who have won freedom and glory for their country by their valour, their toil, and the heavy price of blood.[62]

What is the philosophical basis of the convergence between Machiavelli and Spinoza? The first aspect is that of anthropological realism, or, as Spinoza puts it, 'keeping in mind what [men] really are rather than what we would like them to be'.[63] Machiavelli had developed this in opposition to a long train of classical thought, preaching the need to go straight to the 'effectual truth of the thing rather than to the imagination of it'.[64]

This anthropological concept, so important in Spinoza's reflection, comes from a wider 'ontological realism' that allows Spinoza to develop a concept of law which is strongly original compared to the theoretical framework of the seventeenth century.[65] The law (*jus*), says Spinoza, is nothing else but the 'power' (*potentia*) that each individual has to act in order to preserve his own existence, the primary impulse which characterises each being, human and non-human (the *conatus*). Political theory must therefore recognise that the human world is part of the natural world, not something separate as if it were a 'state within a state' (*imperium in imperio*).[66] Hobbes had described the hyper-conflictual state of nature in those terms of self-preservation, but in moving from the state of nature to one of civilisation, men would be forced to change their human nature. But in Spinoza's view, this theory, in which humans become distinct from nature, an *imperium in imperio*, contradicts reality and is therefore unacceptable.

That is why, commenting on the *Leviathan*, Spinoza does not hesitate to maintain that 'with regard to political theory, the difference between Hobbes and myself [. . .] consists in this, that I always preserve the natural right in its entirety, and I hold that the sovereign power in a State has right over a subject only in proportion to the excess of its power over that of a subject. This is always the case in a state of nature.'[67] The concept of *jus sive potentia* ('right as power'), therefore, concerns the whole of nature, and politics as a part of it. It would be merely a utopian fiction to think that politics can change the natural dimension of relationships between individuals. Spinoza criticises Hobbes and responds to his arguments on his own ground. Sovereignty in his view is absolute, and it can only be such. But this does not imply transcending the natural dimension.

The sovereign is entitled, as in Hobbes's view, to decide about what is right and wrong. But even he is subject to the iron rule of right as power. For example, only the sovereign is a lawful judge and interpreter of the validity of the contract, and no individual can rightfully replace him. However, the sovereign has this right only as long as he has power to exercise it. In fact if

> the laws are such that they cannot be broken without at the same time weakening the commonwealth – that is, without at the same time turning into indignation the common fear felt by the majority of the citizens – then by their violation the commonwealth is dissolved and the contract comes to an end. Thus the contract depends for its enforcement not on civil right but on right of war. So the ruler is bound to observe the terms of the contract for exactly the same reason as a man in the state of nature, in order not to be his own enemy, is bound to take care not to kill himself.[68]

In Spinoza's theory, not civil law but the law of war is at the heart of the state, in the conflicting relationship between subjects and the sovereign.[69] In this passage Spinoza mentions indignation, which is for him one of the fundamental affects in politics. His philosophy has been called philosophy of joy, as he defines it as an increase of power (and therefore, in political terms, of rights) for each individual, while its opposite, sadness, as a loss of power (and thus of rights).[70] Alexandre Matheron points to the ambiguous and yet fruitful status of the affect of indignation, which is defined by Spinoza as 'hatred toward one who has injured another'.[71] On the one hand, as a specific form of sadness, indignation is a loss of power, and therefore a negative affect. On the other hand, unlike Hobbes, for whom conflict is always negative, Spinoza is forced to maintain a fundamental, and thus in some way positive, value of indignation as regards its contribution to the formation of the state.

Men are led more by affects than by reason when they agree to join together and form a community. This is a completely natural step which gathers the multitude around a 'common hope, or common fear, or desire to avenge some common injury'[72] which depends on the affect of indignation. This dimension is not overcome in an artificial manner and remains at the heart of the political construction in the subsequent relationship between sovereign and subjects: 'Matters which arouse the general indignation are not likely to fall within the right of the commonwealth. It is without doubt a natural thing for men to conspire together either by reason of a common fear or through a desire to avenge a common injury. And since the right of the commonwealth is defined by the common power of the multitude [*communi multitudinis potentia*], undoubtedly the power of the commonwealth and its right is to that extent diminished, as it affords reasons for many citizens to join in a conspiracy.'[73]

The violence of the state of nature does not dissolve in the peace of the civil state. On the contrary, for Spinoza, just as for Machiavelli, that violence is kept alive within and through the original right (that is, a power) of resistance that the subjects have against the ruler. In this context we can observe in Spinoza's theory the emergence of a relationship of mutual support, based on conflict (and not on common good), which Machiavelli had developed in *The Prince*, but also of the Machiavellian idea of a constant and productive exercise of conflict. And it is at this point that, making reference to the subject of the return to principles, Spinoza quotes Machiavelli for the second time:

> The primary reason why states of this kind disintegrate is the one noted by that acute Florentine in his Book 3 on Livy, Discourse 1, where he says, 'A state, like the human body, has every day something added to it which some time or another needs to be put right.' It is therefore necessary, he continues, that something should occasionally occur to bring the state back to the original principle on which it was first established. If this does not happen in due time, its defects will develop to such an extent that they cannot be removed without destroying the state itself.[74]

Spinoza does not agree with all the solutions offered by Machiavelli. For instance, he does not believe in the possibility of creating dictatorial power based on the Roman model and avoiding the dangers which are implicitly connected to this office. Even more important seems the emergence of the conflictual dimension of politics, to which institutions must adapt in order to, as Machiavelli would say, give vent to natural humours. Spinoza praises the division that emerges in assemblies and deliberative processes. Against the authoritarianism of the supporters of William of Orange, he writes in his *Political Treatise* that if, on the one hand, '"while the Romans debate, Saguntum is lost", on the other hand when all decisions are made by a few men who have only themselves to please, freedom and the common good are lost'.[75]

Against the absolutist tradition of Hobbes and the pacifying republicanism of Harrington, Spinoza reconsiders Machiavelli from a realistic viewpoint. This leads him to argue that social conflicts are a physiological phenomenon, a natural function, of republics and constitute part of the struggle through which the people constantly defend its freedom:

Thus the quarrels and rebellions [*discordiis et seditionibus*] that are often stirred up in a commonwealth never lead to the dissolution of the commonwealth by its citizens (as is often the case with other associations) but to a change in its form – that is, if their disputes cannot be settled while still preserving the structure of the commonwealth. Therefore, by the means required to preserve a state I understand those that are necessary to preserve the form of the state without any notable change.[76]

Once again, these are means that only Machiavelli had dared to praise and support within his conflictual republicanism.

PIERRE BAYLE AND AMELOT DE LA HOUSSAYE

The reflection on the author of *The Prince* in the seventeenth century is concluded with the publication of the entry on 'Machiavel' in the *Dictionnaire historique et critique* (*Historical and Critical Dictionary*) of Pierre Bayle in 1697. The *Dictionnaire*, a masterful work fundamental for understanding both the seventeenth and the eighteenth centuries, reveals both the genius of its author and the tradition to which it belongs and from which it draws. It is the tradition of erudite and philosophical criticism of philosophy in itself which perceives morality through the prism of mechanism. This current of thought is cultivated by the major libertine minds of the French seventeenth century. Bayle reviews all the biographical material available at that time, in an attempt to reconstruct an image of Machiavelli as being as faithful as possible to the historical truth. With wit and honesty he quotes sources, systematises opinions and debates, and corrects inaccuracies. He undermines the naive interpretation – which will however go on for a long time – according to which Machiavelli wrote *The Prince* to expose the tyrants and inspire a sense of freedom in people. He concludes, however, by saying that Machiavelli 'has shown his republican spirit through his conduct'.[77] The authority of the judgement and the scrupulousness of this work of reconstruction will make this article by Bayle an unquestionable point of reference for the interpretations of the following century – a century which, even more than the previous one, prepares to read Machiavelli in the light of revolutionary passions.

The shift in the political and philosophical issues that accompanied the Enlightenment helped renew the interest in Machiavelli. As we have already seen in the sixteenth and seventeenth centuries, the name of Machiavelli became a real theoretical weapon in political debates that contributed to the creation of cultural conditions which, among other things, would enable the outbreak of the French Revolution. The 'Machiavellian eighteenth century' can be circumscribed by two publications of fundamental importance: the edition of *The Prince* annotated by Amelot de la Houssaye and published in Amsterdam in 1683,[78] and the *Complete Works* translated by Toussaint Guiraudet, released in Paris in 1799 at the very end of the Jacobin period.[79]

Though Amelot's name is absent from some mainstream accounts of the Enlightenment,[80] his importance can hardly be overestimated. Secretary to the French ambassador in Venice in 1669, an admirer of La Rochefoucauld – but also of the Protestant 'heretics' William of Orange and the admiral Coligny – and convinced follower of Tacitus, Amelot published his comments to *The Prince* after releasing the translation of the *History of the Council of Trent* by Paolo Sarpi and before authoring the translation of the *Oráculo manual y arte de prudencia* (as *L'Homme de cour* or *The Art of Worldly Wisdom*) by Baltasar Gracián.[81] Amelot's interpretation intertwines a Tacitean reading of Machiavelli and a Machiavellian reading of Tacitus, shedding new light on *The Prince*, laid out in a fresh and modern French. It is in this version that *The Prince* was read in eighteenth-century Europe, by King Frederick II of Prussia and Voltaire, but also by fine and careful readers such as Queen Christina of Sweden, who, in her own edition, scrupulously annotated both Machiavelli's text and Amelot's comments.[82]

Although presented merely as a translation and a sober comment, the work of Amelot has enormous political significance. This has not always been noticed by modern commentators, although Joseph Macek rightly highlights the interventions that Amelot has made in Machiavelli's text as a translator.[83] These comments to Machiavelli's text – especially when read together with comments to Tacitus,[84] as rightly pointed out by Procacci – shed light on the emergence of a republican Machiavelli. Bayle will positively critique the new edition,[85] which will help revive the interest in Machiavelli across Europe.

FREDERICK II

It is paradoxical, however, that the popularity and longevity of Amelot's Machiavelli is linked to the most important, thorough and well-planned – but ultimately failed – early modern anti-Machiavellian operation. The edition of Amelot, in fact, was included in the *Anti-Machiavel* of Frederick II, king of Prussia, a work in which Voltaire also participated, published in The Hague in 1740. One of the military geniuses of his time, responsible for the successful reorganisation of the Prussian army, Frederick was also a poet and a fine philosopher. Friend of Voltaire and protector of scientists and philosophers like Maupertuis and La Mettrie, Frederick perfectly embodied 'enlightened despotism', aspiring to achieve the ancient dream of a philosopher-king.

It is no coincidence that he prepared his refutation of Machiavelli based on the Tacitean commentary of Amelot. Frederick II worked on the text between 1739 and 1740, gladly accepting the suggestions of Voltaire. The result is a treatise which is quite naive, sometimes even limited, the author of which does not seem to grasp the rhetorical strategy and even the very evident content of some of Machiavelli's metaphors – such as the one of hunting as an exercise preparing for war, which the author reduces trivially to 'one of those sensual pleasures that stir the body but that say nothing to the mind'.[86]

Yet, reading between the lines, one can see that the enlightened prince had grasped something essential from Machiavelli's text. No doubt he noticed the danger of Machiavelli's thought, which he does not hesitate to describe as monstrous and 'epidemic'.[87] It is, however, a thought that seems to triumph effortlessly in the confrontation with Frederick's moralism. Hobbes had raised the need for an antidote to the seditious thought of the Greeks and Romans, and similarly Frederick declares the need for an antidote to Machiavellianism, which should be at least as powerful as the poison itself.[88] And yet the great insight that underlies the entire work, as already suggested by Innocent Gentillet, is that it would ultimately be better to draw a veil of silence over Machiavelli, even at the cost of corrupting and perverting history – just to erase his cursed name for ever.[89]

Notwithstanding his simplistic reduction of Machiavellian *virtù* to vice and moral crime, which does not add anything to the long tradition of Machiavelli's critics, Frederick still manages to notice a few key elements, even while missing the larger issue. For example, in Chapter IX, on 'civil principality', Machiavelli argued that 'two classes are found in every city. And [. . .] the people do not want to be dominated or oppressed by the nobles, and the nobles want to dominate and oppress the people.'[90] The prince, who comes to power with the support of the *grandi* – and this is the radical thesis of Machiavelli – should favour the people, and govern with their support.

Frederick does not seem to grasp at all the crucial point, that is, the popular and democratic foundation of princely power. He merely states that, in reality, no republic will ever voluntarily surrender to the power of a prince, because of its love of independence and freedom. The topic of the division within the city, which is the basic theme of the chapter on 'civil principality', is not addressed. Yet, at the end of the chapter, Frederick mentions the 'overly powerful families' that are the cause of the destruction of any state. This is a clear reference to the 'fatal families' on whom the prince should turn his back, as advised by Machiavelli. Where Machiavelli decomposes the unity of the city, in order to bring out the political and economic divisions, Frederick tries to reconstruct a narrative of the unity of the city which opposes the tyrant.

Frederick uses the same neutralising mechanism in Chapter 20 – a comment on the Machiavellian passages about hereditary principality. Here Frederick once again raises the issue of division and of the policy of the prince towards the conflicting factions. These are unwaveringly condemned in the name of the uncritically assumed unity of the city subject to the reign of the prince: 'Nothing makes the monarchy stronger than the intimate and inseparable union of all its members, the ultimate goal of every wise prince.'[91] In his limited rhetorical arsenal Frederick, backed up by Voltaire, finds nothing better to quote in favour of his statement than the famous apology with which Menenius Agrippa intends to unite the Roman people.

And yet, behind the apparent naivety and limitation of these arguments, once again Frederick grasps something important, which is only hinted at but which will be treated in a more thorough manner in later eighteenth-century readings of Machiavelli. A republic, the author adds, 'must, however, maintain jealousy among its members, because if the parties do not oversee one another, the form of government changes into monarchy'.[92] The conflictual argument of Machiavelli, who was in favour of disunion and believed that the people must continuously keep the *grandi* in check, is here neutralised to the form of the reciprocal control of the different forces present in the republic. Although Frederick does not develop this issue in depth, the subject will be of crucial importance for the future readings of Machiavelli, first and foremost that of Montesquieu, as we shall see in a moment. Montesquieu did not have to draw from the Prussian king in order to develop his theory of the division and mutual control of powers. Frederick II and Voltaire have however formulated a bright, though synthetic, anticipation of the strategy of neutralising the Machiavellian argument about conflicts, from a viewpoint which anticipates some of the seminal concepts of political liberalism of the following decades.

In conclusion, although many future readers, including Hegel, would consider the *Anti-Machiavel* to be little more than a rhetorical exercise, the text soon became influential, more because of the authority of its authors than for the depth of its statements. It prevailed, however, in a paradoxical way. In fact, it added little or nothing to the already existing critical arguments. It did, however, contribute significantly to the revival of interest in Machiavelli and the political significance of his writings, reread and reinterpreted in a context different from that of his era. The presence of the comment, republican in its spirit, written by Amelot de la Houssaye, which Voltaire placed in the centre of his editorial presentation of the text,[93] gives an ambiguous meaning to the entire project. With the support of the French secretary, the Florentine secretary's text easily resists the assault of its royal opponent.

Although playing a fundamental role, Voltaire, in the end, voluntarily remains at the margins of the attempt to denigrate Machiavelli on behalf of absolute despotism. Three of the greatest philosophers of the century – Montesquieu, Diderot and Rousseau – directly engage, on the contrary, with Machiavelli's work in a more open manner. And all of them, using different strategies, attempt to counter the authoritative condemnations of Machiavelli, trying to associate him with different policies: constitutional liberalism and democratic republicanism.

Voltaire accuses Montesquieu of Machiavellianism.[94] This allegation is certainly unjust, from the point of view of what Voltaire means by it, but it is also correct – at least partially – from the point of view of Montesquieu, who does not quote Machiavelli explicitly but who does embrace his teaching, modifying it in an original way and adapting it to his own political taste. This adaptation is, however, also a neutralisation of Machiavelli's thought, especially when we consider some key points such as the conflictual foundation of the political and military power of Rome.

MONTESQUIEU

Charles-Louis de Secondat, Baron de la Brède et de Montesquieu, is one of the most interesting political writers of the eighteenth century. Belonging to the movement of the 'philosophes', and contributing to the development of the enlightened sensibility in politics and culture, Montesquieu lived on the edge of a universe – the *ancien régime* – which was about to collapse, and whose crumbling he perfectly perceives and denounces, for example in his *Persian Letters* (published anonymously in 1721). Like Machiavelli, Montesquieu is interested in the theoretical function of history, and in particular of Roman history. Like Machiavelli, he searches for a principle of explanation of history that avoids transcendental causes and principles. In his masterpiece *L'Esprit des lois* (*The Spirit of the Laws*, also published anonymously in 1748), not only does Montesquieu give a groundbreaking contribution to the genealogy of political sociology, but he also develops, following John Locke and the English model he knows first hand, an original theory of separation of powers.

Montesquieu's interest in Machiavelli goes back at least to the early draft of the *Dissertation sur la politique des Romains dans la religion* (*Dissertation on the Politics of the Romans Concerning Religion*, 1716), in which Montesquieu lays out with great fervour the Machiavellian idea of religion as a tool in the hands of the tyrant.[95] Scholars have reconstructed in detail the genealogy of his interest.[96] The work in which the influence of Machiavelli is most apparent is undoubtedly the *Considérations sur les causes de la grandeur des Romains et de leur décadence* (*Considerations on the Causes of the Greatness of the Romans and their Decline*, 1734), but it is also useful to follow his influence in *L'Esprit des lois*, in which Machiavelli's thought was absorbed and neutralised in the great design of the early liberal constitutionalism.

The rhapsodic and unsystematic style of the *Considérations* has disturbed several contemporary readers.[97] Yet those who read it together with the *Discourses* do not overlook the fact that the strategy of this writing is first and foremost a strategy of thought that was necessary in presenting opposition to unifying theories about ultimate goals or 'providence' in history. As we have seen, Machiavelli pertains to one of the more radical trends of the Western philosophical tradition, that is, Lucretian-Epicurean materialism, and rejects any teleology of historical events and any higher, universal divine design. That unifying design was still alive and influential in the eighteenth century, and counted among its apologists Jacques Bénigne Bossuet, a former historian of Rome (*Discours sur l'histoire universelle* or *Discourse on Universal History* of 1681) and anti-Machiavellian theoretician who in *Politique tirée des propres paroles de l'Écriture sainte* (*Politics Drawn from Holy Scripture*, 1709) tries, in a very Machiavellian manner, to imagine an absolute and yet not arbitrary princely power.

Against the authoritative providentialism of Bossuet, Montesquieu writes his *Considérations* in search of an 'effectual truth' that can be found in the irregular and conflictual movement of history rather than in the dreams of theologians. The aim is to discover the laws, or at least constant rules, which manifest themselves in history, such as those relating to human nature, just as in the teaching of Machiavelli, who claims that 'because men of all times share the same passions, the circumstances that give rise to great changes may vary, but the causes are always the same'.[98]

Machiavelli's name never appears in the *Considérations*, though his influence is evident. In this period, it is still an infamous and accursed name, whose dangerous 'viral' power, threatening pedagogical moralism and Christianised thought, has been fully understood.

Yet Montesquieu can not shy away from addressing the question of Machiavelli and its radical and innovative consequences. For example, in the field of military thought, Montesquieu follows Machiavelli, fully recognising the superiority of infantry – principle of organised defence, discipline and resistance – over the cavalry – principle of disorganised attack, impetus and action.[99] For Machiavelli, however, as we have seen, the superiority of infantry over cavalry is based on a presumption not only of military but also of political importance. Montesquieu also insists on the importance of the link between military discipline and social structure, though with less political complexity:

> The Romans were able to control all peoples, not only through the art of war, but also by means of prudence, wisdom, constance, love of glory and of fatherland. Under the empire, once all of these *virtù* disappeared, what remained was only military art. With its help they defended what they had conquered, in spite of the weakness and the tyranny of their princes. But when corruption took up also in the army, then they fell prey to all other peoples.[100]

The comparison between Machiavelli and Montesquieu provides original and interesting insights on the subject of political conflicts. Montesquieu seems to share the Machiavellian view on the bond between *virtù*, power, freedom and conflict. This view is quite explicit and it is repeated several times in the *Considérations*[101] and *L'Esprit des lois* (also bearing in mind the *Persian Letters*). It is thus possible to reconstruct the evolution of Montesquieu's position, also clarifying the peculiar way in which he adopts the Machiavellian conflictual stand. While in the first work Montesquieu emphasises the need to tolerate riots and conflicts between the plebeians and the Senate in order to give vent to the ambition inscribed in human nature (the famous Machiavellian argument of 'humours'), in *L'Esprit* the principal idea is that of containing conflicts by means of institutions and constitutions, within the framework of a more mature logic of the mutual control of powers.

Montesquieu is a fine reader, and invokes the name of Machiavelli with a certain amount of caution in order to avoid uncomfortable accusations. If considered against the general backdrop of the evolution of his thought, however, his raising of the subject of conflicts and factions does not seem to be simply a more moderate version, but rather an attempt to neutralise the fundamental points, by inscribing the position of Machiavelli, who is openly in favour of the people, into an institutional framework that completely dismounts its constituent revolutionary character. The approach of Montesquieu is not Machiavellian, although it is marked by a moderate Machiavellianism.[102] The factional republicanism is not a consequence of the separation of powers, serving as a solid foundation for the construction of constitutionalism. This political and legal framework through which the author develops his most mature convictions within the liberal paradigm replaces Machiavelli's radical conflictualism. Machiavelli is interested in the people, and in particular in the people as opposed to the *grandi*. For Montesquieu, in turn, everything revolves around the individual, who enjoys peace and security within a paradigm in which exchange and trade have replaced conflict and war.

Montesquieu deprives Machiavelli's theory on conflict of its internal content, using his language within a context that is completely different from and, in fact, antithetical to Machiavelli's political and theoretical stance, which is clearly partial and in favour of the people. The detachment of Montesquieu from Machiavelli is visible, for example, in the fact that the Florentine explicitly condemns the nobility and the *grandi*, while taking a stand in favour of the people and the plebs.[103] This is particularly evident in the references to the passages of Machiavelli's *Istorie fiorentine*[104] that are ambiguous and unworthy of Montesquieu's clever interpretations (for instance in the banal assimilation of Machiavelli and '*machiavélisme*').

Lastly, the importance that Montesquieu progressively ascribes to judicial power does not proceed from Machiavelli, but is rather developed *against* Machiavelli, his praise of power of people's tribunes and, more generally, of the role of the people in taking decisions. Machiavelli argues that law and politics, laws and conflicts proceed recursively, each having an effect on the other.[105] The constitutionalism of Montesquieu is not a moderated version of Machiavelli's thesis, but rather one of the most acute and intelligent attempts to abrogate its revolutionary content and incorporate it into the emerging tradition of liberalism. The aristocratic Montesquieu understands very well Machiavelli and the democratic, and therefore anti-aristocratic and anti-liberal, potential of his thought. His strategy does not consist in rejecting the more radical arguments openly, but in depriving them of their internal content and introducing them into the framework of the new liberal ideology. In this way, paradoxically, Montesquieu converges with Frederick II and his *Anti-Machiavel*, as well as with the attempt to reuse and convert the thought of Machiavelli into a moderate form of conflictual dynamics, compatible with the new role of the rising bourgeoisie.

But this is not the end of ambiguities and paradoxes of the readings of Machiavelli in the Enlightenment. It is generally acknowledged that Denis Diderot is the author of the entry on '*machiavélisme*' in the *Encyclopédie*, which states that it is 'a kind of detestable policy which can be summed up in two words – art of tyrannising'.[106] Yet after having condemned the impious maxims, especially those appearing in Chapters XV and XXV of *The Prince*, the author lays out a series of questions about the 'paradox' represented by Machiavelli and about the implicit suggestion that he would reveal to the readers the true nature of tyranny so that they could defend themselves. Under the veil of a critical judgement, 'in a Machiavellian way' Diderot calls attention to the republican interpretations which bloom throughout the century, and find their most authoritative formulation – although one not deprived of a certain ambiguity – in the thought of Jean-Jacques Rousseau.

JEAN-JACQUES ROUSSEAU

Jean-Jacques Rousseau is probably the most illustrious philosopher, after Spinoza, to talk positively, and yet not without ambiguity, about Machiavelli. Rousseau's works were written a few years before the French Revolution, and largely influence the political climate that immediately precedes the revolutionary outbreak. Besides collaborating, like Montesquieu, on the *Encyclopédie*, Rousseau's production is extremely diverse, including novels and poetry, and touches themes like society, music, botany, pedagogy and, of course, politics. Denouncing the society of the *ancien régime*, Rousseau pleads for a return to the original and natural status of man, uncorrupted by culture and civilisation. His anthropological conception, thus, points to a sphere of human relationships that precedes any conflict, against what natural-law theorists, in particular Hobbes, had maintained, namely an originary conflictual state of nature. Although his use of sources is eclectic and unsystematic, he explicitly quotes Machiavelli several times throughout his major works.

Rousseau's relationship with Machiavelli looks like a paradox, if not a true enigma.[107] If one considers the central theme of social conflicts, the problem can be formulated as follows: the Machiavellian theory is unambiguous in supporting the positive role of conflicts for the freedom and the power of a republic. Rousseau, on the contrary, openly rejects this aspect; especially in the *Social Contract* there is a strong condemnation of factions and partial associations in the name of a process in which individual wills should converge towards a general one – a non-conflictual distillation of individual differences: 'For the general will to be well articulated, it is therefore important that there should be no partial society in the state and that each citizen make up his own mind.'[108] When discussing the specific mechanisms of the exercise of sovereignty, Rousseau goes so far as condemning also the physiological disagreements that are naturally present in any republic: 'The more harmony reigns in the assemblies, that is to say, the closer opinions come to unanimity, the more dominant too is the general will. But long debates, dissensions, and tumult betoken the ascendance of private interests and the decline of the state.'[109]

However – and this is the paradox – in the *Social Contract* Rousseau has words of praise for only two authors, the Marquis d'Argenson and Machiavelli. Moreover, Rousseau quotes the Florentine in a positive context precisely in relation to his theory of conflict and internal dissensions. He uses Book VII of the *Florentine Histories*, which concerns the differences between the useful and the harmful divisions in republics,[110] and, while commenting on Machiavelli's text, adds:

> Riots and civil wars may greatly disturb the leaders, but they are not the true misfortunes of the people, who may even have a reprieve while people argue over who will tyrannize them. It is their permanent condition that causes real periods of prosperity or calamity [. . .]. It seemed, says Machiavelli, that in the midst of murders, proscriptions, and civil wars, our republic became more powerful; the *virtù* of its citizens, their mores, and their independence did more to reinforce it than all its dissensions did to weaken it. A little agitation gives strength to souls, and what truly brings about prosperity for the species is not so much peace as liberty.[111]

Freedom here is an attribute not of peace but of prosperity, when it comes with (a certain amount of) conflict. How to interpret this seeming contradiction?[112]

Rousseau comes to know Machiavelli through the commentary of Amelot de la Houssaye[113] and his interpretation generally follows Bayle and Diderot, filling the spaces of ambiguity that the latter had left open between the lines of his façade condemnation in the *Encyclopédie*. But there is no doubt that, through its authority, the republican interpretation of Machiavelli clarifies and strengthens itself also through the ambiguous passages of the *Social Contract*. To fully understand the rhetorical strategy of Rousseau, and the seemingly paradoxical use he makes of Machiavelli's thought, as is the case for Montesquieu, the *Social Contract* should be read in the light of other political works and in the broader context of the evolution of Rousseau's thought.

It is in the *Discourse on the Origin of Inequality*, where the name of Machiavelli does not appear, that we find the most Machiavellian pages written by Rousseau. And this happens in the context of one of the topics that, as we have seen, is central to the thought of the author of *The Prince*, when he condemns the classical concept of the common good as a deception. Rousseau demonstrates to the reader the origins of the division of property, in a style that closely resembles some pages of the *Florentine Histories*, even in the writing strategy, for example in the fictional dialogue, brief but dazzling, between a rich man and a poor man:

> 'I am the one who built that wall; I have earned this land with my labor.'
> In response to them it could be said: 'Who gave you the boundary lines? By
> what right do you claim to exact payment at our expense for labor we did
> not impose upon you? Are you unaware that a multitude of your broth-
> ers perish or suffer from need of what you have in excess, and that you
> needed explicit and unanimous consent from the human race for you to help
> yourself to anything from the common subsistence that went beyond your
> own?'[114]

The rich are afraid. Conscious of the original violence related to the establishment of property, they know that their rights are based solely on the original strength and prevarication. And so they invent the common good and concord as an ideological mask for the 'ugliness' – as Machiavelli would say – of their income:

> 'Let us unite [. . .] in order to protect the weak from oppression, restrain the
> ambitious, and assure everyone of possessing what belongs to him. Let us
> institute rules of justice and peace to which all will be obliged to conform,
> which will make special exception for no one, and which will in some way
> compensate for the caprices of fortune by subjecting the strong and the weak
> to mutual obligations. In short, instead of turning our forces against our-
> selves, let us gather them into one supreme power that governs us according
> to wise laws, that protects and defends all the members of the association,
> repulses common enemies, and maintains us in eternal concord.'[115]

Peace and justice cast a dark shadow on the original freedom. Concord and union, which will have a far greater role in Rousseau's later works, appear here in all their arbitrariness. We can clearly hear the echo of Machiavelli's thought in these pages, and one who wants to fully understand his cumbersome presence in the *Social Contract* should start from here. In the *Discourse on the Origin of Inequality*, the spirit of conflict inspired by Machiavelli is clearly visible. When, in the *Social Contract*, the constituent moment takes the upper hand, Rousseau is forced to make a choice: to completely obliterate the inconvenient name of Machiavelli, or to invoke it explicitly, trying to integrate his more radical theories. He chooses the latter. But, just as for Montesquieu, it is not easy for him to domesticate the radical Machiavellian theory, and particularly the partial and conflicting nature of politics.

A certain social dynamism is still to be found in the *Social Contract*, when Rousseau seems to remember that peace and freedom do not necessarily coexist, but rather that peace and justice often establish themselves *against* the original freedom. And yet the Machiavellian conflictual stance is unacceptable alongside the *Social Contract*'s geometric and harmonising notion of the general will. Herein lies the cause of the tension between Rousseau and Machiavelli. Rousseau has not misunderstood or only partly understood Machiavelli, as many modern scholars claim. On the contrary, he understands Machiavelli quite well, especially in the most radical points of his theory. And yet, in the climate of the middle of the eighteenth century, largely favourable to republicanism, following Bayle, Amelot and Diderot as well as the strategy used by Montesquieu, and having objectives that justify an unscrupulous and not always consistent use of sources, Rousseau counts the inconvenient position of Machiavelli amongst the precursors of his republicanism. This is where his peculiar version of unanimist republicanism, which will horrify pluralists and liberals of the next century, originates.

This is the Machiavelli that will be passed on to the men of the French Revolution. The philosophical ideas of Montesquieu, Diderot and especially Rousseau will affect their more strictly political readings. Condorcet, for example: in the *Esquisse d'un tableau historique des progrès de l'esprit humain* (*Outlines of a Historical View of the Progress of the Human Mind*, 1795) he reconstructs the conflict between the two pillars of thought, the utopian one of Plato and More, in which, with great clarity, he also includes Hobbes, and the realistic one of Machiavelli and of those who 'in the deep examination of the historical facts search for the rules by which it would be possible to control the future'.[116] As a philosopher of history, Condorcet understands all too well that Machiavelli's historiography, and its theoretical consequences, are fully political. Chateaubriand, Sieyès, Guiraudet and many others will follow. Perhaps, pronouncing words that seem to come directly from Amelot de la Houssaye, Robespierre is not too far from the truth when he writes that 'the plan for the French Revolution was clearly written in the works of Tacitus and Machiavelli'.[117]

8. Nationalism and Class Conflict (Nineteenth to Twentieth Centuries)

It is difficult to summarise the politics of an entire century in just one or a few theoretical categories. And it is difficult, if not impossible, to summarise in a few categories the interpretations of Machiavelli's thought put forward by the intellectuals of an entire century. We can say, however, that the image of the Florentine, released from the burden of the theoretical debates of the two previous centuries and following the incentive of great revolutions, establishes itself in the nineteenth century based on two major themes: nationalism and internationalism. It is mainly in the German and French context where these movements assume proportions that will prove crucial for all of European history (but I shall leave aside the other national areas only for reasons of conciseness). This is also where one encounters the most lucid interpretations and most heated debates around the figure of Machiavelli.

GEORG WILHELM FRIEDRICH HEGEL

Georg Wilhelm Friedrich Hegel is the main exponent of German idealism. He knew one of the most troubled periods of German and European history, which deeply influences his political opinions. These opinions are coherently developed, though, within a grandiose and methodical systematisation of philosophy in all fields of thought, from logic to philosophy of history, from aesthetics to ethics, from philosophy of law to philosophy of religion and history. A profound connoisseur of Greek philosophy, he is also influenced by the new philosophy, and in particular by Rousseau, Lessing and Kant. Within the new Romantic movement, Hegel develops a conception of nationalism that is at the same time cultural and political. Through this idea, he becomes interested in Machiavelli's thought and in what Machiavelli represents for the early genealogy of the Italian nation and its spirit.

In his essay on the German Constitution of 1802, Hegel unambiguously maintains that Machiavelli's thought can be understood
only if one grasps the immediate political aims typical of his own
historical time. Machiavelli's goal is to unify into a single nation-state
the multitude of small states scattered throughout the Italian territory.
Machiavelli points to the moon, but his detractors, in Hegel's opinion,
can see only the finger. The problem of adequacy of means to ends is
not a question here. For Machiavelli, as for Hegel, the only possible
means are 'drastic' ones, and they are the only ones necessary to reor-
ganise a 'life which is close to decay', because 'gangrenous limbs cannot
be cured by lavender-water'.[1]

The unity of the nation, therefore, is the element that is dear to
Machiavelli and that Hegel places at the very centre of his reading.
When Machiavelli urges a virtuous and 'excellent' prince to take action,
he expresses 'idealistic demands [. . .] which have probably never been
fulfilled by any princes since his times (not even by the one who refuted
him)'. But the denunciation of the naive criticism of Frederick II is not
of primary importance to Hegel. The German philosopher develops
a very strong reading that fully embraces the lesson of Machiavelli's
realism. He does not attempt to reject accusations of anti-moralism
raised against Machiavelli by appealing to a superior morality. The goal
is rather to reverse the paradigm of traditional morality, in order to cast
'a very different light' on the whole issue:

> What would indeed be abhorrent if done by one private individual to
> another, or by one state to another (or to a private individual), is now [seen
> to be] a just punishment. The promotion of anarchy is the ultimate – or
> perhaps the only – crime against the state; for all crimes which the state has
> to deal with tend in this direction.[2]

It is important to emphasise once again that Hegel consciously
follows Machiavelli's realism, within the intrinsic necessity of politics,
and turning against the abstract rules of extrinsic morality. One knows
how important morality is for Hegel. This is the necessary shift that
Hegel proposes: the concrete realisation of morality occurs in and
through politics. Therefore morality must accept the tools of politics
and everything that their usage entails in terms of violence. Hence the
interpretation developed by Hegel is marked by the union between
necessity and contingency, just as Machiavelli had taught. Necessity
guides the action of the state and for the state which, in turn, is constantly exposed to the contingencies of human actions, and hence to the
'entangled' ways of politics.

The memory of Machiavelli will not fade even in Hegel's most
mature works such as the *Philosophy of Right* (1821), in which the

dialectical relationship between the particular and the universal, between existence and essence, is subject to contingency, precisely as it was for Machiavelli. This is where the 'universal mind' whose right is the 'highest' emerges from:

> Since states function as *particular* entities in their mutual relations, the broadest view of these relations will encompass the ceaseless turmoil not just of external contingency, but also of passions, interests, ends, talents and *virtù*, violence, wrongdoing, and vices in their inner particularity. In this turmoil, the ethical whole itself – the independence of the state – is exposed to contingency.[3]

The Machiavellian spirit of these pages written by Hegel is evident. It should be noted, however, that the interpretation developed by Hegel is fully original, and Machiavelli's thought is bent for the purpose of constructing the Hegelian system. Once again, Machiavelli is used as a theoretical-political tool. Hegel turns to Machiavelli to develop the core of his theory of history, but this core remains the central and determining element. The unitary and unifying element becomes absolute in Hegel's philosophy of law and of state. Machiavelli's and Hegel's contingency are not one and the same thing. While the first of the two exposes, in a productive manner, the fact that the nature of conflicts occurring in the state is connected to fortune, the second perceives them in the category of chaos and anarchy. The people must be united in the state and this unity represents rationality and morality, which are finally accomplished within a higher purpose.

JOHANN GOTTLIEB FICHTE

Like Hegel, Johann Gottlieb Fichte is also one of the main interpreters of German nationalism, developed as a reaction against the French military enterprise and the campaigns of Napoleon. His major political work, the *Addresses to the German Nation* (1808), gathers the political sermons pronounced by Fichte during the terrible years of the war with France, when Germany had to acknowledge military defeat. In this critical period, Fichte looks for the conditions needed to breathe new life into the spirit of the German people, in order to resist the oppressor and find again the way toward freedom and independence. Within these circumstances, the figure of Machiavelli appears to him charged with a prophetic message.

The interpretation of Machiavelli set out by Fichte in his paper 'On Machiavelli as an Author' (1807) is clearly a nationalist one.[4] But, first of all, it is a reading which brings Machiavelli closer to current circumstances. After the initial enthusiasm for the French Revolution, Fichte witnessed the expansionist wars of Napoleon's *Grande Armée* and the taking of Berlin in 1806. Significantly, therefore, Fichte's text carries the subtitle 'Aspects in which the policy of Machiavelli is still applicable in our time'. This is the perspective in which Fichte acknowledges the full political weight of Machiavelli's military considerations on the superiority of infantry over cavalry and artillery. Fichte also supports this argument, giving voice to the opinions of many German reformers who saw in the liberation of the peasants from servitude a prerequisite for rebuilding an armed power which would be able to resist the revolution which Napoleon had implemented in France, precisely in the military field.

Fichte, therefore, does not differ much from Hegel in his view that Machiavelli's theories – seemingly evil – are intrinsically ethical ones. Machiavellian realism, as well as his theory of chance as *fortuna*, are interpreted by Fichte as an invitation for the German people and the Prussian monarchy to be courageous and to resist. The same can be said of the anthropological assumption on the general wickedness of human nature, the true foundation of Machiavellian politics according to Fichte. Every legislator must keep this hypothesis in mind. This leads to embracing the more extreme principles of Machiavellian realism, but also to pushing them in the direction of a justification of expansionism and adopting power politics by states:

> Unless he is your natural ally against a power which is hostile to you both, your neighbour will always be quick to seize the opportunity to expand at your expense, as soon as he can do it without any risk. If he is prudent, he must do so, and he will not fail to do so, even if he were your brother. It is not enough to defend your territory, you must watch out for everything that might affect your position. You must not tolerate any changes in your area of influence which might be unfavourable to you, nor waste any moment when you can change things to your advantage, because you can be sure that others will act this way as soon as they can. If you do not act, others will anticipate. Who does not expand, weakens, while others in turn grow in power.[5]

This is how Fichte sums up – simplifying beyond measure – the complex position of Machiavelli on the necessity of power politics. In this way, once again, the theories of Machiavelli are bent to fit a discourse that is not part of its original nucleus and that, as it has been written, with exaggeration, 'will become one of the mainstays of fascism and nazism'.[6] It is interesting, however, to notice that Fichte's realism never becomes a part of the unifying and pacifying movement of history, and that the Hegelian idea of unity of the people within a state which embodies the highest morality and the most noble freedom is not part of Fichte's interpretation of Machiavelli. For him, without any ambiguity, the lesson learnt from the Florentine is clear: the state remains a *Zwanganstalt*, a coercive institution, and a *Notstaat*, a state of necessity which is based not on the common good, but on the repression of the individual and on his incorporation into a mechanism which is foreign to any ethical evaluation.[7]

Acute readers of Machiavelli would become more numerous in the nineteenth century, from Nietzsche to Clausewitz, from Ferrari to Quinet, from Mundt to Marx and Sismondi. And yet, despite the appreciation, none of these authors attempts a direct confrontation with the works of the Florentine. Paradoxically, those, too, who recognise the revolutionary character of the man who has played '*la Marseillaise* of the sixteenth century' (as Quinet writes in 1848 in *The Revolutions of Italy*, where he also defines *The Prince* as an 'incredible war machine'[8]) do not undertake a thorough analysis of the work of Machiavelli. To find such deep and direct involvement with the Machiavellian text, one has to wait for the following century.

ANTONIO GRAMSCI

Antonio Gramsci is not only one of the greatest Marxist authors, but also one of the greatest philosophers of the twentieth century. Emigrating from poor and rural Sardinia to the advanced and capitalist city of Turin to study Humanities in 1911, he became more and more engaged in politics, first as a Socialist, and eventually as one of the founders of the new Italian Communist Party in 1921. The Fascist regime saw in him one of its strongest enemies. Arrested in 1927, he was condemned to twenty years in prison for conspiracy against the regime. He spent the rest of his life in prison, in very precarious health, dying in 1937. Nevertheless, during his imprisonment, he was able to write several works ranging from philosophy to political theory, history, sociology, pedagogy and literary criticism, eventually collected in his *Prison Notebooks* (published in a critical edition in 1975).

Gramsci's 'Noterelle' on Machiavelli starts with a portrait of the metaphorical prince which represents the symbol of the 'collective will'. The modern prince is not and cannot be 'a real person, a concrete individual', but rather a 'complex element' that expresses a 'collective will'. According to Gramsci, 'this organism [. . .] is the political party – the first cell in which there come together germs of a collective will tending to become universal and total'.[9] The Jacobins – this is a parallel drawn by Gramsci – were a 'categorical incarnation' of Machiavelli's prince, and the 'theory' of the new prince should contain a section on political and collective will, on its actual forming, on its historical affirmation.

The prince, therefore, just like *fortuna*, is an allegory that Machiavelli uses to increase the rhetorical impact of its revolutionary theses. It is precisely this that makes *The Prince* a '"live" work'.[10]

This argument demonstrates to what degree the Gramscian reading of Machiavelli is an attempt to bring his thought closer to the present. Gramsci, once again, uses Machiavelli as a theoretical tool in the ideological struggle of his own time. But at the same time, this interpretation is extremely interesting also from a historiographical point of view, as it shows that the prince for Machiavelli is a partial element of and actor in the struggle. The *virtù* consists for Machiavelli not in a higher principle that operates above the social conflicts that are to be organised and solved, but a radically immanent principle that operates *in and through* conflict. The prince is necessarily a partial principle, one among and against many others. It is a plural, manifold, collective and conflictual principle. And because it does not *represent* the people (by reducing it to a unity as in the case of the Hobbesian sovereign), the prince *becomes* the people *against* the *grandi*. This is the way Gramsci thinks about the political party as the new prince.

Gramsci also reads Machiavelli within the context of a broader concept of history and the possibilities of altering it – a subject dear to every Marxist.[11] Once again, his interpretation is extremely thoughtful, as it develops Machiavelli's insights on a *virtù* that is seen not as a transcendent principle, but as an immanent element and as a political practice of intervening in the historical situation. For instance, on the topic of military organisation Gramsci writes:

> The decisive element in every situation is the permanently organised and long-prepared force [. . .]. Therefore the essential task is that of systematically and patiently ensuring that this force is formed, developed, and rendered ever more homogeneous, compact, and self-aware. This is clear from military history, and from the care with which in every period armies have been prepared in advance to be able to make war at any moment. The great Powers have been great precisely because they were at all times prepared to intervene effectively in favourable international conjunctures – which were precisely favourable because there was the concrete possibility of effectively intervening in them.[12]

One can hardly imagine a description closer to the Machiavellian idea of *virtù* as an intervention in the existing conjuncture. The whole Machiavellian reflection on the relationship between politics and war, expressed especially in the *Art of War*, is meant to develop the idea of preparing the best conditions (never the perfect ones, but the best possible) enabling active intervention in the possibilities of history. One uncovers here the 'utopian' character of *The Prince* – utopian, for Gramsci, not because unrealistic, but because it does not yet exist in Italian historical reality:[13] only by following certain means will it be possible to achieve certain ends.

Machiavelli's political ends are therefore at the centre of Gramsci's interpretation. On this basis, for the first time in the history of Machiavellian historiography, Gramsci is able to go beyond the naive interpretations of the earlier centuries' republican moralism. Those interpretations did not go beyond the acknowledgement of an intrinsic morality of Machiavelli as a man, opposed to the apparent evil of his teachings, especially those contained in *The Prince*. The aim of Machiavelli, according to Gramsci, was not to unveil the logic of the behaviour of tyrants, nor to uncover their methods in order to educate and warn people. The teaching of Machiavelli is not 'negative' but 'positive', as it shows the necessity of adopting 'certain means, even if they are typical of tyrants' by those who want to achieve a certain goal – that is, democracy.

The use of the term 'democracy' by Gramsci should be understood in all its political and revolutionary senses. Democracy is not just one of the possible forms of government, but signifies the *rule* of the people against aristocracy. And, in the historical conditions in which Machiavelli writes, the people can achieve this goal only through the prince. The question becomes the recognition of the necessarily partial and conflicting nature of modern politics, within which one must take one's own stand.

Gramsci sees clearly the centrality of the conflict between the people and the nobles in the Machiavellian political discourse, and approves of it. This interpretation also produces effects on his philosophical reading of Machiavelli.[14] For example, Gramsci's interpretation goes against the liberal reading of Benedetto Croce, who reflects on a broader conception of philosophy, taking even the figure of Marx into consideration. As a philosopher, according to Croce, Machiavelli has discovered the autonomy of politics from morality. They are governed by different laws and it would be futile to interpret and act in one field according to the laws of the other.[15] In this sense, according to Gramsci, Croce has cleared the field by removing a series of false problems, such as the supposed immorality of Machiavelli. Croce, however, has limited the scope of the Machiavellian 'revolution' to the domain of theory and speculation. This would correspond to the undertaking of Marx, who has been defined by Croce as the 'Machiavelli of the proletariat'.

As Eugenio Garin explains, however, Gramsci wants to reverse this perspective and see in Machiavelli the 'Marx of the people'.[16] For Gramsci, Machiavelli has actually made a philosophical discovery and actually created a political philosophy. He did so, though, because he intended to revolutionise the real world and intervene in the conjuncture in a political way, in this way also influencing morality and philosophy. The theoretical and philosophical thought of Machiavelli is completely immersed in the concrete analysis of the present. This means that philosophy is not previously processed, in order to be later applied to practical reality. On the contrary – it is designed within and through a political situation. This is why it can be called philosophy of praxis.[17]

LEO STRAUSS

Leo Strauss is one of the most important conservative philosophers of the twentieth century. Born in Germany, in an Orthodox Jewish family, Strauss developed his career mainly in the United States, where he emigrated in 1938 to escape the rise of Nazism. Strauss is one of the strongest critics of modernity and the crisis of classic values. Against modern rationalism and historicism, his philosophy is centred on ancient virtue and political principles. Analysing the genealogy of modernity and the loss of philosophical and political meaning that this represents, Strauss focuses on authors like Aristotle, Plato, Thucydides, Hobbes, Spinoza and, of course, Machiavelli. Within his critique of modernity, Strauss writes his *Thoughts on Machiavelli* (1958) precisely to demonstrate the evil nature of his doctrine.

Let us examine some examples, such as the exhortation to liberate Italy, addressed to the new prince in Chapter XXVI of Machiavelli's masterpiece, on which many of the authors analysed in the previous pages focused their attention. Strauss reads the chapter as the sign of an exchange of favours and political opportunism, through which Machiavelli was trying to raise his personal position. Machiavelli, in his low position, and Lorenzo, the prince to whom the text is dedicated, would stand 'at the opposite ends of the scale of Fortuna', and they would be 'born to supplement each other'. Machiavelli 'desires to receive something in return [for the knowledge that he bestows on the prince]. [. . .] Looking forward to the end of the book, we may say that he desires to better his fortune by showing Lorenzo how to better his fortune through becoming Prince of Italy.'[18] The passage that has allowed Gramsci to identify in Machiavelli the inventor of a new philosophical method is reduced by Strauss to an expression of a trade-off with which the ignoble politician tries to ingratiate himself with the noble sovereign.

The passages of Machiavelli which were scandalous for the most acute philosophers of previous centuries are for Strauss a sign of servile prudence. Machiavelli, according to Strauss, deeply respects power and 'expresses with the greatest boldness such views as are tolerable to one party but he is very cautious in regard to views which have no respectable support whatever. [...] Machiavelli does not go to the end; he does not reveal the end; he does not fully reveal his intention; [he only intimates] what he is unable to state.'[19] As far as sources are concerned, Machiavelli would not reveal particular originality, as his writings are to a large extent based on Livy: 'For Machiavelli, Livy's work was authoritative, as it were, his Bible. His way of reading Livy was nearer to the way in which all theologians of the past read the Bible than to our way of reading either Livy or the Bible.'[20] Hence, Strauss does not recognise any depth in the Machiavellian strategy of reading classical and modern authors, not only Livy.

It is this last judgement on Livy as the 'Bible' of Machiavelli, however, that allows us to move to a further and more interesting level of the interpretation of Strauss's critical reading.[21] Since the 1920s, Strauss had focused his philosophical inquiry on the theologico-political subject and the analysis of the greatest philosophers who had written on this topic, from Plato to Aristotle, from Maimonides to Hobbes and Spinoza. Where do we find Machiavelli in this picture? In the fracture in Western thought that, according to Strauss's central thesis, opened between faith and reason, between religion and philosophy, between old reason, based on the natural values, and modern reason, based on artificiality. Machiavelli is part of – to use the beautiful expression quoted by Strauss – the contrast between Jerusalem and Athens.

What is blameworthy for Strauss, within this series of oppositions, is on the contrary elevated by Machiavelli in the context of a new ethics of politics – an ethics that, in Strauss's view, is responsible for the fatal fact that men have lost the ability to discern between the values: right and wrong, good and evil. This is the 'crisis of modernity' that proceeds as a triple 'wave', from Machiavelli through Rousseau and Nietzsche, coming down to us through the centuries. If the theory of liberal democracy, as well as communism, has its origin in the first and second waves of modernity, history has shown that the political implication of the third one is fascism.[22]

Livy becomes a Bible, not only because he has been closely followed, but also because Machiavelli dares to put history in the place of religion, and politics in the place of morality, reinventing the status of politics in the universe of Western values. Hence Machiavelli is an immoral author. But even in this case, the conclusion should be read on a double level. On the most obvious one, Strauss reverses the republican interpretations, arguing that the alleged patriotism of Machiavelli was actually a strategy – surely a Machiavellian one – aimed at putting through his arguments in favour of tyranny. But what are these arguments? Once again, they are not only the most obvious ones, concerning the necessary use of force or deception, but also the more intrinsically philosophical theses, indirectly emerging from his conscious destruction of traditional values, on the ruins of which modernity will be built.

Strauss has the courage to face the true Machiavelli, by denouncing his wicked character. Strauss openly acknowledges some of the basic theses of the Florentine's philosophy that not even his defenders had the capacity or the strength to recognise. For example, in an important page of his *Thoughts*, Strauss develops the thesis that Machiavelli is not defending the 'empty' name of freedom, but that he unambiguously stands on the side of the people. In the name of the multitude, he denounces the alleged superiority of the elite and supports the democratic order of the Romans against the oligarchy of the Spartans. With rare insight, Strauss reaches the crux of the matter, highlighting that

> this is one reason why the argument of the *Discourses* consists partly of a movement away from republics toward principalities and even toward tyrannies, why Machiavelli appears in some discourses to be completely neutral in the conflict between free states and tyrannies, or why he sometimes seems to blur the distinction among tyrannies, principalities, and republics. It is no accident, I believe, that the most shocking or the most 'Machiavellian' passage of the *Florentine Histories* is the speech addressed by a Florentine plebeian in the year 1378 to the Florentine plebs.[23]

Even today there are but a few commentators who dare to go so far. Strauss does not hesitate in the face of these scandalous pages, tracing the origin of this philosophical revolution in the method through which Machiavelli separates himself from the classical thought, which is so dear to Strauss. The cosmological premises of the author of the *Discourses* seem to recall Aristotle, and yet Machiavelli moves away precisely from Aristotle when, following ancient materialists (particularly Democritus), he introduces 'chance' as a force opposed to prudence.[24] Machiavelli separates himself even more from Aristotle, and from a certain classical tradition, when he destroys the concept of common good. He continues to use this expression, but he employs it in a new and revolutionary way:

> The common good claims to be the good of everyone. But since the common good requires that innocent individuals be sacrificed for its sake, the common good is rather the good of the large majority, perhaps even the good of the common people as distinguished from the good of the nobles or of the great.[25]

Significantly, these acute considerations appear on the pages of one of the most important and influential critics of Machiavelli, in the name of a conservatism that however does not hesitate to grant the honours of war to Machiavelli. The republican defenders of Machiavelli had rarely assigned such an important role to his philosophy, in the context of the modern revolution of Western thought.

LOUIS ALTHUSSER

Louis Althusser is one of the most important Communist French philosophers of the twentieth century. His theoretical work, especially before the upheavals of May 1968, is a powerful interpretation of Marxism as an anti-humanist and anti-dialectical philosophy. In later years, Althusser developed a theory of materialism that involves an original reading of the history of Western philosophy, as well as a new theory of history, radically opposed to every idea of an end in human affairs, thus wiping away the illusion of a necessary final triumph of Communism.

Althusser's reworking of Marxism is deeply rooted in early modern philosophy. There is a group of authors who, according to Althusser, constitute an 'Underground Current of Materialism', as he writes in his later works, which includes an element of the unpredictable into materialism. This circle includes Marx, of course, but also Spinoza, Hobbes, Epicurus, Rousseau, Darwin and, finally, Machiavelli. In many fragments that Althusser devotes to this current of thought, Machiavelli is counted among the founders of a great philosophical project, which is not completely free from ambiguity and blind spots: the development of a new form of materialism that breaks away from the traditional bipolar division between deterministic materialism and idealism which is characteristic of the entire history of Western metaphysics.[26] The theoretical elements of this new materialism have been developed by the authors of an 'underground' current of Western thought. These elements make it possible to think of a materialism based not on the stiffness of cause-effect causality, but on contingency, on the unpredictable, on occasion – all of these being central concepts of Machiavellian philosophy.[27]

The encounter between Machiavelli and Althusser is somewhat paradoxical. Although the Florentine is one of the most important authors for the development of the underground current of materialism, many of Althusser's previous thoughts on Machiavelli do not reveal particular originality. When directly commenting on his thought, Althusser writes for example that Machiavelli is a theoretician of the mixed state, a concrete element that interrupts Polybius's endless cycle of the three classic forms of government.[28] After acknowledging the distance between Machiavelli and classical philosophy,[29] Althusser writes that the new prince, in Aristotelian terms, is an absolute ruler, a person appointed by history to give 'form' to existing 'matter', which aspires to become a nation.[30]

In Althusser's more mature pages, however, the role of Machiavelli is quite different. The thought of the Florentine, and in particular his conception of politics and history, is used for the purpose of the construction of a materialism that includes the element of chance. The presence of Machiavelli is even more apparent here than that of Marx, not because it is more important, but because in Althusser's view Marx himself, with his philosophy and conception of history, is at stake in the debate against the anti-teleological and deterministic interpretations prevailing in Marxism in those years. By interpreting Machiavelli's thought in such a way, and within a completely new context, Althusser joins those who, in previous centuries, had recognised the existence of an accomplished theory and philosophy within Machiavellian historiography.

Althusser highlights the fact that Machiavelli has analysed the necessary conditions for the construction of a nation-state in sixteenth-century Italy. He has also scrutinised the potential actors of this political change and the contribution they could offer, finally discarding them all because of the impossibility of identifying the 'subject' of this process of unification, as if it were possible to identify a specific cause for a specific effect. On the contrary:

> using the example of Cesare Borgia, [Machiavelli] moves on to the idea that unification will be achieved if there emerges some nameless man who has enough luck [*chance*] and *virtù* to establish himself somewhere, in some nameless corner of Italy, and, starting out from this atomic point, gradually aggregate the Italians around him in the grand project of founding a national state. This is a completely aleatory line of reasoning, which leaves politically blank both the name of the Federator and that of the region which will serve as starting point for the constitution of this federation. Thus the dice are tossed on the gaming table, which is itself empty (but filled with men of valour).[31]

Whereas Gramsci had found a modern name for this 'subject' – that is, the political party – Althusser instead finds in the 'emptiness' the random encounter between *virtù* and *fortuna*. For Althusser, then, the lure that Valentino had in the eyes of Machiavelli was more philosophical than political: 'a man of nothing who has started out of nothing starting out from an unassignable place' who can fill the 'emptiness' of the political conditions of Italy of the time. Machiavelli thus becomes a philosopher of 'occasion' and his philosophy is seen as an instrument for redefining the content of a non-determinist Marxism. Althusser seems to share and appreciate the political and cultural project of Gramsci when he writes that 'this is how, in the dark night of Fascism, Machiavelli "speaks" to Gramsci: in the future tense. And the Modern Prince then casts its light on the New Prince. Gramsci writes calmly that *The Prince* is a "manifesto" and a "revolutionary utopia".'[32] On occasion and conjuncture, however, Althusser's reading differs from Gramsci's, to finally reach the highest originality and theoretical strength:

> What does it mean *to think in the conjuncture*? [It] is not to think *on* the conjuncture, as one would reflect on a set of concrete data. To think under the conjuncture is quite literally to submit to the problem introduced and imposed by its case: the political problem of national unity and the constitution of Italy into a national state. [...] Machiavelli merely registers in his theoretical position a problem that is objectively, historically posed by the case of the conjuncture: not by simple intellectual comparisons, but by the confrontation of existing class forces and their relationship of uneven development – in fact, by their aleatory future.[33]

The conflict, once again, takes centre stage. It is a conflict within which the construction of a new materialism is at stake – a materialism able to claim the most compelling elements of this lively tradition of thought. It is precisely these pages that make us fully aware of the lively force of Machiavelli's thought.

CONCLUSION

In the first and second parts of this book, the reader has seen the diverse nature of Machiavelli's thought. Such a variety largely depends on the themes developed by the Florentine to put in place his study of politics and history. It also depends on the diverse nature of works that Machiavelli has decided to write, or has been required to write, following the concrete circumstances of his life and career. It is, though, the history of the reception of Machiavelli's thought across the centuries that better illustrates the origin of such a diversity of interpretations. Through the history of Machiavelli's influence, the reader is now able to perceive not the unity but the multiplicity of points of view required to grasp his thought. Not one but many Machiavellis are now available and open to the reader's interpretation.

Yet Machiavelli has not been tamed, diluted or neutralised into this multiplicity. The diversity of points of view and perspectives is not only the work of the centuries; it was implied since the beginning in Machiavelli's methodology. This apparently centrifugal movement goes along an opposed return toward a few thematic cores with which all political theorists and philosophers after Machiavelli have been forced to engage. All authors analysed in the third part of this book – and many other authors that I have not been able to deal with for reasons of conciseness – keep going back to the themes and topics that Machiavelli put at the heart of his diverse political production. And this is true for authors who either claim the wickedness of his theories or maintain his sincere and ultimately moral intention in unveiling the wickedness of princes and of politics itself. These thematic cores are recognisable under the plethora of interpretations after his death and still in our time.

Machiavelli, in this sense, has won his battle. Not so much the battle for glory and fame, about which I think he personally did not care much. The battle, rather, to influence and change the very meaning of political thought at the dawn of modernity. Machiavelli has sometimes introduced these themes in the philosophical debate for the first time. Sometimes he has impressed a new turn to discussions already existing, moving away from traditional positions and forcing readers and political actors to look at them in a completely new way. The history of political thought has never been the same since Machiavelli. His thought is still producing its effects in our reality and in the way we interpret politics today.

In this introductory book, I have discussed the thematic cores in Machiavelli's works and I have suggested a pattern to read their influence on the political theorists of the following centuries. These thematic cores are the role and meaning of social conflict in politics, the relationship between domestic and foreign politics, the division among citizens and the conception of justice, shared or disputed by different members of the political community, and the meaning of history and the role it plays in the knowledge and prevision of human affairs.

The history of Machiavelli's reception has become inseparable from the history of Machiavelli's thought itself. This is probably the destiny of all classic authors, be they novelists, poets, philosophers or political theorists. This does not mean, however, that their original thought is lost forever. On the contrary, as I have suggested in this book, this means that the diversity and richness of interpretations impose on the modern reader the necessity of keeping the text at the centre of the stage and considering it as an indispensable compass. Rather than dismissing the author's original voice, the diversity of political and philosophical uses that have been made of Machiavelli suggests the necessity of continuing to go back to him and listen to him directly. This book has been conceived as a contribution and a proposal in that sense. Conscious of its partiality, I do not intend to suggest a *truth* on Machiavelli, but rather to suggest the necessity of a *true* reading of his works, that can come only from a direct engagement with Machiavelli's thought.

Chronology

1297 Venice: *Serrata* of the Great Council

1378 Florence: *ciompi* uprising

1434 Cosimo de' Medici assumes power in Florence

1462 Foundation of the Accademia Platonica

1464 1 August: Cosimo de' Medici dies

1469 3 May: birth of Machiavelli

1478 26 April: Pazzi conspiracy against the Medici

1480 Marsilio Ficino, *Theologia platonica*

1482 Girolamo Savonarola arrives in Florence

1486 Giovanni Pico, *De hominis dignitate*

1489 Savonarola preaches against the Medici

1492 Conquest of Granada and reunification of Spain

1492 February: edict of expulsion against the Jews of Spain

1492 8 April: Lorenzo de' Medici dies

1492 11 August: Cardinal Rodrigo Borgia succeeds Innocent VIII as Pope Alexander VI

1492 October: Christopher Columbus lands on an island he names San Salvador

1494 September: French invasion of Italy under Charles VIII; expulsion of the Medici from Florence; Pisa becomes free; establishment of the Great Council in Florence

1497 Machiavelli copies the *De rerum natura* of Lucretius

1497 13 May: Savonarola is excommunicated by Alexander VI

1498 Savonarola, *Treatise on the Constitution and Government of the City of Florence*

1498 23 May: Savonarola is burned at the stake in the Piazza della Signoria

1498 15 June: Machiavelli is elected chancellor of the Second Chancery of the Republic

1498 17 August: Cesare Borgia is named Duke of Valentinois by King Louis XII of France

1500 July: Machiavelli's first legation to the French court

1501 August: Machiavelli's marriage to Marietta Corsini

1501 Cesare Borgia is created Duke of Romagna

1502 24 June: Machiavelli's first legation to Cesare Borgia

1502 22 September: Piero Soderini is elected lifetime Standard-bearer of Justice

1502 5 October: Machiavelli's second legation to Cesare Borgia

1502 9 October: Cesare Borgia kills Oliverotto da Fermo and Vitellozzo Vitelli and, eventually, Paolo and Francesco Orsini, the lieutenants who conspired against him

1503 18 August: Pope Alexander VI dies

1503 October: Giuliano della Rovere is elected Pope Julius II

1503 November: fall of Cesare Borgia

1504 January: Machiavelli's second legation to France

1506 January: Machiavelli is sent to the countryside to raise troops for the new militia

1506 March: Machiavelli, *La cagione dell'ordinanza*

1507 January: Machiavelli becomes chancellor of the militia's Nine

1507 December: Machiavelli's legation to Maximilian I

1508 December: League of Cambrai (Maximilian I, Ferdinando the Catholic, Louis XII, Julius II) against Venice

1509 14 May: Battle of Agnadello; Venice is defeated

1509 8 June: fall of Pisa; Machiavelli is among the Florentine negotiators

1509 June: Pisa surrenders to Florence

1510 February: peace between Julius II and Venice; Julius II turns against France

1510 June: Machiavelli's third legation to France

1511 Julius II forms the Holy League (with Spain and Venice) against France

1512 11 April: France defeats the League's army at Ravenna

1512 August: the League sends a Spanish army against Florence; sack of Prato; the Medici return to Florence; Machiavelli is dismissed from all his posts and confined out of town for one year

1513 February: Boscoli and Capponi's plot against the Medici; Machiavelli is arrested and tortured. He is set free after Giovanni de' Medici is elected Pope Leo X. Machiavelli is confined to his family domain, the 'Albergaccio' at Sant'Andrea in Percussina, near San Casciano Val di Pesa; here, he probably started to write *The Prince*. Lorenzo de' Medici the younger controls Florence's government.

1515 Louis XII dies; Francis I is new king of France. Machiavelli hopes to be able to go back in office. He probably starts to attend the *Orti Oricellari*'s discussions, where he reads parts of the *Discorsi*.

1516 May: Erasmus, *Institutio principis christiani*

1516 June: Leo X conquers Urbino, and Lorenzo becomes the new duke of the city; Machiavelli dedicates *The Prince* to Lorenzo

1516 Thomas More, *Utopia*; Ariosto, *Orlando Furioso*

1518 Machiavelli, *Mandragola*

1519 Giuliano de' Medici controls Florence after Lorenzo's death; Machiavelli finishes writing the *Art of War*

1519 28 June: Charles (V) of Augsburg is elected emperor

1520 15 June: Leo X's bull *Exsurge Domine* against Martin Luther

1520 August: Machiavelli writes the *Life of Castruccio Castracani*

1520 December: Machiavelli, *Discursus florentinarum rerum*

1521 May: Machiavelli is sent by the Eight of Ward of Florence to the Franciscan Friars Chapter (the so-called 'Repubblica degli Zoccoli') at Carpi; during the mission he gets in touch with Francesco Guicciardini, governor of Modena

1521 August: the *Art of War* is published in Florence

1521 1 December: Leo X dies; Adrian of Utrecht is elected Pope Adrian VI

1522 May: anti-Medicean plot of Zanobi Buondelmonti, Luigi Alamanni, Antonio Brucioli and other members of the *Orti Oricellari* group

1523 Agostino Nifo, *De regnandi peritia*

1523 19 November: Giulio de' Medici is elected Pope Clement VII

1525 24 February: at the battle of Pavia, Francis I is defeated and imprisoned by Charles V

1525 May: Machiavelli presents the *Florentine Histories* to Clement VII

1526 Francis I is released by Charles V; League of Cognac (France, Rome, Venice, Milan, Genoa and Florence) against the emperor

1526 April: Machiavelli is appointed Chancellor of the Walls, to prepare the defence of Florence

1526 July: the Spanish army occupies Milan

1526 September: Machiavelli is sent by the Eight of Ward to the field of the Holy League (September 1526), then to Modena (November 1526), and finally to Parma (February 1527), in order to discuss the role of the Florentine Republic in the League, and the conduct of military operations, with the Governor of the Papal Army Francesco Guicciardini

1527 6 May: sack of Rome

1527 17 May: the Medici are expelled from Florence; the Republic and the Great Council are restored

1527 21 June: Machiavelli dies

1531 First printing of the *Discourses on Livy*

1532 First printing of *The Prince* and the *Florentine Histories*

Notes

INTRODUCTION

1. *Il Novellino, The Hundred Old Tales,* LXXXIV.
2. See, for example, J. G. A. Pocock, *The Machiavellian Moment,* Quentin Skinner, *Machiavelli: A Very Short Introduction,* Maurizio Viroli, *Machiavelli,* or Philip Pettit, *Republicanism: A Theory of Freedom and Government.*
3. Italo Calvino, 'Why Read the Classics?' Curiously, the English translator has added a question mark to the much less ambiguous Italian title 'Perché leggere i classici'.
4. Especially when one is able to read the original Italian text. As is the case for Aristotle and Spinoza, Descartes and Hegel, a direct reading of the original will help in overcoming the minor inaccuracies and the major mistakes in several of the existing English translations of Machiavelli.
5. A new 'translation' of Machiavelli's *The Prince* has just appeared: a translation in modern Italian. See Machiavelli, *Il Principe. Edizione del cinquecentennale.*

CHAPTER 1

1. Ludovico Ariosto, *Orlando Furioso,* XII.
2. Jane Everson and D. Zancani (eds), *Italy in Crisis: 1494.*
3. Hans Baron, *The Crisis of the Early Italian Renaissance.*
4. John R. Hale, *Renaissance Venice.*
5. André Chastel, *Le grand atelier d'Italie.*
6. John M. Najemy, *A History of Florence.*
7. Piero Parenti, *Storia fiorentina,* I.
8. Bartolomeo Cerretani, *Storia fiorentina.*
9. Andrea Guidi, *Un Segretario militante.*
10. Paolo Giovio, *Elogia clarorum virorum,* c. 55v.
11. Eugenio Garin, 'I cancellieri umanisti della repubblica fiorentina

da Coluccio Salutati a Bartolomeo Scala', and Demetrio Marzi, *La Cancelleria della Repubblica Fiorentina*.

12. Lodi Nauta, *In Defense of Common Sense*.
13. Lorenzo Valla, *On the Donation of Constantine*.
14. Oreste Tommasini, *La vita e gli scritti di Niccolò Machiavelli*, II, 151.
15. D II, 5. Throughout this book I cite the following translations of Machiavelli's works: *Discourses on Livy* (trans. Harvey C. Mansfield and Nathan Tarcov), abbreviated as D; *The Prince* (trans. Harvey C. Mansfield), abbreviated as P; *Florentine Histories* (trans. Laura F. Banfield and Harvey C. Mansfield), abbreviated as FH; *Art of War* (trans. Christopher Lynch), abbreviated as AW.
16. Donald Weinstein, *Savonarola and Florence*.
17. Luca Landucci, *Diario fiorentino*.
18. Najemy, *A History of Florence*, 378–80.
19. Francesco Guicciardini, *Storie fiorentine*.
20. Jean-Louis Fournel and Jean Claude Zancarini, *La politique de l'expérience. Savonarole, Guicciardini et le républicanisme florentin*.
21. P, dedicatory letter.
22. P III.
23. Letter to the *Dieci*, 26 June 1502, signed Franciscus Soderinus Episcopus Volaterrarum, in Machiavelli, *Legazioni, Commissarie, Scritti di governo*, II, 125.
24. Guidi, *Un Segretario militante*.
25. *1512. La cagione dell'ordinanza, dove la si truovi, et quel che bisogni fare Post Res Perditas*. This text was not written in 1512 (the title was added later) but rather during the period when Machiavelli was actively working on his project of a citizen militia. See Machiavelli, *I primi scritti politici (1499–1512)*.

CHAPTER 2

1. See for example Charles B. Schmitt and Quentin Skinner (eds), *The Cambridge History of Renaissance Philosophy*, 430–42.
2. D I, preface.
3. For example Claude Lefort, *Le travail de l'oeuvre Machiavel*.
4. For example Leo Strauss, *Thoughts on Machiavelli*.
5. P XV. This is one of the weakest points of Skinner and Price's edition of *The Prince*. They translate the passage as 'It seems to me better to concentrate on what really happens rather than on theories and speculations.' The *'verità effettuale'* is certainly linked to what 'really' happens. By employing the term *'verità'*, however, Machiavelli points out something that has a stronger ontological reality, linked with both the 'factual' and the 'effectual', whose meaning must be preserved in the translation. Mansfield opts for a better choice: 'It has appeared to me more fitting to go directly to the effectual truth of the thing than to the imagination of

it.' Mansfield's choice is also better for the second term of the opposition: the imagination of truth has a much deeper philosophical meaning than what is implied by the couple 'theories' and 'speculations'.

6. See for example Maurizio Zanardi, 'Note su Machiavelli filosofo'.

7. Felix Gilbert, *Machiavelli and Guicciardini: Politics and History in Sixteenth-Century Florence*, 193, and Francesco Bausi, 'Introduzione', in Machiavelli, *Discorsi* (2001), ix–xliv.

8. See Emanuele Cutinelli-Rèndina, *Introduzione a Machiavelli*, 112.

9. See Luigi Zanzi, *I «segni» della natura e i «paradigmi» della storia.*

10. See Nicola Badaloni, 'Natura e società in Machiavelli', Giovanni Di Napoli, 'Niccolò Machiavelli e l'Aristotelismo del Rinascimento', and Bernard Guillemin, 'Machiavel, lecteur d'Aristote'.

11. *Discursus florentinarum rerum.*

12. D I, 17: 'Where the matter is not corrupt, tumults and other scandals do not hurt; where it is corrupt, well-ordered laws do not help unless indeed they have been put in motion by one individual who with an extreme force ensures their observance so that the matter becomes good.'

13. Machiavelli's *virtù*, therefore, is not the typical *virtù* of man as *animal politicum* of the Aristotelian tradition, as John G. A. Pocock maintains, and the political organisation of life is not, as he suggests, 'the form in which human matter developed its proper virtue, and it was the function of virtue to impose form on the matter of *fortuna*'. See J. G. A. Pocock, *The Machiavellian Moment: Florentine Political Thought and the Atlantic Republican Tradition.*

14. D I, 35.

15. This is Pocock's interpretation: 'It is noteworthy how often in his treatment of corruption Machiavelli employs teleological language: laws and constitutions, even structures of virtue, are *forma*, and the legislator and law-enforcer (not to mention the reformer) seek to impose form on the *materia* of the republic, which is of course its human constituent matter.' See Pocock, *The Machiavellian Moment*, 207.

16. It is true, as Zanzi claims, that this approach to the study of the world and its changing nature largely derives, in the late Renaissance, from the Aristotelian revaluation of the possibility of knowing the corruptible realm of nature (see especially Aristotle, *De partibus animalim*). The Aristotelian move, however, is not intended to completely overcome the Platonic transcendence of the world of ideas. This transcendence is embodied by the forms and their action upon matter or, in other words, by teleology. It is precisely from this scheme of thought that Machiavelli intends to differentiate himself by challenging *any* form of transcendence, and this is only possible through a profound transformation of the Aristotelian concepts of form and matter. See Zanzi, *I «segni» della natura e i «paradigmi» della storia.*

17. See Gian Mario Anselmi, *Ricerche sul Machiavelli storico.* Anselmi maintains that naturalism allows Machiavelli to develop a secular and

materialist interpretation of history. This interpretation, according to Anselmi, echoes Sallust's theory of history in the ancient culture, and Pomponazzi's Aristotelianism in the modern culture. The dynamic relationship between human and natural in Sallust's historiography definitely has a strong impact on Machiavelli's methodology. I am less convinced, however, that Machiavelli also follows the Paduan Aristotelianism; in fact, on the contrary, I would say that he intends to differentiate himself from it, precisely by a reworking of the concepts of form and matter.

18. Miguel Vatter powerfully grasps this new attitude, at the same time theoretical and political, by saying that 'Machiavelli decenters the instance of form within political life [. . .] The priority of the situation over the norm, of the event over the form, articulates one of the fundamental aspects in which Machiavelli breaks with classical political thought and inaugurates political modernity: the question of how to change the political form has overtaken the question of what is the right form' (see *Between Form and Event*, 34).

19. D II, 3, or P VII.

20. The famous 'long experience with modern things and a continued reading of ancient ones'. P, dedicatory letter.

21. P III.

22. D I, preface.

23. D I, preface.

24. D III, 1.

25. The 'beginnings', then, do not represent the dusk of the possibility of imitating the ancient, as Giorgio Inglese maintains. See Giorgio Inglese, *Per Machiavelli. L'arte dello stato, la cognizione delle storie*, 106. See also Vatter, *Between Form and Event*.

26. As is the case in the theory of humours developed in the *Discourses*. See below for the political meaning and role of humours.

27. On political action, see Oliver Feltham, *Anatomy of Failure*.

28. *La cagione dell'ordinanza* (1512), in *L'arte della guerra, scritti politici minori*.

29. D III, 9.

30. Polybius, *The Histories*, VI.

31. According to a thesis that has been widely criticised. See Gennaro Sasso, *Machiavelli e gli antichi*, and Eugenio Garin, *Machiavelli fra politica e storia*. Inglese, *Per Machiavelli*, 109, maintains that Machiavelli read Polybius in the translation of Giano Lascaris or Zephyrus. But he also correctly suggests that Polybius's VI book was already known by Bernardo Rucellai.

32. Arnaldo Momigliano, 'Polybius' Reappearance in Western Europe', 114.

33. Tommasini, *La vita e gli scritti di Niccolò Machiavelli*, II, 1, 36, correctly points out that, following his rhetorical education, Machiavelli does not fall into the narrow and sterile debates often characterising the culture of the time.

34. Polybius, *The Histories*, VI, 4.
35. Polybius, *The Histories*, VI, 9.
36. See Maurizio Zanardi, *Il corpo rigenerato*.
37. D I, 2.
38. Both Gilbert, *Machiavelli and Guicciardini*, 137, and Maurizio Viroli, *How to Read Machiavelli*, 50, on the contrary, see Machiavelli closely following Polybius's circular notion of history.
39. D I, 2.
40. On Machiavelli and Lucretius see Zanardi, *Il corpo rigenerato*, Chauncey E. Finch, 'Machiavelli's Copy of Lucretius', Roberto Ridolfi, 'Del Machiavelli, di un codice di Lucrezio e di altro ancora', Sergio Bertelli, 'Noterelle machiavellian. Un codice di Lucrezio e di Terenzio', Sergio Bertelli, 'Noterelle machiavelliane II. Ancora su Lucrezio e Machiavelli', Roberto Ridolfi, 'Erratacorrige machiavelliana', and, more recently, Alison Brown, *The Return of Lucretius to Renaissance Florence*, and Paul A. Rahe, 'In the Shadow of Lucretius'.
41. See Michel Serres, *La naissance de la physique dans le texte de Lucrèce: fleuves et turbulences*, Jean Salem, *Tel un dieu parmi les hommes. L'éthique d'Épicure*, Jean Salem, *La mort n'est rien pour nous. Lucrèce et l'éthique*, Jean Salem, *Démocrite. Grains de poussière dans un rayon de soleil*, and David N. Sedley, *Lucretius and the Transformation of Greek Wisdom*.
42. Dante, *The Divine Comedy*, Inferno IV.
43. Cf. Leon Robin, 'Sur la conception aristotélicienne de la causalité', William D. Ross, *Aristotle*, and Wolfgang Wieland, *Die aristotelische Physik*.
44. Salem, *Démocrite*.
45. Salem, *Démocrite*.
46. See Lucretius, *De rerum natura*, II, 216ff.: 'While the first bodies are being carried downwards by their own weight in a straight line through the void, at times quite uncertain and uncertain places, they swerve a little from their course, just so much as you might call a change of motion. For if they were not apt to incline, all would fall downwards like raindrops through the profound void, no collision would take place and no blow would be caused amongst the first-beginnings: thus nature would never have produced anything.'
47. Lucretius, *De rerum natura*, II, 251ff.: 'If all motion is always one long chain, and new motion arises out of the old in order invariable, and if the first-beginnings do not make by swerving a beginning of motion such as to break the decrees of fate, that cause may not follow cause from infinity, whence comes this free will in living creatures all over the earth, whence I say is this will wrested from the fates by which we proceed whither pleasure leads each, swerving also our motions not at fixed times and fixed places, but just where our mind has taken us?'
48. Lucretius, *De rerum natura*, II, 303ff.: '[No power can] change the sum

total of things; for there is no place without into which any kind of matter could flee away from the all; and there is no place whence a new power could arise to burst into the all, and to change the whole nature of things and turn their motions.'

49. Cf. Salem, *La mort n'est rien pour nous*.

50. Inglese, *Per Machiavelli*, 111, acknowledges the fact that Machiavelli uses the concept of chance against Polybius's rigid necessity. Yet he does not link Machiavelli's chance with the Lucretian background and the Epicurean theory of freedom and human action. On the contrary, he intends the Epicurean *clinamen* as a synonym of 'natural necessity', embodied in the fall and clash of atoms. The fall of Rome, in this sense, should be considered as a natural and necessary event in Machiavelli's mind (p. 124), rather than a historical event linked with political, economic and military circumstances.

51. In this sense, Machiavelli's reflection moves away from the humanist positions, exclusively considered by Quentin Skinner, *Machiavelli: A Very Short Introduction*, 33, through the classic positions of Seneca in ancient times, or Enea Silvio Piccolomini in modern times. Although aware of the enormous importance that both Latin classics and Christian humanists such as Cicero, Boetius, Petrarch or Pontano concede to fortune, and the accepted image of it as a capricious but controllable goddess, Machiavelli undeniably introduces an original and powerful dimension, thanks to the philosophical elements drawn from Lucretius.

52. See Gérard Colonna d'Istria and Roland Frapet, *L'art politique chez Machiavel*.

53. It is true, then, that Machiavelli shrinks the realm of liberty and strongly focuses on necessity. Not in the same sense, though, as what Hegel will call *Weltlauf* in his *Phenomenology of the Spirit*, namely the 'world course' whereby necessity progressively swallows liberty. If Machiavelli insists on necessity, following Lucretius, it is precisely for the sake of grounding an effective and pregnant notion of freedom.

54. D I, 1. See Raymond Polin, 'Les régimes politiques et l'imitation des anciens chez Machiavel'.

55. The secondary literature devoted to the Machiavellian dialectic between *virtù* and *fortuna* is extremely wide. Works specifically devoted to this theme are Hannah F. Pitkin, *Fortune Is a Woman: Gender and Politics in the Thought of Niccolò Machiavelli*, Oded Balaban, 'The Human Origin of Fortuna in Machiavelli's Thought', Gianni Nicoletti, 'Caso-causa o fortuna nel machiavellismo', Alessandro Fontana, 'Fortune et décision chez Machiavel', and Cary J. Nederman, 'Amazing Grace: Fortune, God and Free Will in Machiavelli's Thought'.

56. Plutarch, *De fortuna Romanorum*, Moralia, IV, 318b–19b.

57. D II, 1. For various descriptions of *fortuna* in Machiavelli's own time and in the Florentine literature, see Gilbert, *Machiavelli and Guicciardini*, 43 ff.

58. P VI, translation modified.
59. P XXV.
60. *Capitolo dell'Occasione*, in *Lust and Liberty: The Poems of Machiavelli*, 128.
61. Maurizio Viroli's description of *Fortuna* as 'the capricious and malignant goddess who takes pleasure in tormenting the good and rewarding the wicked' is definitely underestimating the complexity of Machiavelli's concept. See Viroli, *How to Read Machiavelli*, 52.
62. Louis Althusser, *Machiavelli and Us*, speaks of a 'philosophical theory of the encounter' between *fortuna* and *virtù* in Machiavelli's thought.
63. P XXV, translation slightly modified.
64. D II, 29.
65. Cf. Althusser, *Machiavelli and Us*, 18: 'I believe it is not hazardous to venture that Machiavelli is the first theorist of the conjuncture or the first thinker consciously, if not to think the concept of conjuncture, if not to make it the object of an abstract and systematic reflection, then at least consistently – in an insistent, extremely profound way – to think *in* the conjuncture: that is to say, in its concept of an aleatory, singular case. What does it mean *to think in the conjuncture*? To think about a political problem under the category of conjuncture? It means, first of all, taking account of all the determinations, all the existing, concrete *circumstances*, making an inventory, a detailed breakdown and comparison of them.'
66. D III, 31.
67. Lucretius, *De rerum natura*, II, 581ff.: 'This is also herewith you would do well to guard sealed and treasured in memory, that there is none of those things which are in plain view before us which consists only of one kind of element, nothing which does not consist of various seeds commingled; and the more a thing has in itself many powers and faculties, so it shows that there are within it most kind of elements and varied shapes.'
68. P XXIV.
69. P XXIV.

CHAPTER 3

1. See Federico Chabod, *Machiavelli and the Renaissance*.
2. See Felix Gilbert, 'The Composition and Structure of Machiavelli's *Discorsi*'.
3. See Bausi, 'Introduzione', in Machiavelli, *Discorsi* (2001).
4. On the *Orti Oricellari* see Felix Gilbert, 'Bernardo Rucellai and the Orti Oricellari: A Study of the Origin of Modern Political Thought', and Rudolf von Albertini, *Das florentinische Staatsbewusstsein im Übergang von der Republik zum Prinzipat*.
5. John McCormick recently insisted on the importance of the dedication in order to understand the very nature and political character of the *Discourses*. See John P. McCormick, *Machiavellian Democracy*.

6. Gilbert, *Machiavelli and Guicciardini*, 80.

7. P, dedicatory letter.

8. See Tommasini, *La vita e gli scritti di Niccolò Machiavelli*, II, 147.

9. See Alessandro Fontana, 'Introduction', in Machiavelli, *Discours* (2004), 12.

10. D I, 4.

11. On Machiavelli and social conflict see Filippo Del Lucchese, *Conflict, Power, and Multitude in Machiavelli and Spinoza*. See also Marie Gaille-Nikodimov, *Conflit civil et liberté*, and Gabriele Pedullà, *Machiavelli in tumulto*.

12. D I, 4. For an analysis of who the 'many' are to whom Machiavelli refers, see Sasso, *Machiavelli e gli antichi*.

13. D I, 4.

14. In both directions. Not only are political thinkers interested in medical concepts, but also authors of medical treatises such as Taddeo Alderotti and Pietro Torrigiani refer to political works, such as Aristotle's *Nicomachean Ethics*, in order to explain the Galenic notion of humours' complexion. See Laurent Gerbier, 'Histoire, médecine et politique. Les figures du temps dans le *Prince* et les *Discours* de Machiavel'.

15. Gerbier, 'Histoire, médecine et politique'.

16. Anthony Parel underlines the Galenic framework of this chapter and its importance for understanding Machiavelli's philosophy. Yet he does so in order to stress, against Strauss, the premodern approach of Machiavelli to politics: the theory of humours, for him, shows how Machiavelli was more interested in premodern medical concepts than in the modern building of a political science. In doing so, though, he does not recognise the originality of Machiavelli's reworking of traditional ideas. See Anthony J. Parel, *The Machiavellian Cosmos*. J. G. A. Pocock, *The Machiavellian Moment*, 194, also underestimates Machiavelli's powerful and conscious reflections when he writes that 'if union arises from disunion, it comes about through irrational rather than rational action. Of this the inscrutable workings of fortune seem the only possible explanation.'

17. D I, 37.

18. D I, 37.

19. D I, 37.

20. Aristotle, *Politics*, III, 5, 7, 209–11.

21. D I, 5.

22. D I, 5.

23. D I, 55.

24. See the *Rapporto delle cose della Magna* of 1508 and the *Discorso* as well as the *Ritratto delle cose della Magna* of 1509 in Machiavelli, *L'arte dela guerra, scritti politici minori*.

25. D I, 55.

26. It is important to stress that, although political and economic conflict can

be distinguished and are not necessarily the same thing for Machiavelli, he always has both dimensions clearly in mind, and in fact they are inextricably linked to each other, and this explains the peculiar situation – both political and economic – of Tuscany. J. G. A. Pocock, *The Machiavellian Moment*, 209, on the contrary, maintains that '"inequality" [. . .] connotes neither inequality of wealth nor inequality of political authority'.

27. D I, 6.
28. D I, 6.
29. D I, 6.
30. J. G. A. Pocock, *The Machiavellian Moment*, 197, underestimates this point when he writes that the choice for empire 'involves a preference for a more popular form of government'. Pocock also excessively reduces the breadth of Machiavelli's consideration, narrowing it – as well as the whole Book I of the *Discourses* – to the 'concern, typical of his generation, with the republic's ability to control its external environment'.
31. *1512. La cagione dell'ordinanza*, in Machiavelli, *L'arte della guerra, scritti politici minori*.
32. D I, 21.
33. D I, 43.
34. See Umberto Mazzone, *'El buon governo.' Un progetto di riforma generale nella Firenze savonaroliana*. See also Chapter 6 below.
35. D II, 10.
36. D II, 18.
37. D I, 11.
38. D I, 13.
39. D I, 13.
40. See Machiavelli's letter to Ricciardo Becchi of 9 March 1498, in *Machiavelli and His Friends: Their Personal Correspondence*.
41. Machiavelli, letter to Becchi, 9 March 1498, in *Machiavelli and His Friends*.
42. D I, 14.
43. D II, 2.
44. D II, 2.
45. It is difficult to agree with Maurizio Viroli, *Machiavelli*, 165: 'Machiavelli's patriotism is not irreligious and not even antichristian; it is just anticlerical, as Florentine patriotism had been since the end of the fourteenth century.' In fact, Machiavelli is not only criticising the Roman Church, but also the moral and ideological ideas that form the ground of the Christian religion.
46. D I, 12.
47. D I, 12.
48. D I, 12.
49. D I, 12.
50. In Lucretius, but also in Plato, Aristotle and Polybius.

51. D II, 5.
52. D II, 5.
53. D II, 5.
54. It is important, I believe, to insist on the philosophical ground of Machiavelli's criticism, because this explains his denunciation of Christianity qua religion, and makes any further argument claiming Machiavelli's sincere religiousness inconsistent. A few modern authors have claimed not only that Machiavelli had genuine religious beliefs, but also that, despite his open denunciation, he was in fact truly a Christian. One of the most authoritative scholars to support such a reading is Roberto Ridolfi in *Vita di Niccolò Machiavelli*, but I would like to mention at least Alberto Tenenti, 'La religione di Machiavelli', Sebastian de Grazia, *Machiavelli in Hell*, and Maurizio Viroli, *Machiavelli's God*. With different arguments these scholars claim either a personal religiousness of Machiavelli, distinct from the 'public' position of his major written works, or a 'Republican Christianity' of Machiavelli, emerging also from his major works. Whereas the former aspect mainly is of interest for the reconstruction of Machiavelli's morality, the latter aspect concerns the interpretation of his political philosophy. Now this philosophy, as I have been showing, is deeply rooted in a rereading of ancient Lucretian materialism. The powerful critique of Christianism in the name of pagan values stems from those philosophical roots as well as from a political reasoning about what can be learned, for Machiavelli, from the ancient Roman experience and applied in modern times. Machiavelli never claims that these values, which contribute for him to political *virtù*, can be linked to Christianity or to the figure of Christ himself. Machiavelli's sincere Christianity is a striking thesis that does not have, in my view, a strong ground in Machiavelli's texts. For an erudite and meaningful criticism of the whole question concerning Machiavelli's religion see Emanuele Cutinelli-Rèndina, *Chiesa e religione in Machiavelli*.
55. Simone Weil, *The Iliad, or the Poem of Force*.

CHAPTER 4

1. See below, Part III.
2. Letter to Francesco Vettori, 10 December 1513, in Machiavelli, *The Prince*.
3. The anecdote is in Machiavelli, *Lettere familiari*. See Ridolfi, *Vita di Niccolò Machiavelli*, 258, and Inglese, *Per Machiavelli*, 50.
4. Machiavelli, *Machiavelli and His Friends*, 264.
5. P, dedicatory letter.
6. P, dedicatory letter.
7. Machiavelli's claim about his own experience is proudly illustrated, for example, in P III, when he writes about the encounter with George d'Amboise, the powerful cardinal of Rouen in 1500, 'when Valentino

[. . .] was occupying Romagna. [. . .] when the Cardinal of Rouen said to me that the Italians do not understand war, I replied to him that the French do not understand the state, because if they understood, they would not have let the Church come to such greatness.'

8. See Gennaro Sasso, *Niccolò Machiavelli*.

9. AW VII, 235: 'Before they tasted the blows of the ultramontane wars, our Italian princes used to believe that it was enough for a prince to know how to think of a sharp response in his studies, to write a beautiful letter, to show wit and quickness in his deeds and words, to know how to weave a fraud, to be ornamented by gems and gold, to sleep and eat with greater splendor than others [. . .].'

10. P, dedicatory letter.

11. See Gilbert, *Machiavelli and Guicciardini*, 192: '[His] conception of man gave Machiavelli's political utopia its unique character. For Machiavelli *was* the creator of an utopia; with his image of Roman politics he made his contribution to the body of literature in which perfect societies are constructed.' Nor is he a realist whose realism resembles more an idealism, according to Maurizio Viroli, *How to Read Machiavelli*, 20.

12. See Augustin Renaudet, *Machiavel*.

13. See Chabod, *Machiavelli and the Renaissance*.

14. Gennaro Sasso, *Niccolò Machiavelli*, 365–79, has clearly and strongly pointed this out.

15. See Jack H. Hexter, *The Vision of Politics on the Eve of Reformation*, especially Chapter 4.

16. See Viroli, *Machiavelli*.

17. Gennaro Sasso, *Niccolò Machiavelli*, 382, is once again clear and correctly unambiguous on this point.

18. P V. Addressed to a Medici in 1513, these words do not certainly testify of Machiavelli's opportunism or even prudence.

19. See below, Part III. See also Romain Descendre, 'È certo che vale più la pratica che la teorica'.

20. Gennaro Sasso, *Niccolò Machiavelli*, 399ff., underlines the risk of uncritically endorsing the 'scientific' attitude of Machiavelli, and points out a meaningful reading of the 'scientific' character of his method.

21. P XXVI.

22. P XXVI.

23. Sasso, *Niccolò Machiavelli*.

24. Viroli, *How to Read Machiavelli*, 4.

25. P XV.

26. P VIII.

27. P VIII.

28. P VIII.

29. P VIII.

30. Tommasini, *La vita e gli scritti di Niccolò Machiavelli*, II, 1, 124.

31. P VII.

32. P VII.
33. Inglese, *Per Machiavelli*, 62.
34. Machiavelli, *The Legations*, in *The Chief Works and Others*, I.
35. P VII.
36. P VII.
37. See *A Description of the Method Used by Duke Valentino in Killing Vitellozzo Vitelli, Oliverotto da Fermo, and Others [at Sinigaglia]*, in *The Chief Works and Others*.
38. P VII.
39. P XIII.
40. P XIII.
41. P XVII.
42. P XVII.
43. D I, 9.
44. P XVIII.
45. 'There never was a man', Machiavelli maintains about Alessandro, 'with greater efficacy in asserting a thing, and in affirming it with greater oaths, who observed it less.' And another 'prince of present times', Ferdinando the Catholic, 'never preaches anything but peace and faith, and is very hostile to both'.
46. P XVIII.
47. See Cicero, *De Officiis* I, 2, 34 and 13, 41.
48. P XVIII. See Dimitris Vardoulakis, *Sovereignty and Its Other*.
49. P XVIII, translation modified.
50. Strauss, *Thoughts on Machiavelli*.
51. As Gennaro Sasso has maintained. See Sasso, *Niccolò Machiavelli*, I, 384.
52. P IX.
53. D III, 3. The chapter discusses Soderini's weakness and irresolution. Stating that 'he would have needed to take up extraordinary authority and break up civil equality together with the laws', 'he should', however, 'never allow an evil to run loose out of respect for a good, when that good could easily be crushed by that evil'.
54. P IX.
55. P IX.
56. Hans Baron, 'Machiavelli', maintains on the contrary that 'principatus civilis here means one-man rule established with the consent of the citizens in a former republic, and the chapter presents a discussion not of the harmfulness, but of the suitable moment for the introduction, of absolute rule'. See the remarks of Gennaro Sasso in *Niccolò Machiavelli*, I, 389.

CHAPTER 5

1. Machiavelli started thinking about Castruccio as a possible source for this piece of work during a mission in the city of Lucca, in 1520, where

he also prepared the *Sommario delle cose della città di Lucca*, on the political organisation of the city.

2. *The Life of Castruccio Castracani*, in *The Chief Works and Others*, II, 533–4.

3. And together with *The Prince*, it is presented in the first printed edition by Bernardo Giunta, in 1532.

4. *The Life of Castruccio Castracani*, in *The Chief Works and Others*, II, 552.

5. Letter to Francesco Vettori, 10 December 1513.

6. On the political importance of the choice between Latin and Italian see Mario Martelli, 'Firenze'.

7. Letter to Francesco Guicciardini, 30 August 1524, in *The Chief Works and Others*, II, 978.

8. FH, preface.

9. FH, preface.

10. See for example Sasso, *Niccolò Machiavelli*, or Inglese, *Per Machiavelli*.

11. Cutinelli-Rèndina, *Introduzione a Machiavelli*, 121.

12. FH, preface.

13. See Anselmi, *Ricerche sul Machiavelli storico*.

14. Giovanni Villani, *Cronica*.

15. See Tommasini, *La vita e gli scritti di Niccolò Machiavelli*, II, 1, 53.

16. Aristotle, *Politics*, I, 2, 1252a 30ff.

17. Aristotle, *Nicomachean Ethics*, IX, 6, 1167a. See also VIII, 11, 1159b and *Politics*, II, 4, 1262b.

18. See the letter to Ricciardo Becchi of 9 March 1498: '[. . .] though earlier he sought only to unite his party by speaking evil of his adversaries and to frighten them with the name of tyrant, now – believing that he no longer needs to do so – he has changed his cloak. So, encouraging them to share in the union that has begun, and making no further mention of the tyrant and of their wickedness, he tries to set all of them against the Supreme Pontiff and, biting them, says of him what could be said of the wickedest man you can think of. Thus, according to my judgement, he keeps on working with the times and making his lies plausible.'

19. Girolamo Savonarola, *Prediche sopra Aggeo, con il Trattato circa il reggimento e governo della città di Firenze*, XIII.

20. Hans Baron has described the role played by this ideological debate in the fight against the Visconti in Milan. See Baron, *The Crisis of the Early Italian Renaissance*.

21. Savonarola, *Prediche*, XIV.

22. Savonarola, *Prediche*, XV.

23. FH II, 35.

24. FH II, 26.

25. FH VI, 1.

26. FH IV, 4.

27. FH IV, 7.

28. FH IV, 14.
29. FH IV, 14.
30. Literally 'beard of gold'.
31. FH IV, 27.
32. FH IV, 27.
33. For this interpretation see for example Sasso, *Niccolò Machiavelli*, and Inglese, *Per Machiavelli*.
34. Filippo Del Lucchese, 'Crisis and Power'. See also Yves Winter, 'Plebeian Politics', and Martin Breaugh, *L'expérience plébéienne*.
35. FH III, 11.
36. FH III, 13.
37. FH III, 13.
38. FH III, 13.
39. FH III, 1.
40. FH III, 1.
41. D I, 55.
42. Fabio Raimondi, 'Il paradigma-Firenze nel Discursus florentinarum rerum di Machiavelli'.
43. See McCormick, *Machiavellian Democracy*.
44. *Discursus*, in *The Chief Works and Others*, I.
45. See Alessandro de' Pazzi, *Discorso al Cardinale Giulio de' Medici*.

CHAPTER 6

1. Matteo Bandello, *Novelle*, I, 46.
2. See for example Piero Pieri, *Il Rinascimento e la crisi militare italiana*.
3. Laurence Arthur Burd, 'Le fonti letterarie di Machiavelli nell'"Arte della guerra"'.
4. C. C. Bayley, *War and Society in Renaissance Florence*.
5. AW I, 82–4.
6. AW I, 171–3.
7. *Cagione dell'ordinanza*.
8. AW, preface.
9. AW VII, 236–7.
10. Together with other strategic organs involved in the financial policy of the Republic. See Jérémie Barthas, *L'argent n'est pas le nerf de la guerre*.
11. See Guidi, *Un Segretario militante*.
12. It is probably even more important than the nomination of Miguel de Corella, Cesare Borgia's former lieutenant, upon which scholars have traditionally focused. See for example Carlo Dionisotti, 'Machiavelli, Cesare Borgia e don Micheletto', in *Machiavellerie*.
13. See *Provvisioni per il Magistrato de' Nove*, 1506.
14. AW II, 29.
15. See Piero Pieri, 'Introduzione', in Machiavelli, *L'arte della guerra*, xv.
16. See Pieri, *Il Rinascimento e la crisi militare italiana*.

17. The most famous example of this evolution is probably the death of the legendary Medicean general Giovanni delle Bande Nere, killed by a falconet ball fired by the Landsknechts of Georg von Frundsberg on 25 November 1526.
18. AW VII, 179.
19. AW VII, 212–24.
20. D I, 21.
21. See Bayley, *War and Society in Renaissance Florence*.

INTRODUCTION TO PART III

1. Benedetto Croce, *Theory and History of Historiography*.
2. Benedetto Croce, 'Una questione che forse non si chiuderà mai. La questione del Machiavelli'.
3. For example, I think that Machiavelli's theory of social conflict is one of his strongest contributions to Western political modernity. Many authoritative scholars would disagree with this, in particular both the conservative Straussian and the progressive Republicans affiliated with the 'Cambridge School'. Now, if I can show that social conflict and political struggles in Machiavelli's thought have *already* been the main concern of Machiavelli's interpreters since the sixteenth century, and I can also show that these interpreters happen to be some of the most important Western political philosophers, then my sometimes unconventional approach has some ground.

CHAPTER 7

1. Francesco Vettori, *Viaggio in Alamagna*, in *Scritti storici e politici*, 14.
2. Francesco Vettori, *Sommario della Istoria d'Italia (1511–1527)*, in *Scritti storici e politici*, 145–6.
3. Francesco Guicciardini, *Considerations*, in *The Sweetness of Power*, 422, slightly adapted.
4. Guicciardini, *Considerations*, 393.
5. Alberico Gentili, *De legationibus libri tres*, II, 156.
6. Alberico Gentili, *The Wars of the Romans*, II, 2, 151.
7. Louis Le Roy, *Les politiques d'Aristote*, 288.
8. Louis Le Roy, *De l'Origine*, 33.
9. Innocent Gentillet, *Anti-Machiavel*, 32.
10. Gentillet, *Anti-Machiavel*, 191.
11. Gentillet, *Anti-Machiavel*, 555.
12. Gentillet, *Anti-Machiavel*, 540–1.
13. Luigi Amabile, *Fra Tommaso Campanella*, III, 141.
14. Ugo Dotti, *Machiavelli rivoluzionario*, 125–60, and Gilberto Sacerdoti, *Sacrificio e sovranità: teologia e politica nell'Europa di Shakespeare e Bruno*, 259–64.

15. Francis Bacon, *De augmentis*, VII, 2, in *Works*, V, 17.

16. Francis Bacon, 'Of Goodnesse and Goodnesse of Nature', in *Essays*, *Works*, VI, 403–5.

17. Francis Bacon, 'Of Fortune', in *Essays*, *Works*, VI, 472–3.

18. Bacon, 'Of Fortune', in *Essays*, *Works*, VI, 472–3.

19. Francis Bacon, 'Of the True Greatness of Kingdoms and Estates', in *Essays*, *Works*, VI, 44–52. See Barthas, *L'argent n'est pas le nerf de la guerre*.

20. Francis Bacon, 'Of Seditions and Troubles', in *Essays*, *Works*, VI, 406–13.

21. Bacon, 'Of Seditions and Troubles', in *Essays*, *Works*, VI, 406–13.

22. Francis Bacon, 'Typhon, sive rebellis', in *De sapientia veterum*, *Works*, VI, 630–1.

23. However, in his influential work on the reception of Machiavelli in modern thought, Felix Raab seems to consider the comparison between Machiavelli and Hobbes relevant only in the light of the effects it produces on the seventeenth-century English republican James Harrington's reception of Machiavelli. See Raab, *The English Face of Machiavelli*.

24. Roberto Esposito, *Ordine e conflitto*.

25. Christian Lazzeri, 'Les racines de la volonté de puissance'.

26. Thomas Hobbes, *Behemoth*, in *The English Works*, III, 343.

27. Thomas Hobbes, *Human Nature, or the Fundamental Elements of Policy*, in *The English Works*, IV, *The Epistle Dedicatory*.

28. Thomas Hobbes, *Of Liberty and Necessity*, in *The English Works*, IV, 250–1.

29. Thomas Hobbes, *De Corpore Politico*, in *The English Works*, IV, 226.

30. Thomas Hobbes, *Leviathan*, XXVII, in *The English Works*, III, 282.

31. Hobbes, *Leviathan*, XV, in *The English Works*, III, 132.

32. Hobbes, *Leviathan*, XIV, in *The English Works*, III, 127.

33. Hobbes, *Leviathan*, XLVI, in *The English Works*, III, 683.

34. Hobbes, *Leviathan*, XVII, in *The English Works*, III, 154.

35. Hobbes, *Leviathan*, XLVI, in *The English Works*, III, 669.

36. Hobbes, *Leviathan*, XXIX, in *The English Works*, III, 314–15.

37. Hobbes, *Leviathan*, XLVI, in *The English Works*, III.

38. Hobbes, *Leviathan*, XXV, in *The English Works*, III, 247.

39. Hobbes, *Leviathan*, Review and conclusion, in *The English Works*, III, 706–7.

40. Carl Schmitt, *The Leviathan in the State Theory of Thomas Hobbes*.

41. See Paul A. Rahe, 'Machiavelli in the English Revolution', in *Machiavelli's Liberal Republican Legacy*, 9–35.

42. James Harrington, *The Commonwealth of Oceana*, 69.

43. Harrington, *Oceana*, 9.

44. Harrington, *Oceana*, 33.

45. Harrington, *Oceana*, 13.

46. FH VI, 1, 230.
47. Harrington, *Oceana*, 30.
48. Harrington, *Oceana*, 30.
49. D I, 4.
50. Harrington, *Oceana*, 23.
51. Harrington, *Oceana*, 36–7.
52. See Rahe, 'Machiavelli in the English Revolution'.
53. Harrington, *Oceana*, 22.
54. Harrington, *Oceana*, 23–4.
55. J. G. A. Pocock, 'Introduction', in *The Political Works of James Harrington*, 74–5.
56. Christopher Hill, *Puritanism and Revolution*, 280.
57. See Luca Baccelli, *Critica del repubblicanesimo*.
58. See Warren Montag and Ted Stolze (eds), *The New Spinoza*. See also Pierre-François Moreau, *Spinoza. L'expérience et l'éternité*.
59. Baruch Spinoza, *Political Treatise*, V, 7, in *Complete Works*, 700.
60. Baruch Spinoza, *Theologico-Political Treatise*, XVIII, in *Complete Works*, 556.
61. Spinoza, *Theologico-Political Treatise*, XVII, in *Complete Works*, 546.
62. Spinoza, *Theologico-Political Treatise*, XVII, in *Complete Works*, 545.
63. Spinoza, *Political Treatise*, I, 1, in *Complete Works*, 680.
64. P XV.
65. Laurent Bove, *La stratégie du conatus*.
66. Antonio Negri, *The Savage Anomaly*.
67. Spinoza, Letter 50, in *Complete Works*, 891–2.
68. Spinoza, *Political Treatise*, IV, 6, in *Complete Works*, 698.
69. See Del Lucchese, *Conflict, Power, and Multitude in Machiavelli and Spinoza*, and Vittorio Morfino, *Il tempo e l'occasione* and *Plural Temporality*.
70. See Baruch Spinoza, *Ethica*, III, 11 *scholia*, in *Complete Works*.
71. Spinoza, *Ethica*, III, 22 *scholia*, in *Complete Works*. See Alexandre Matheron, *Études sur Spinoza*.
72. Spinoza, *Political Treatise*, VI, 1, in *Complete Works*, 700.
73. Spinoza, *Political Treatise*, III, 9, in *Complete Works*, 693.
74. Spinoza, *Political Treatise*, X, 1, in *Complete Works*, 747.
75. Spinoza, *Political Treatise*, IX, 14, in *Complete Works*, 746.
76. Spinoza, *Political Treatise*, VI, 2, in *Complete Works*, 701.
77. Bayle, *Dictionnaire historique et critique*, s.v. 'Machiavel', 21.
78. *Le Prince de Nicolas Machiavel sécretaire et citoyen de Florence traduit et commenté par A. N. Amelot sieur de la Houssaye*.
79. *Oeuvres de Machiavel*. On Guiraudet's translation see Bernard Gainot, 'Lectures de Machiavel à l'époque du Directoire et du Triennio jacobin', in Paolo Carta and Xavier Tabet (eds), *Machiavelli nel XIX e XX secolo/ Machiavel au XIXe et XXe siècles*, 17–48.
80. For example Jonathan Israel, *The Radical Enlightenment*.

81. See Baltasar Gracián, *L'Homme de cour*, and Paolo Sarpi, *Histoire du concile de Trente*.
82. See Jacob Soll, *Publishing 'The Prince'*.
83. See Joseph Macek, *Machiavelli e il machiavellismo*, 223.
84. Tacitus, *Les six premiers livres des Annales*.
85. Soll, *Publishing 'The Prince'*, 15.
86. Frédéric II, *Anti-Machiavel*, 66.
87. Frédéric II, *Anti-Machiavel*, 37.
88. Frédéric II, *Anti-Machiavel*, 7.
89. Frédéric II, *Anti-Machiavel*, 8 and 37.
90. P IX.
91. Frédéric II, *Anti-Machiavel*, 96.
92. Frédéric II, *Anti-Machiavel*, 96.
93. Soll, *Publishing 'The Prince'*, 116.
94. Voltaire, *Oeuvres complètes*, V, 5. Ironically, though, Frederick II personally congratulates Montesquieu on his most Machiavellian work, the *Considérations sur les causes de la grandeur des Romains et de leur décadence*. See Montesquieu, *Oeuvres complètes*, 435.
95. Montesquieu, *Dissertation*, in *Oeuvres complètes*, 39–43.
96. See Ettore Levi-Malvano, *Montesquieu e Machiavelli*, and Robert Shackleton, 'Montesquieu and Machiavelli'.
97. 'It is – Voltaire maintains – nothing more than a clever table of contents written in Roman style, rather than a real book.' See Montesquieu, *Oeuvres complètes*, 435.
98. Montesquieu, *Considérations*, in *Oeuvres complètes*, 436.
99. Montesquieu, *Considérations*, in *Oeuvres complètes*, 473.
100. Montesquieu, *Considérations*, in *Oeuvres complètes*, 473.
101. Montesquieu, *Considérations*, in *Oeuvres complètes*, 453. Among modern scholars, only Paul Carrese has grasped the fundamental importance of this theoretical argument. See 'The Machiavellian Spirit of Montesquieu's Liberal Republic', in Paul A. Rahe, *Machiavelli's Liberal Republican Legacy*, 121–42.
102. This is Carrese's thesis.
103. Montesquieu, *Considérations*, Chapters VIII and XIV, in *Oeuvres complètes*.
104. Especially in FH III, 1, when Machiavelli maintains that the most radical conflicts had beheaded the Florentine nobility and brought the city to a 'wonderful equality', as Laura F. Banfield and Harvey C. Mansfield translate, and not to a 'shameful degree', as Carrese incorrectly translates.
105. See Del Lucchese, *Conflict, Power, and Multitude in Machiavelli and Spinoza*.
106. Denis Diderot, *Encyclopédie*, s.v. 'Machiavélisme'.
107. On Machiavelli and Rousseau see Yves Lévy, 'Les parties et la démocratie', Paolo M. Cucchi, 'Rousseau lecteur de Machiavel', Roger Payot, 'Jean-Jacques Rousseau et Machiavel', Lionel A. McKenzie, 'Rousseau's

Debate with Machiavelli in the Social Contract', and Maurizio Viroli, 'Republic and Politics in Machiavelli and Rousseau'.

108. Jean-Jacques Rousseau, *On the Social Contract*, II, 3, in *Basic Political Writings*, 156.

109. Rousseau, *On the Social Contract*, IV, 2, in *Basic Political Writings*, 205.

110. Rousseau, *On the Social Contract*, II, 3, footnote, in *Basic Political Writings*, 156.

111. Rousseau, *On the Social Contract*, III, 9, footnote, in *Basic Political Writings*, 191.

112. Modern scholars do not agree on this question. Payot maintains that Rousseau has fully understood Machiavelli, without explaining why. Lévy and Cucchi maintain that Rousseau has misunderstood Machiavelli, and therefore has quoted him inappropriately, while McKenzie and Viroli think that Rousseau has only partially understood Machiavelli, because whereas Rousseau mentions only one kind of division, Machiavelli supports some kinds while blaming others.

113. See Soll, *Publishing 'The Prince'*, 114.

114. Jean-Jacques Rousseau, *Discourse on the Origin of Inequality*, II, in *Basic Political Writings*, 69, to be compared in particular with FH III, 11 and 13.

115. Rousseau, *Discourse on the Origin of Inequality*, II, in *Basic Political Writings*, 69.

116. Condorcet, *Esquisse d'un tableau historique des progrès de l'esprit humain*, 200–1.

117. Maximilien Robespierre, 'Report on the Principles of Political Morality', in *Virtue and Terror*, 109.

CHAPTER 8

1. G. W. F. Hegel, *The German Constitution*, in *Political Writings*, 80.

2. Hegel, *The German Constitution*, in *Political Writings*, 81.

3. G. W. F. Hegel, *Elements of the Philosophy of Right*, par. 340, 371.

4. J. G. Fichte, 'Ueber Machiavell, als Schriftsteller', in *Werke 1806–1807*.

5. Fichte, 'Ueber Machiavell, als Schriftsteller', in *Werke 1806–1807*, 242.

6. Macek, *Machiavelli e il machiavellismo*, 312.

7. Jean-Michel Buée, 'Les lectures de Machiavel en Allemagne dans la première moitié du XIXème siècle', in Carta and Tabet (eds), *Machiavelli nel XIX e XX secolo*, 49–65.

8. Edgar Quinet, *Oeuvres complètes. Les Révolutions d'Italie*, II, 13.

9. Antonio Gramsci, *The Modern Prince*, in *Selection from the Prison Notebooks*, 129.

10. Gramsci, *The Modern Prince*, in *Selection from the Prison Notebooks*, 125.

11. Peter D. Thomas, *The Gramscian Moment*.

12. Gramsci, *The Modern Prince*, in *Selection from the Prison Notebooks*, 185.
13. Antonio Gramsci, *Quaderni del carcere*, 1,556.
14. Fabio Frosini, *Gramsci e la filosofia*.
15. Benedetto Croce, *Machiavelli e Vico – La politica e l'etica*, in *Elementi di politica*, 205.
16. Eugenio Garin, 'Gramsci nella cultura italiana', 415–16.
17. Gramsci, *Quaderni*, 657.
18. Strauss, *Thoughts on Machiavelli*, 75.
19. Strauss, *Thoughts on Machiavelli*, 34–5.
20. Strauss, *Thoughts on Machiavelli*, 29–30.
21. Silvio Suppa, 'Riflessioni sul Machiavelli di Leo Strauss, Isaiah Berlin e Raymond Aron', in Luigi Marco Bassani and Corrado Vivanti (eds), *Machiavelli nella storiografia e nel pensiero politico del XX secolo*, 277–98.
22. Leo Strauss, *The Three Waves of Modernity: An Introduction to Political Philosophy*.
23. Strauss, *Thoughts on Machiavelli*, 127.
24. Strauss, *Thoughts on Machiavelli*, 221–2.
25. Strauss, *Thoughts on Machiavelli*, 259–60.
26. See Filippo Del Lucchese, 'On the Emptiness of an Encounter', and Mikko Lahtinen, *Politics and Philosophy*.
27. Louis Althusser, 'The Underground Current of the Materialism of the Encounter', in *Philosophy of the Encounter*. See Vittorio Morfino, 'An Althusserian Lexicon'.
28. Louis Althusser, *Politique et histoire*, 243.
29. Althusser, *Politique et histoire*, 208.
30. Althusser, *Machiavelli and Us*, 55.
31. Althusser, 'The Underground Current of the Materialism of the Encounter', in *Philosophy of the Encounter*, 172.
32. Althusser, *Machiavelli and Us*, 13.
33. Althusser, *Machiavelli and Us*, 18.

References

PRIMARY SOURCES

Works by Machiavelli

Machiavelli, Niccolò, *Dell'arte della guerra*, ed. Piero Pieri (Rome: Edizioni Roma, 1937).

Machiavelli, Niccolò, *L'arte della guerra, scritti politici minori* (Rome: Salerno Editrice, 2001).

Machiavelli, Niccolò, *Art of War*, ed., trans. and with a commentary by Christopher Lynch (Chicago: University of Chicago Press, 2003).

Machiavelli, Niccolò, *The Chief Works and Others*, trans. Allan Gilbert (Durham, NC, and London: Duke University Press, 1989).

Machiavelli, Niccolò, *Discorsi sopra la prima deca di Tito Livio* (Rome: Salerno Editrice, 2001).

Machiavelli, Niccolò, *Discourses on Livy*, trans. Harvey C. Mansfield and Nathan Tarcov (Chicago and London: University of Chicago Press, 1996).

Machiavelli, Niccolò, *Discours sur la première décade de Tite-Live*, trans. Alessandro Fontana and Xavier Tabet (Paris: Gallimard, 2004).

Machiavelli, Niccolò, *Florentine Histories*, new translation by Laura F. Banfield and Harvey C. Mansfield (Chicago: University of Chicago Press, 1988).

Machiavelli, Niccolò, *Legazioni, Commissarie, Scritti di governo*, ed. Fredi Chiappelli (Bari and Rome: Laterza, 1971–85).

Machiavelli, Niccolò, *Lettere familiari*, ed. Edoardo Alvisi (Florence: Sansoni, 1883).

Machiavelli, Niccolò, *Lust and Liberty: The Poems of Machiavelli*, translated into verse with notes and introduction by Joseph Tusiani (New York: Ivan Obolensky, 1963).

Machiavelli, Niccolò, *Machiavelli and His Friends: Their Personal Correspondence*, ed. and trans. James B. Atkinson and David Sices (DeKalb: Northern Illinois University Press, 1996).

Machiavelli, Niccolò, *I primi scritti politici (1499–1512). Nascita di un pensiero e di uno stile* (Padua: Antenore, 1975).

Machiavelli, Niccolò, *The Prince*, translated and with an introduction by Harvey C. Mansfield (Chicago: University of Chicago Press, 1985).

Machiavelli, Niccolò, *Le Prince de Nicolas Machiavel sécretaire et citoyen de Florence traduit et commenté par A. N. Amelot sieur de la Houssaye* (Amsterdam: chez Henry Wetstein, 1683).

Machiavelli, Niccolò, *Il Principe. Edizione del cinquecentennale*, with a translation in modern Italian by Carmine Donzelli, ed. and intro. by Gabriele Pedullà (Rome: Donzelli, 2013).

Further Works

Althusser, Louis, *Machiavelli and Us*, ed. F. Matheron, trans. G. Elliott (London: Verso, 1999).

Althusser, Louis, *Philosophy of the Encounter: Later Writings, 1978–1987*, ed. F. Matheron and O. Corpet, trans. G. M. Goshgarian (London: Verso, 2006).

Althusser, Louis, *Politique et histoire, de Machiavel à Marx. Cours à l'École normale supérieure 1955–1972*, ed. F. Matheron (Paris: Seuil, 2006).

Ariosto, Ludovico, *Orlando Furioso*, trans. with intro. by Guido Waldman (Oxford: Oxford University Press, 2008).

Aristotle, *Nicomachean Ethics*, trans. H. Rackham (Cambridge, MA: Harvard University Press, 1934).

Aristotle, *Politics*, trans. H. Rackham (Cambridge, MA: Harvard University Press, 1932).

Bacon, Francis, *Works*, ed. J. Spedding, R. L. Ellis and D. D. Heath (London: Longman, 1858–74).

Bandello, Matteo, *Novelle* (Milan: Rizzoli, 1990).

Bayle, Pierre, *Dictionnaire historique et critique* (Paris: Desoer, 1820).

Cerretani, Bartolomeo, *Storia fiorentina*, ed. G. Berti (Florence: Olschki, 1994).

Cicero, *De Officiis*, trans. W. Miller (Cambridge, MA: Harvard University Press, 1913).

Condorcet, *Esquisse d'un tableau historique des progrès de l'esprit humain* (Paris: Flammarion, 1988).

Croce, Benedetto, *Elementi di politica* (Bari and Rome: Laterza, 1981).

Croce, Benedetto, 'Una questione che forse non si chiuderà mai. La questione del Machiavelli', *Quaderni della Critica* 14 (1949): 1–9.

Croce, Benedetto, *Theory and History of Historiography* (London: Harrap, 1921).

Dante, *The Divine Comedy* (London: Penguin Classics, 2002).

Diderot, Denis, 'Machiavélisme', in *Encyclopédie ou dictionnaire raisonné des sciences, des arts et des métiers*, IX (Neuchâtel: Faulche, 1765), p. 793.

Fichte, J. G., 'Ueber Machiavell, als Schriftsteller, und Stellen aus seines Schriften', in *Gesamtausgabe der Bayerischen Akademie der Wissenschaften*,

Bd. 9. Werke 1806–1807, ed. Reinhard Laut and Hans Gliwitzky (Stuttgart: Friedrich Frommann Verlag (Günther Holzboog), 1995), pp. 215–75.

Frédéric II, roi de Prusse, *Anti-Machiavel. Oeuvres philosophiques* (Paris: Fayard, 1985).

Gentili, Alberico, *De legationibus libri tres*, trans. Gordon J. Laing (New York: Oxford University Press, 1924).

Gentili, Alberico, *The Wars of the Romans: A Critical Edition and Translation of 'De armis Romanis'*, ed. B. Kingsbury, trans. D. Lupher (Oxford: Oxford University Press, 2011).

Gentillet, Innocent, *Anti-Machiavel* (Geneva: Librairie Droz, 1968).

Giovio, Paolo, *Elogia clarorum virorum* (Venice: Tramezzino, 1546).

Gracián, Baltasar, *L'Homme de cour* (Paris: La Veuve Martin and Boudot, 1684).

Gramsci, Antonio, *Quaderni del carcere* (Turin: Einaudi, 1975).

Gramsci, Antonio, *Selection from the Prison Notebooks*, ed. and trans. Q. Hoare and G. Nowell Smith (London: Lawrence and Wishart, 1971).

Guicciardini, Francesco, *Storie fiorentine*, ed. A. Montevecchi (Milan: Rizzoli, 1998).

Guicciardini, Francesco, *The Sweetness of Power: Machiavelli's 'Discourses' and Guicciardini's 'Considerations'*, trans. J. B. Atkinson and D. Sices (DeKalb: Northern Illinois University Press, 2002).

Harrington, James, *'The Commonwealth of Oceana' and 'A System of Politics'* (Cambridge: Cambridge University Press, 1992).

Hegel, G. W. F., *Elements of the Philosophy of Right*, ed. Allen W. Wood, trans. H. B. Nisbet (Cambridge: Cambridge University Press, 1991).

Hegel, G. W. F., *Phenomenology of Spirit*, trans. E. V. Miller (Oxford: Oxford University Press, 1977).

Hegel, G. W. F., *Political Writings*, ed. Laurence Dickey and H. B. Nisbet, trans. H. B. Nisbet (Cambridge: Cambridge University Press, 2004).

Hobbes, Thomas, *The English Works*, ed. W. Molesworth (London: John Bohn, 1839–45).

Il Novellino, The Hundred Old Tales, trans. from the Italian by Edward Storer (New York: E. P. Dutton & Co, 1925).

Landucci, Luca, *Diario fiorentino dal 1450 al 1516*, ed. J. Del Badia (Florence: Sansoni, 1883).

Le Roy, Louis, *De l'Origine, antiquité, progrès, excellence et utilité de l'art politique* (Lyon: Benoist Rigaud, 1568).

Le Roy, Louis, *Les politiques d'Aristote* (Paris: Ambroise Drouart, 1599).

Lucretius, *De rerum natura*, trans. W. H. D. Rouse, rev. M. Ferguson Smith (Cambridge, MA: Harvard University Press, 2006).

Montesquieu, *Oeuvres complètes* (Paris: Seuil, 1964).

Parenti, Piero, *Storia fiorentina. I (1476–78, 1492–96)*, ed. A. Matucci (Florence: Olschki, 1994).

Parenti, Piero, *Storia fiorentina. II (1496–1502)*, ed. A. Matucci (Florence: Olschki, 2005).

Pazzi, Alessandro de', *Discorso al Cardinale Giulio de' Medici* [1522], *Archivio Storico Italiano* 1 (1842): 420–32.

Plutarch, *De fortuna Romanorum, Moralia*, IV (Cambridge, MA, and London: Harvard University Press, 1936).

Polybius, *The Histories*, trans. W. R. Paton (Cambridge, MA, and London: Harvard University Press, 2003).

Quinet, Edgar, *Oeuvres complètes. Les Révolutions d'Italie* (Paris: Germer-Baillière, 1874 [1857]).

Robespierre, Maximilien, *Virtue and Terror* (London: Verso, 2007).

Rousseau, Jean-Jacques, *Basic Political Writings*, ed. and trans. D. A. Cress (Indianapolis and Cambridge, MA: Hackett Publishing Co., 1987).

Sarpi, Paolo, *Histoire du concile de Trente* (Amsterdam: G. P. and J. Blaeu, aux dépens de la Compagnie, 1683).

Savonarola, Girolamo, *Prediche sopra Aggeo, con il Trattato circa il reggimento e governo della città di Firenze* (Rome: Angelo Belardetti Editore, 1965).

Spinoza, Baruch, *Complete Works*, ed. M. L. Morgan, trans. S. Shirley (Indianapolis and Cambridge, MA: Hackett Publishing Co., 2002).

Strauss, Leo, *Thoughts on Machiavelli* (Glencoe: The Free Press, 1958).

Strauss, Leo, *The Three Waves of Modernity: An Introduction to Political Philosophy*, ed. Hilail Gildin (Detroit: Wayne State University Press, 1989).

Tacitus, *Les six premiers livres des Annales* (Paris: Boudot and Martin, 1692).

Valla, Lorenzo, *On the Donation of Constantine* (Cambridge, MA: Harvard University Press, 2007).

Vettori, Francesco, *Scritti storici e politici* (Bari and Rome: Laterza, 1972).

Villani, Giovanni, *Cronica* (Rome: Multigrafica, 1980).

Voltaire, *Oeuvres complètes* (Paris: Furne, 1835).

Weil, Simone, *The Iliad, or the Poem of Force*, ed. and trans. James P. Holoka (New York: Peter Lang, 2006).

SECONDARY SOURCES

Albertini, Rudolf von, *Das florentinische Staatsbewusstsein im Übergang von der Republik zum Prinzipat* (Bern: Francke, 1955).

Amabile, Luigi, *Fra Tommaso Campanella. La sua congiura, i suoi processi, la sua pazzia* (Naples: Morano, 1882).

Anselmi, Gian Mario, *Ricerche sul Machiavelli storico* (Pisa: Pacini, 1979).

Baccelli, Luca, *Critica del repubblicanesimo* (Bari and Rome: Laterza, 2003).

Badaloni, Nicola, 'Natura e società in Machiavelli', *Studi Storici* 10 (1969): 675–708.

Balaban, Oded, 'The Human Origin of Fortuna in Machiavelli's Thought', *History of Political Thought* 9 (1990): 21–36.

Balibar, Étienne, *Écrits pour Althusser* (Paris: La Découverte, 1991).

Baron, Hans, *The Crisis of the Early Italian Renaissance: Civic Humanism* and *Republican Liberty in an Age of Classicism and Tyranny* (Princeton: Princeton University Press, 1966).

Baron, Hans, 'Machiavelli: The Republican Citizen and the Author of *The Prince*', *English Historical Review* 76 (1961): 217–53.

Barthas, Jérémie, *L'argent n'est pas le nerf de la guerre. Essai sur une prétendue erreur de Machiavel* (Rome: École Française de Rome, 2011).

Bassani, Luigi Marco, and Corrado Vivanti (eds), *Machiavelli nella storiografia e nel pensiero politico del XX secolo* (Milan: Giuffrè Editore, 2006).

Bayley, C. C., *War and Society in Renaissance Florence: The 'De Militia' of Leonardo Bruni* (Toronto: University of Toronto Press, 1961).

Benner, Erica, *Machiavelli's Ethics* (Princeton and Oxford: Princeton University Press, 2009).

Benner, Erica, *Machiavelli's 'Prince': A New Reading* (Oxford: Oxford University Press, 2013).

Berns, Thomas, *Violence de la loi à la Renaissance: L'originaire du politique chez Machiavel et Montaigne* (Paris: Kimé, 2000).

Bertelli, Sergio, 'Noterelle machiavelliane. Un codice di Lucrezio e di Terenzio', *Rivista Storica Italiana* 73 (1961): 544–55.

Bertelli, Sergio, 'Noterelle machiavelliane II. Ancora su Lucrezio e Machiavelli', *Rivista Storica Italiana* 76 (1964): 774–92.

Bove, Laurent, *La stratégie du conatus. Affirmation et résistance chez Spinoza* (Paris: Vrin, 1996).

Breaugh, Martin, *L'expérience plébéienne. Une histoire discontinue de la liberté politique* (Paris: Payot, 2007).

Brown, Alison, *The Return of Lucretius to Renaissance Florence* (Cambridge, MA: Harvard University Press, 2010).

Burd, Laurence Arthur, 'Le fonti letterarie di Machiavelli nell'"Arte della guerra"', *Atti della R. Accademia dei Lincei. Classe di Scienze Morali, Storiche e Filologiche*, s.v., vol. IV, a. CCXCIII (1896): 188–261.

Calvino, Italo, 'Perché leggere i classici', in *Perché leggere i classici* (Milan: Mondadori, 1991), pp. 11–19; English translation by P. Creagh, 'Why Read the Classics?', in *The Uses of Literature: Essays* (San Diego: Harcourt Brace Jovanovich, 1987), pp. 125–34.

Carta, Paolo, and Xavier Tabet (eds), *Machiavelli nel XIX e XX secolo/ Machiavel au XIXᵉ et XXᵉ siècles* (Milan: Cedam, 2007).

Chabod, Federico, *Machiavelli and the Renaissance* (London: Bowes & Bowes, 1958).

Chastel, André, *Le grand atelier d'Italie* (Paris: Gallimard, 1965).

Colonna d'Istria, Gérard, and Roland Frapet, *L'art politique chez Machiavel* (Paris: Vrin, 1980).

Cucchi, Paolo M., 'Rousseau lecteur de Machiavel', in M. Launay (ed.), *Jean-Jacques Rousseau et son temps. Politique et littérature au XVIIIᵉ siècle* (Paris: Librairie A.-G. Nizet, 1969), pp. 17–35.

Cutinelli-Rèndina, Emanuele, *Chiesa e religione in Machiavelli* (Pisa and Rome: Istituti Editoriali e Poligrafici Internazionali, 1998).

Cutinelli-Rèndina, Emanuele, *Introduzione a Machiavelli* (Bari and Rome: Laterza, 1999).

de Grazia, Sebastian, *Machiavelli in Hell* (Princeton: Princeton University Press, 1989).

Del Lucchese, Filippo, *Conflict, Power, and Multitude in Machiavelli and Spinoza: Tumult and Indignation* (London and New York: Continuum, 2009).

Del Lucchese, Filippo, 'Crisis and Power: Economics, Politics and Conflict in Machiavelli's Thought', *History of Political Thought* 30 (2009): 75–96.

Del Lucchese, Filippo, 'Freedom, Equality and Conflict: Rousseau on Machiavelli', *History of Political Thought* 35 (2014): 29–49.

Del Lucchese, Filippo, 'On the Emptiness of an Encounter: Althusser's Reading of Machiavelli', *Décalages* 1 (2013), available at <http://scholar.oxy.edu/decalages/vol1/iss1/5> (last accessed 17 October 2014).

Descendre, Romain, '"È certo che vale più la pratica che la teorica": premières remarques sur l'expérience comme enjeu du savoir au début du XVIe siècle (Léonard, Vespucci, Machiavel)', in J.-L. Fournel, H. Miesse, P. Moreno and J.-C. Zancarini (eds), *Catégories et mots de la politique à la Renaissance italienne* (Brussels: P. Lang, 2014), pp. 179–98.

Di Napoli, Giovanni, 'Niccolò Machiavelli e l'Aristotelismo del Rinascimento', *Giornale di Metafisica* 25 (1970): 215–64.

Dionisotti, Carlo, *Machiavellerie* (Turin: Einaudi, 1980).

Dotti, Ugo, *Machiavelli rivoluzionario: vita e opere* (Rome: Carocci, 2003).

Esposito, Roberto, *Ordine e conflitto. Machiavelli e la letteratura politica del Rinascimento italiano* (Naples: Liguori, 1984).

Everson, Jane, and D. Zancani (eds), *Italy in Crisis: 1494* (Oxford: Legenda, 2000).

Feltham, Oliver, *Anatomy of Failure: Philosophy and Political Action* (London: Bloomsbury, 2013).

Finch, Chauncey E., 'Machiavelli's Copy of Lucretius', *Classical Journal* 56 (1960): 29–32.

Fontana, Alessandro, 'Fortune et décision chez Machiavel', *Archives de philosophie* 62 (1999): 255–68.

Fournel, Jean-Louis, and Jean Claude Zancarini, *La politique de l'expérience. Savonarole, Guicciardini et le républicanisme florentin* (Alessandria: Edizioni dell'Orso, 2002).

Frosini, Fabio, *Gramsci e la filosofia. Saggio sui 'Quaderni del carcere'* (Rome: Carocci, 2003).

Gaille-Nikodimov, Marie, *Conflit civil et liberté: la politique machiavélienne entre histoire et médecine* (Paris: Honoré Champion, 2004).

Garin, Eugenio, 'I cancellieri umanisti della repubblica fiorentina da Coluccio Salutati a Bartolomeo Scala', in *Scienza e vita civile nel Rinascimento italiano* (Bari and Rome: Laterza, 1965), pp. 1–32.

Garin, Eugenio, 'Gramsci nella cultura italiana', in *Studi gramsciani. Atti del convegno tenuto a Roma nei giorni 11–13 gennaio 1958* (Rome: Editori Riuniti, 1958), pp. 395–418.

Garin, Eugenio, *Machiavelli fra politica e storia* (Turin: Einaudi, 1993).

Gerbier, Laurent, 'Histoire, médecine et politique. Les figures du temps dans le *Prince* et les *Discours* de Machiavel', unpublished doctoral dissertation, University of Tours, 1999.

Gilbert, Felix, 'Bernardo Rucellai and the Orti Oricellari: A Study of the Origin of Modern Political Thought', *Journal of the Warburg and Courtauld Institute* 12 (1949): 101–31.

Gilbert, Felix, 'The Composition and Structure of Machiavelli's *Discorsi*', *Journal of the History of Ideas* 14 (1953): 136–56.

Gilbert, Felix, *Machiavelli and Guicciardini: Politics and History in Sixteenth-Century Florence* (Princeton: Princeton University Press, 1965).

Guidi, Andrea, *Un Segretario militante. Politica, diplomazia e armi nel Cancelliere Machiavelli* (Bologna: Il Mulino, 2009).

Guillemin, Bernard, 'Machiavel, lecteur d'Aristote', in P. Aquilone (ed.), *Platon et Aristote à la Renaissance: XVIe colloque international de Tours* (Paris: Vrin, 1976), pp. 163–73.

Hale, John R., *Renaissance Venice* (Totowa, NJ: Rowman and Littlefield, 1973).

Hexter, Jack H., *The Vision of Politics on the Eve of Reformation* (New York: Basic Books, 1973).

Hill, Christopher, *Puritanism and Revolution: Studies in Interpretation of the English Revolution of the 17th Century* (New York: St. Martin's Press, 1997).

Inglese, Giorgio, *Per Machiavelli. L'arte dello stato, la cognizione delle storie* (Rome: Carocci, 2006).

Israel, Jonathan, *The Radical Enlightenment* (Oxford: Oxford University Press, 2001).

Lahtinen, Mikko, *Politics and Philosophy: Niccolò Machiavelli and Louis Althusser's Aleatory Materialism* (Leiden: Brill, 2009).

Lazzeri, Christian, 'Les racines de la volonté de puissance: le "passage" de Machiavel à Hobbes', in Y. C. Zarka and J. Bernhardt (eds), *Thomas Hobbes. Philosophie première, théorie de la science et politique* (Paris: Presses Universitaires de France, 1990), pp. 225–46.

Lefort, Claude, *Le travail de l'oeuvre Machiavel* (Paris: Gallimard, 1972); English translation by Michael B. Smith, *Machiavelli in the Making* (Evanston, IL: Northwestern University Press, 2012).

Levi-Malvano, Ettore, *Montesquieu e Machiavelli* (Paris: Honoré Champion, 1912).

Lévy, Yves, 'Les parties et la démocratie', *Le contrat social* 3 (1959): 79–86 and 217–21.

McCormick, John P., *Machiavellian Democracy* (Cambridge: Cambridge University Press, 2011).

Macek, Joseph, *Machiavelli e il machiavellismo* (Florence: La Nuova Italia, 1980).

McKenzie, Lionel A., 'Rousseau's Debate with Machiavelli in the Social Contract', *Journal of the History of Ideas* 43 (1982): 209–28.

Martelli, Mario, 'Firenze', in A. Asor Rosa (ed.), *Letteratura Italiana. Storia e geografia. L'età moderna* (Turin: Einaudi, 1988), pp. 25–201.

Marzi, Demetrio, *La Cancelleria della Repubblica Fiorentina* (Rocca San Casciano: Capelli, 1910).

Matheron, Alexandre, *Études sur Spinoza et les philosophes de l'âge classique* (Lyon: ENS Éditions, 2011).

Mazzone, Umberto, *'El buon governo.' Un progetto di riforma generale nella Firenze savonaroliana* (Florence: Leo S. Olschki Editore, 1978).

Momigliano, Arnaldo, 'Polybius' Reappearance in Western Europe', in *Sesto contributo alla storia degli studi classici e del mondo antico* (Rome: Edizioni di Storia e Letteratura, 1980), pp. 103–23.

Montag, Warren, *Louis Althusser* (New York: Palgrave Macmillan, 2003).

Montag, Warren, and Ted Stolze (eds), *The New Spinoza* (Minneapolis: University of Minnesota Press, 1997).

Moreau, Pierre-François, *Spinoza. L'expérience et l'éternité* (Paris: Presses Universitaires de France, 1994).

Morfino, Vittorio, 'An Althusserian Lexicon', *Borderlands* 4 (2005), available at <http://www.borderlands.net.au/vol4no2_2005/morfino_lexicon.htm> (last accessed 17 October 2014).

Morfino, Vittorio, *Plural Temporality: Transindividuality and the Aleatory Between Spinoza and Althusser* (Leiden: Brill, 2014).

Morfino, Vittorio, *Il tempo e l'occasione. L'incontro Spinoza-Machiavelli* (Milan: L.E.D., 2002).

Najemy, John M., *A History of Florence: 1200–1575* (Oxford: Blackwell, 2006).

Nauta, Lodi, *In Defense of Common Sense: Lorenzo Valla's Humanist Critique of Scholastic Philosophy* (Cambridge, MA: Harvard University Press, 2009).

Nederman, Cary J., 'Amazing Grace: Fortune, God and Free Will in Machiavelli's Thought', *Journal of the History of Ideas* 60 (1999): 617–38.

Negri, Antonio, *L'anomalia selvaggia. Saggio su potere e potenza in Baruch Spinoza* (Milan: Feltrinelli, 1981); English translation by Michael Hardt, *The Savage Anomaly: The Power of Spinoza's Metaphysics and Politics* (Minneapolis: University of Minnesota Press, 1991).

Nicoletti, Gianni, 'Caso-causa o fortuna nel machiavellismo', in *Il tema della Fortuna nella Letteratura francese e italiana del Rinascimento. Studi in memoria di Enzo Giudici* (Florence: Olschki, 1990), pp. 343–53.

Parel, Anthony J., *The Machiavellian Cosmos* (New Haven and London: Yale University Press, 1992).

Payot, Roger, 'Jean-Jacques Rousseau et Machiavel', *Les Études Philosophiques* 26 (1971): 209–23.

Pedullà, Gabriele, *Machiavelli in tumulto. Conquista, cittadinanza e conflitto nei 'Discorsi sopra la prima deca di Tito Livio'* (Rome: Bulzoni, 2012).

Pettit, Philip, *Republicanism: A Theory of Freedom and Government* (Oxford: Oxford University Press, 1999).

Pieri, Piero, *Il Rinascimento e la crisi militare italiana* (Turin: Einaudi, 1952).

Pitkin, Hannah F., *Fortune Is a Woman: Gender and Politics in the Thought of Niccolò Machiavelli* (Berkeley: University of California Press, 1984).

Pocock, J. G. A., 'Introduction', in *The Political Works of James Harrington* (Cambridge: Cambridge University Press, 1977), pp. 1–152.

Pocock, J. G. A., *The Machiavellian Moment: Florentine Political Thought and the Atlantic Republican Tradition* (Princeton: Princeton University Press, 1975).

Polin, Raymond, 'Les régimes politiques et l'imitation des anciens chez Machiavel', in *Platon et Aristote à la Renaissance* (Paris: Vrin, 1976), pp. 155–62.

Raab, Felix, *The English Face of Machiavelli: A Changing Interpretation (1500–1700)* (London: Routledge & Kegan Paul, 1964).

Rahe, Paul A., 'In the Shadow of Lucretius', *History of Political Thought* 28 (2007): 30–55.

Rahe, Paul A. (ed.), *Machiavelli's Liberal Republican Legacy* (Cambridge: Cambridge University Press, 2006).

Raimondi, Fabio, 'Il paradigma-Firenze nel Discursus florentinarum rerum di Machiavelli: in principio sono i conflitti, i conflitti governano', in M. Scattola (ed.), *Figure della guerra. La riflessione su pace, conflitto e giustizia tra medioevo e prima età moderna* (Milan: Franco Angel, 2003), pp. 145–75.

Renaudet, Augustin, *Machiavel* (Paris: Gallimard, 1942).

Ridolfi, Roberto, 'Del Machiavelli, di un codice di Lucrezio e di altro ancora', *La Bibliofilia* 65 (1963): 249–59.

Ridolfi, Roberto, 'Erratacorrige machiavelliana', *La Bibliofilia* 70 (1968): 137–41.

Ridolfi, Roberto, *Vita di Niccolò Machiavelli* (Florence: Sansoni, 1954).

Robin, Leon, 'Sur la conception aristotélicienne de la causalité', *Archiv für Geschichte der Philosophie* 33 (1910): 1–28 and 184–210.

Ross, William D., *Aristotle* (London: Methuen & Co., 1923).

Sacerdoti, Gilberto, *Sacrificio e sovranità: teologia e politica nell'Europa di Shakespeare e Bruno* (Turin: Einaudi, 2003).

Salem, Jean, *Démocrite. Grains de poussière dans un rayon de soleil* (Paris: Vrin, 1996).

Salem, Jean, *La mort n'est rien pour nous. Lucrèce et l'éthique* (Paris: Vrin, 1990).

Salem, Jean, *Tel un dieu parmi les hommes. L'éthique d'Épicure* (Paris: Vrin, 1989).

Sasso, Gennaro, *Machiavelli e gli antichi e altri saggi* (Naples: Ricciardi, 1987–88).

Sasso, Gennaro, *Niccolò Machiavelli* (Bologna: Il Mulino, 1993).

Schmitt, Carl, *Der Leviathan in der Staatslehre des Thomas Hobbes. Sinn und Fehlschlag eines politischen Symbols* (Hamburg: Hanseatische Verlaganstalt AG, 1938); English translation by George Schwab and Erna Hilfstein, *The Leviathan in the State Theory of Thomas Hobbes: Meaning and Failure of a Political Symbol* (Westport, CT: Greenwood Press, 1996).

Schmitt, Charles B., and Quentin Skinner (eds), *The Cambridge History of Renaissance Philosophy* (Cambridge: Cambridge University Press, 1988).

Sedley, David N., *Lucretius and the Transformation of Greek Wisdom* (Cambridge: Cambridge University Press, 1988).

Serres, Michel, *La naissance de la physique dans le texte de Lucrèce: fleuves et turbulences* (Paris: Éditions de Minuit, 1977); English translation by Jack Hawkes, *The Birth of Physics* (Manchester: Clinamen Press, 2001).

Shackleton, Robert, 'Montesquieu and Machiavelli: A Reappraisal', *Comparative Literature Studies* 1 (1964): 1–13.

Skinner, Quentin, *Machiavelli: A Very Short Introduction* (Oxford: Oxford University Press, 2000).

Soll, Jacob, *Publishing 'The Prince': History, Reading, and the Birth of Political Criticism* (Ann Arbor: University of Michigan Press, 2005).

Tenenti, Alberto, 'La religione di Machiavelli', *Studi Storici* 10 (1969): 709–48.

Thomas, Peter D., *The Gramscian Moment: Philosophy, Hegemony and Marxism* (Leiden: Brill, 2009).

Tommasini, Oreste, *La vita e gli scritti di Niccolò Machiavelli nella loro relazione col machiavellismo* (Turin: E. Loescher, 1883–1911).

Torres, Sebastián, *Vida y tiempio de la república. Contingencia y conflicto político en Maquiavelo* (Buenos Aires: Universidad Nacional de General Sarmiento, 2013).

Vardoulakis, Dimitris, *Sovereignty and Its Other* (New York: Fordham University Press, 2013).

Vatter, Miguel, *Between Form and Event: Machiavelli's Theory of Political Freedom* (Dordrecht: Kluwer Academic, 2000).

Vatter, Miguel, *Machiavelli's 'The Prince'* (London: Bloomsbury, 2013).

Viroli, Maurizio, *How to Read Machiavelli* (London: Granta, 2008).

Viroli, Maurizio, *Machiavelli* (Oxford: Oxford University Press, 1996).

Viroli, Maurizio, *Machiavelli's God* (Princeton and Oxford: Princeton University Press, 2010).

Viroli, Maurizio, 'Republic and Politics in Machiavelli and Rousseau', *History of Political Thought* 10 (1989): 405–20.

Weinstein, Donald, *Savonarola and Florence: Prophecy and Patriotism in the Renaissance* (Princeton: Princeton University Press, 1970).

Wieland, Wolfgang, *Die aristotelische Physik* (Göttingen: Vandenhoeck & Ruprecht, 1962).

Winter, Yves, 'Plebeian Politics: Machiavelli and the Ciompi Uprising', *Political Theory* 40 (2012): 736–66.

Zanardi, Maurizio, 'Il corpo rigenerato', *Il Centauro* 5 (1982): 68–9.

Zanardi, Maurizio, 'Note su Machiavelli filosofo', *Il Centauro* 11–12 (1984): 243–55.

Zanzi, Luigi, *I «segni» della natura e i «paradigmi» della storia: il metodo del Machiavelli* (Manduria: Lacaita, 1981).

Index